HISTORY

OF THE

TRANQUEBAR MISSION

HISTORY

OF THE

TRANQUEBAR MISSION

WORKED OUT FROM THE ORIGINAL PAPERS

J. FERD. FENGER

GYAN

Published by

GYAN

Gyan Publishing House
5, Ansari Road
Daryaganj, New Delhi-110002
Phone: 011-47034999, 9811692060
E-mail: books@gyanbooks.com

Distribution Network
gyanbooks.com
India, USA, Canada, UK, Australia, France

ISBN: 978-81-212-8953-5 (PB)
First Published, 1863

2nd Impression 2023

Printed at: Gyan Press, Delhi.

HISTORY OF THE TRANQUEBAR MISSION

AUTHOR: J. FERD. FENGER

HISTORY

OF THE

TRANQUEBAR MISSION

WORKED OUT FROM THE ORIGINAL PAPERS

BY

J. FERD. FENGER,

LICENTIATE OF THEOLOGY, AND PASTOR OF LIUNGE AND BRAABY NEAR SORÖ.

TRANQUEBAR,

EVANGELICAL LUTHERAN MISSION PRESS.

1863.

TRANSLATOR'S PREFACE.

The pleasure which every true Christian must feel in the spread of his Saviour's religion is of itself a sufficient cause for making known the labours of the earliest Missionaries in India; for the man who has learnt from Christianity to love God with all his heart and his neighbour as himself rejoices to see its inestimable blessings declared "to every creature." It is true that the picture has its dark shades; who see here the almost insuperable difficulties that impede the conversion of the Hindùs, amongst which, alas! the carless or profane lives of many Europeans stand prominently forth, but though it is still "the day of small things," any one who has heard, as I have, converted natives of irreproachable lives praying earnest scriptual prayers, giving extemporaneous sermons of remarkable clearness and force, or writing such books as "The Dawn in the East,"* must feel that it is a work blessed of the Lord in spite of any weakness or short comings in the feeble instruments He deigns to use. Pastor Fenger has shown a manly honesty in his account of the failings of the Missionaries, but while we grieve over the unworthy, the labours of such men as Ziegenbalg and Schwartz, which are indeed beyond all praise, should fill us with a noble ambition to follow them "in all virtuous and godly

* "The Dawn in the East;" Edinburgh, Johnstone and Hunter. 1854.

living." We are not called to share their trials in the comparative exile in which they lived, and in the want of sympathy shown to them at home when they wished to return to repair their constitutions shattered by the wearing deadening influence of a tropical climate, but we are called on, each and all, to make some sacrifices for the sake of spreading the kingdom of our blessed Saviour, if only to contribute of our worldly goods towards it.

Pastor Fenger, who was President of the Danish Missionary Society in 1842 when this book was written, had very good opportunities for examining into the history of Missions, and spared no pains in hunting up manuscripts and any documents that could throw light on the subject, always examining them carefully and impartially. He concludes his preface by a suggestion which might be carried out with advantage to English as well as to Danish Church History:—"This book has occupied my leisure hours during the last five or six years, I now publish it with the hope that many of my ministerial brethren may by it be induced to work out separate pieces of our modern Church History. It is high time that the Lutheran period of Denmark's Church should have found its historian, but many parts of that period are so little known that it is extremely desirable that careful monographs should be prepared, which will ease the work for him who feels himself called upon to write the Ecclesiastical History of Denmark since the Reformation. I recommend this book to the kindness of my reader, as an attempt of this sort towards clearing up a remarkable portion of modern Church-historv of our father-land."

CHAPTER I.

THE DANES SETTLE IN THE EAST INDIES. TRACES OF MISSIONARY ACTIVITY AMONGST THE DANES IN THE 17TH CENTURY.

It was during the palmy days of King *Christian IV.* that the Danes first turned their attention to the East Indies, in order to form alliances with that distant country, and thus to appropriate some of the advantages of the rich trade which other seafaring countries had then enjoyed for some time. An East India Company was established in the year 1616, at which time circumstances were particularly favourable to the Danish designs, for the power of the Portuguese was tottering, and the Dutch who were always ready to come forward to drive them off the Indian seas, were not powerful enough to attack them in all their possessions and therefore were quite unable to oppose the Danes if they should also come in to give a blow to the Portuguese here and there. As there had been Danish sailors in the first Dutch expedition to the East Indies, so now Dutch sailors and merchants were quite ready to enter the Danish service, for we find a number of Dutch names amongst those who contributed to the establishment of the Danish East India Company. Amongst these we must particularly mention *Roelant Crape*, who was well acquainted with India and had doubtless been at the Court of Tanjore in his early youth, which induced him to draw the attention of Christian IV. to that part. But the Danes had also an inducement to turn their eyes to the Island of Ceylon. The King of Candy, generally called the Emperor of Ceylon, had in former times called in the Dutch to help him against the Portuguese, and a Dutch merchant, *Marcelis Boshouwers*, had rendered him such signal services that he had created him Prince of Migomme and also made him an Admiral. In the year 1615 when the Emperor was again in difficulties, this Prince of Migomme was dispatched to seek assistance for him from the Dutch, or *from some other nation.* Boshouwers first visited the Dutch possessions in the East Indies and then Holland itself, but without being able to succeed in his aim, for the Dutch were not then in a position to be able to interfere with any advantage in the affairs of Ceylon. There he heard of the establishment of the Danish East India Company and started for Denmark where he arrived in November 1617, had an audience with the King at Frederiksborg and opened new prospects for the Company. It was quite true that Boshouwers was Prince of Migomme, and that the Emperor of Ceylon had sent him to ask for help against the Portuguese, promising great trading advantages to the nation which should give it, but he had not been provided with proper credentials, and when he found that they would be very useful to him, he prepared them for himself;—they were considered as authentic in Denmark, and a treaty for Aid and for Commerce was arranged between Christian IV. and the Emperor of Ceylon in the year 1618, to last for seven years. The equipment of an East Indian Fleet was now carried on with all diligence. One ship, the Oeresund, started first with Roelant Crape on board in August 1618:—it reached Ceylon in safety and informed the Emperor that assistance would soon follow, but Crape allowed himself to be persuaded by the Emperor into an imprudent declaration of hostilities against the Portuguese, by whom he was attacked on the coast of Coromandel. His ship was stranded, and he escaped with only thirteen men to the Naik of Tanjore, who took him under his protection. The remainder of the crew were killed or taken prisoner by the Portuguese and two were executed as pirates. Meanwhile the Fleet, under the command of Admiral *Ove Gedde*, had started about three months after Crape. Fleet and Admiral—it sounds well, but shrinks up on closer examination, for the Fleet consisted of two men-of-war, the Elephant and the David, contributed by the King, and three merchant ships contributed by the Company; the Admiral was but 24 years old, and though he had been a short time in the Dutch service, he knew as little of maritime affairs as he did of East Indian trade; however what he wanted in experience, he made up in zeal and ability, so that even in this case, Christian IV. proved that he knew how to choose his men.* In November 1618 the Indian Fleet sailed from the Sound. Various rendezvous were appointed on the long and dangerous voyage which lay before them, but Gedde had more to contend with in the license of his crew then in the elements, which he met however with a firmness and severity quite surprising. Gedde has been reproached with being over-severe, and that he thus embittered

* It is true that Gedde was called Admiral, but he called himself Commander, and that he was far from pretending to be an Admiral is proved by his being satisfied in 1624 to be Captain of a Company of Infantry which he himself had levied against the Emperor. Before this, immediately on his return from the East Indies, he had been appointed by the King as his Feudary (Governor) in Norway and in one of his Districts (Fiefs) Numedalen, the important Kongsberg-Silvermine was discovered in 1623, a discovery which the King immediately followed up with great zeal. In 1642 he was made Lieutenant Colonel of the Aggerhus Regiment, but still kept his fief; and in the beginning of the year 1645 he was made a member of Council and Admiral of the kingdom without however having any opportunity of distinguishing himself, as the Peace of Brömsebro was concluded that same year. It is remarkable enough that the youthful Admiral of the little Indian fleet should finally become an Imperial Admiral of Denmark.

his inferiors and made the service unendurable to them, but those who did this, have not sufficiently considered the difficulty of the position in which he found himself. The King had been obliged to employ a number of Dutch, in order to secure experienced people as sailors and traders; but for commanders of the ships and of the troops he had chosen Danish nobles, as *Ove Gedde*, *Niels Rosenkrands*, *Thyge Stygge* and *Erik Grubbe*, on whom he could depend. It is therefore easy to imagine how difficult it was to keep up any unanimity between the Danish nobles and the Dutch merchants, and as the good Prince of Migomme wished to play a very great part and could not get the upper hand over Ove Gedde, he joined his Dutch compatriots, and caused the Admiral all sorts of trouble. If the whole was not to fall to pieces, it was necessary to use severity against those who seemed to consider the commanders appointed by the King as unnecessary ballast, only fit to be thrown overboard to make room for professional merchants and sailors.

The ships, which had met at the Cape, were separated during the latter part of the voyage and the Prince of Migomme, who was not with Gedde on board the Elephant but on board the David, died; the Admiral arrived in Ceylon in May 1620, where he assembled his ships by degrees. There he heard of Crape's misfortune, of Boshouwer's death, and what was still worse, he found that the Emperor of Ceylon was not the powerful potentate they had supposed him to be in Denmark, but a weak man, who of late years had been so oppressed by the Portuguese that he was quite unequal to pay the heavy sum for the Danish assistance to which Boshouwer's Treaty obliged him, a Document however which he declared to be invalid in every particular. Now it is really very remarkable to observe the activity and skill which Gedde displayed in his almost desperate circumstances. Zealously anxious for the advantage of the King and of the Company, he did all that was possible to induce the Emperor to pay the stipulated sum, which was most necessary for him to enable him to buy the cargoes which he wished to send home. But finding that there was nothing to be obtained, he made use of the Emperor's great desire to win the Danes, to draw up a Treaty in 24 Articles, quite as advantageous as the Treaty of Boshouwers, and by which Trincomalee, which had not fallen into the possession of the Portuguese and which was in a very important position, was formally ceded to the Danish crown, so that the King and his successors were to govern there after their own pleasure, just as in their own kingdom of Denmark. After these arrangements had been made, in August 1620 Gedde bade adieu to the Emperor, who presented him with some precious stones and an elephant, and sailed away to the Coromandel Coast.

There Roelant Crape had been for some time maintained by the Prince of Tanjore, and had exerted himself greatly to the advantage of the East India Company having come into the possession of Tranquebar, so that undeniably the way was smoothed for Ove Gedde. The negociations very nearly made shipwreck on Crape's mistrust of Gedde, who was represented to him by the Dutch merchants as a hard and obstinate man, from whom on account of his loss of the ship Oeresund he had nothing to expect but the gallows and the wheel. Crape therefore received Gedde with the greatest suspicion, and when the latter had come into Tanjore, and had himself opened communication with the Naik, they worked for sometime against one another to the detriment of their common cause; but as both were active men and zealous in their work (Crape afterwards did great service towards the foundation of the Danish trade in India and was raised by the King to the rank of a noble) it was not difficult to them for each to give way a little and lay their *personnel* aside for the public good. The Treaty was concluded in November 1620. It was advantageous for Danish trade and was lasting while the more advantageous Treaty of Ceylon was never carried into execution.

Immediately on the conclusion of the Treaty Gedde began to lay the foundation of the fortress of *Dansborg*, to the erection of which the Naik had consented, though without obliging himself to furnish either lime or stone. Crape received the highest appointment in the new Colony. *Henrik Hess* was made Commandant of the Fortress, and the first Pastor of the Church in the Fort (of which Gedde laid the foundation before his departure) was *Peder Sörensen Aale*, who died some years afterwards in Tranquebar. Gedde went first to Ceylon, and on the last day of May 1621, sailed in his ship, the Elephant, for Europe, after spending above a year in India, and planting the Danish flag in that place where it has since waved for more then 200 years. His return was much quicker than his outward voyage, not only because he had learned greater experience in sea matters, but because he returned with only one ship, whereas he had sailed out with a fleet which he had tried to keep together. The Elephant reached Copenhagen in March 1622, while the other man-of-war, the David commanded by Niels Rosenkrands, which with Gedde's consent had left India before him, did not arrive till a month later.

A remarkable circumstance in Gedde's voyage is that he kept an exact Diary of all that happened to him both at sea and in India; — Schlegel says:* "I very much doubt whether in the

* T. H. Schlegel "Sammlung zur dänischen Geschichte, 1. Bd. 2. Stck. S.51". Schlegel has not only published Gedde's manuscript Diary which he gave to the

whole voluminous collection of voyages and travels published in England there is a similar example of the account of the first voyage of a nation to the East Indies being written by the Admiral's own hand."

Thus far have I thought it necessary to describe the foundation of the Danish Colony in Tranquebar, and I will now leave the 17th Century to run out in order to come at once to a point when those at home began to think of something besides increasing trade and making money, when they began to take steps for bringing the blessings of Christianity amongst the Heathen who lived on Danish ground in the East Indies, though for a long time the idea was faint and undetermined. It is true that at first there was one Pastor, and afterwards two, for the Danish congregation in Tranquebar, and that most of the ships had a Chaplain on board, but there is scarcely a trace that any of them had turned their attention to the Natives. So much the more careful must we be in following out the few traces that are to be seen. I cannot therefore here pass over a Danish Preacher and Poet who died about the end of the century in Tranquebar, and is called in his Epitaph "the Danish Apostle of India." I mean the well-known master of Arts *Jacob Worm.*

He was born in Kirke-Helsinge, where his father Peder Jacobsen Worm was Pastor, on the 8th of December 1642, and received his first instruction in his father's house, and afterwards in the Gymnasium at Slagelse, whence he entered the University

Chancellor Friis in 1623, but has also worked out the early history of the Danish East Indian trade with great care. There are many particulars of this voyage in the funeral sermon on Ove Gedde by the Copenhagen Pastor Michael Henriksen, published in the collection of his funeral sermons (Copenhagen 1706) and translated into German in the Mission Reports of Halle (Th. 1. Cont. VII). If any one wishes to inquire into Malabar sources with regard to Gedde's arrival in Tranquebar, see the above named Report Th. 1. Cont. XI. S. 883, but the result is very unimportant.

in 1663. He soon showed himself a clever man, wrote verses and not only held Latin disputations, but preached in Latin at the court, where he was in great favour, and where his work on the right of Kings to appoint Pastors was graciously received. He received a promise of the theological lectureship at Viborg as soon as it should be vacant, but was quite satisfied when he was appointed Rector of the school at Slangerup;*—there he remained for six years, till in 1677 he was appointed Pastor of the Church of the Greyfriars in Viborg. Here he married the daughter of his predecessor, Miss Abel Achton. His conduct was irreproachable, his preaching earnest, but the very attention which he could call forth, and the power which he had in lashing vices and crimes, seems to have been ruinous to himself, as he thought himself called upon to become a reformer of his country, and to give counsel in affairs of state. He took up the common rumours of the faults of the great in Copenhagen, and found fault with them from his pulpit at Viborg, round which the poorer classes gladly assembled to hear their superiors satirized. The more severely he preached, the more willingly his hearers listened, for they could easily bear a cutting discourse which was not likely to touch themselves : but Worm proved that he had no call to the office of reformer, by his want of courage and honesty. What he did not dare to say from the pulpit, he wrote in abusive verses in Danish, which were quietly circulated from hand to hand. In these verses not only the faults of the Church, especially in the choice of pastors, were denounced, but the misconduct of the war in Schonen and even the highest

* Pontoppidan says Slagelse for Slangerup in the 4th Part of his Annals P. 607. The same assertion is found in Nyerup History of Danish Poetry, Part 3, P. 262, and in the life of Worm in the Journal of Politics for 1812; but it is incorrect. See Alb. Thura "valvae scholarum regni Danici apertae" P. 230 (amongst the manuscripts of the University Library).

courts of law and the King's Privy Council were brought satirically before the public. "The complaining Student" and the "King's Clock" are the most notable of his verses, which were accompanied by coarse libels in prose, as for example "Abraham's Vision" and "Jeroboam's Idols," in which the King and his ministers were clearly pointed out, and accused of the gravest crimes. His Bishop, Dr. Sören Glud, the brother-in-law of the powerful Privy Counsellor Moth, warned him often, but could not effect any change, as Worm denied that these widely spread satires were his work, and continued to shoot his arrows against the Bishop and his highly connected family. Such lines as those in "The complaining Student":

"Simon Magus, Tæver, Tisper
Kalder Præster, Provster, Bisper"

must have struck hard indeed on Sören Glud, who had been for many years the village pastor in Höie-Taastrup, but through the influence of the Moth family had been made a Doctor of Divinity and Bishop of Viborg and raised to the rank of a noble. But the complete rupture between the Bishop and Worm took place in 1680 on the King's birthday. At the dinner given by the Bishop, the health of the Royal family was drunk, and finally the health of the (illegitimate) children of the King was proposed;—in this Worm would not join, and when he was asked his reason, he designated the children by a very impolite, but well known name. This was naturally made known at Copenhagen, together with information about his various satires. An officer of justice was sent to Viborg to search Worm's house for such papers as would justify a legal prosecution, for the history of the toast was a ticklish affair, which no one wished to stir up. The officer showed Worm the royal commands; he gave up his keys with the greatest indifference, apologizing for not going round with him, as he had to preach the next day and must therefore remain in his chair in his study. The officer searched everywhere, and was much displeased that he found nothing.

But it was not enough for Worm to have made a fool of the officer of justice, he must let all the world know how it had been done. When he preached the next day he began his sermon with the 34th and 35th verses of the 31st Chapter of the Book of Genesis, where it tells that Rachel *sat* upon her father's images so that Laban sought them in vain. This striking text led the officer of justice who was one of the congregation to leave the Church immediately, go to Worm's house and search the chair on which he had sat the day before;—under it he found a drawer, filled with the condemned satires. Worm was now in a sad condition, for suspension and arrest were simultaneously made known to him. From his prison he wrote a defence to the King, and as he could no longer deny, he tried the power of excuses:—he had but spoken the words of scripture;—he could not help it if people would apply to individuals what he had only said of mankind in general;—he had never meant to injure the King's counsellors and servants by his hard words, but only to warn and encourage them;—he had taken much from the printed writings of others &c. But this helped him nothing; the commissioners took away his living and gave him up to the temporal power, which pronounced that he had forfeited honour, life and estates, that his libels should be burnt by the hangman, that he should be punished for perjury by the loss of three fingers, and finally have his head struck off by the sword.

This sentence was not, however, carried out: for the unlucky poet being in danger of death was untiring in sending verses to the King, to Gyldenlöve and any influential people from whom he could expect intercession. Among those who spoke in his favour is mentioned the husband of his stepmother, Dr. Thomas Kingo, who had been first vicar to his father and had then succeeded him in his living. So he escaped with his life, but was transported in the first ship that sailed for Tranquebar, where he acted for some time as Director of the Choir in the Church. In his Adieu to his Fatherland, he says :—

> " Da Lykken slog mig feil, da lærte jeg at kjende
> Min Gud, min Ven, mig selv; men allermeest min Fjende.
> Min Fjende var mig gram, min Ven mig og forlod,
> Selv var jeg skröbelig,—Gud var alene god. " *

It is not easy to say what he did in Tranquebar for the conversion of the heathen. Some declare that he translated the Bible, others that he occupied himself with translating the New Testament only into Tamil, others that he preached to the Natives in the public street, and that on one occasion their idol's car fell to pieces and could not be moved from the spot, while others relate that he was preaching in the Christian Church one Sunday when a large heathen procession passed and his congregation wished to run out to look at it; Worm exhorted them to remain in the Church, assuring them that they would be quite in time to see the ceremony after Divine Service was concluded, and his words came true by the car falling to pieces and remaining on the spot until his sermon was over. It is said that this occurrence gave Worm great influence over the Natives and that after his death (on the 17th Dec. 1691) his corpse did not decay. Be that as it may, not a trace remained in after years of his translation of the Bible, nor of any congregation founded by him, so that he is very

* Others ascribe these lines to Griffenfeldt, and say that he wrote them on a window in his prison; Rask, Amusing Lectures for the Danish People 1841. No. 9. My warrant is taken from a Manuscript collection of Worm's poems, pag. 201. (Amongst the M. S. of the University Library fol. Add. No. 160.)

improperly called the Danish Apostle of India in his Epitaph. This Epitaph runs thus: "The lover of truth, the enemy of vice, the prophet of his fatherland, the Danish apostle of India, *Magister Jacob Worm*, who knew not how to deceive, but knew well how to punish sin and vice, who taught the erring and the unbelieving both by his pen and by his mouth, rests in this place for the truth's sake; for though banished from his native country, he was not burned by the heat of the sun, but naturally and happily, after his sea-voyage, short stay in India, and much building up amongst the Natives, he was received by Christ into the heavenly kingdom."

With the exception of Jacob Worm's efforts, there is nothing in the 17th century which resembles any Missionary activity on the part of the Danes amongst the heathen of the East Indies, unless the fact be taken into the account that during the long war between the Danes in Tranquebar and their neighbours in Bengal which was principally carried on by privateering, it was their custom to take the crews of the privateers as slaves, to baptize them and sell them at a price varying from 5 to 10 piasters. This unworthy commerce is a stain on the Danish honour in the East, which Niebuhr tries in vain to wash out with the remark that it must be attributed to the century and not to the persons. We long to see nobler characters appear than those who could allow the heathen to be baptized in order to sell them for a few piasters. I need scarcely add that this custom did not originate with the Danish Government, which on the contrary had considered the spiritual welfare of its heathen subjects before the regular beginning of any Mission, for when the New East India Company, which was formed in 1670, received a Charter for 40 years, dated from the 20th of November 1670, the 5th

Paragraph runs thus:—"As it is to be hoped that many of the Indians, when they shall be properly instructed will be turned from their heathen errors, there shall always be Priests in the ships and in the territory belonging to the Company, and the King promises to promote such Priests as have been in the service of the Company;"—but this royal promise had no effect in promoting the conversion of the heathen. Moreover though there is no trace of the Government having been aware of the traffic in baptized Natives, there is also no trace of its having done any thing to oppose it.

CHAPTER II.

FREDERIC IV.—LUETKENS.—THE YOUTH OF ZIEGENBALG.

It is no rare occurrence in Denmark to be able to say when any thing good, noble, or beautiful is set on foot: "This originates with the King;" and the heart of every patriot rejoices when it can he said with truth. That the man who opened the road to Evangelical Missionary activity in the 18th and 19th centuries was a Danish King, is a fact which has been acknowledged and appreciated throughout Europe. It was not the passing impression of an idle hour which induced *Frederic* IV. to seek for evangelical messengers to send forth to the heathen of India. He had meditated on the subject for many years; even when he was Crown Prince the cause of the heathen lay very near his heart and he wondered much that no one in the Evangelical Church had thought of helping them. As soon as he ascended the throne of Denmark and Norway these thoughts returned so often that they awoke the resolution of making an attempt. The first person whom he consulted in the affair was his confessor, the Norwegian *Dr. Peder Jespersen*, whom he requested to find two suitable men to make known the Gospel to the Laplanders in Finmark. In the same way the King spoke to his German court-preacher *Dr. Masius*, begging him to seek for Missionaries for another heathen people. It was not till 1704, however, when *Dr. Lütkens* came to Copenhagen as court-preacher, that Frederic IV. found a man who entered earnestly into what lay so near his heart, and who, to use his own expression, carried wood with joy, when he saw such a fire begin to blaze.

Franz Julius Lütkens was the son of a miller in the Duchy of Lauenburg, had occupied posts in schools and churches in various places in Germany, and was Pastor of St. Peter's Church in Berlin, when Frederic IV. called him to Copenhagen as preacher to the court. As soon as he had been commissioned by the King to look for Missionaries to send to Tranquebar, he consulted with the Bishop of Zealand, *Dr. Bornemann*, as to whether he knew any one fit for the undertaking and finding that he did not, Lütkens wrote to his former colleagues in Berlin, Pastors *Lysius* and *Campe*, who in their turn consulted Prof. *Francke* of Halle, and soon received the desired answer that he knew of two men who feared God from their hearts, and were willing to go to the heathen. This was the beginning of that union between Copenhagen and Halle in Missionary affairs which lasted so many years with much satisfaction on both sides. The King was so much pleased with the first two Missionaries, that when they asked for assistants, he turned to Lütkens saying: "Provide people for us, Doctor."

The two first Missionaries were *Heinrich Plütschau* from Wesenberg in Mecklenburg, and *Bartholomäus Ziegenbalg* from Pulsnitz in Upper-Lausitz, and as the latter was not only one of the founders of the Mission and worked for it with undiminished zeal to his latest breath, but also a remarkable man on many accounts, we must pause a little to consider the history of his life, which we are acquainted with from his own accounts.

He was born on St. John's Day, 24th June 1683. His father, a merchant in Pulsnitz, was named like himself Bartholomäus, his mother Catharina; but he lost both his parents at such an early age, that he knew but little of them. And yet one occurrence of his mother's dying hours was never forgotten by him. When she felt her death approaching she gathered her family round her bed, and said to them: "Dear children, I have collected a great treasure for you; a very great treasure have I collected for you." When the eldest daughter asked: "Dear Mother, where is the treasure", the dying woman answered: "Seek it in the Bible, my dear children, there you will find it. I have watered every page with my tears." This hour, says Ziegenbalg, went to our hearts, and we pledged ourselves to remind each other of it often.—His father's death was remarkable also. The old Ziegenbalg lay ill, when a fire broke out in the town and reached his house;—in their hurry and fright his friends did not know how to arrange to save the dying man, when they thought of his own coffin, which he had had for some time in readiness. He was carried out in it, and died in it in the open air in the market place. Young Ziegenbalg was thus left under the care of his eldest sister, who kept him diligently to a regular attendance at school and to reading the Bible. An extraordinary earnestness characterized his childhood. He meditated on Heaven and Hell, felt severe reproaches from conscience whenever he had done any thing wrong, and when he heard of the death of any one he thought: "Where may that soul now be, and what change has it experienced?" He was placed in the school at Kamenz, and afterwards in the Gymnasium at Görlitz where he was exposed to temptations and passed some time idly, but the first impressions of childhood were soon refreshed. He was about sixteen years old when one day a pious student came to him as he was amusing himself with music, and expressed his opinion on music being a noble art, but added that none could understand or practise it, who were not in a spiritual harmony with God and with themselves;—the mind of man, he said, had been entirely disordered by the Fall and must be brought into a completely different condition before it can attain to real harmony. This speech struck Ziegenbalg; he took a great fancy to this student, offered him his friendship, and they afterwards met daily, partly for prayer and for reading God's Word, and partly for walking out into the country to read the goodness of God in the book of Creation. Thus Ziegenbalg showed his care for his soul, and withdrew from all other society. When the other scholars observed this, they made him such a target for their ridicule that his friend proposed that they should undertake a journey together:—it took place, and had such a favourable influence on Ziegenbalg, that he returned to Görlitz so strengthened as to bear courageously the scorn not only of his fellow students, but also of many others. "My soul," said he, "had tasted such sweetness and joy in God that she was willing not only to give up all the pleasures of this world, but cheerfully to bear its hatred and contempt."

But he soon had to endure a harder trial than the ridicule of the world. We will let him speak for himself:—"When I had been for some time in the enjoyment of the perceptible grace of God, and had thereby gained many victories over the devil, the world and my sinful flesh and blood—behold, the hardest temptations beset me, and I felt as if abandoned by God, for I could no longer feel his consolatory communion with my soul; on the contrary, I saw in myself and in all mankind nothing but misery, grief and heart-ache. Then my eyes were first opened to behold the entire ruin of the children of men, and my astonishment was great to see on the one side the long-suffering of God who reigns with so much forbearance over a guilty world instead of striking it at once with the rod of his justice, and on the other the great wickedness of men in remaining so proud, shameless and secure in the midst of their misery. I had no one to whom I could speak on this deep-seated grief of my heart (his above-mentioned friend had gone away), and could not make known my condition to a single soul, for every one thought that it arose simply from melancholy, which ought to be driven away by amusement. I loathed all earthly things, and could not find rest or pleasure in any thing. My tutors saw me wandering about in great depression both of mind and body and could not at all comprehend it, though they were much kinder to me than I deserved. When however I had suffered this anguish of heart for nine months, and God had tried and purified me by trials, the joyous and healing light of the holy Gospel dawned once again on my soul, and I was restored to a truly evangelical cheerfulness. But now I had to combat with myself, for I could not determine whether it was advisable to pursue the study of theology, both on account of the heavy responsibility, and of the great corruption which I now perceived had crept into the clerical profession. But I soon overcame this temptation and decided that it was the more necessary to study theology as the sincere workers were so few. When I meditated on God's mercies to my soul during the last twelve months, I acknowledged myself bound to dedicate myself entirely to his service, and to seek nothing in the world but the magnifying of his holy name; and I soon perceived that this could only be done by so teaching my neighbours that they might also be saved and brought into communion with the Triune God. But here I perceived also how necessary it was that I should make myself fit for performing such a service to God and my neighbour. I therefore began to carry on my studies with great earnestness: they all appeared easy to me, for my mind was quite in another condition before God from what it had been before. I arranged my studies in what I considered the best way for attaining my aim. For this I began a correspondence with pious, wise and learned theologians, confided to them my experiences, and asked good counsel of them, and by their letters I became more and more awakened and encouraged in my studies."

Amongst the men with whom Ziegenbalg thus entered into correspondence we must particularly mention Prof. *August Hermann Francke* of Halle, whose Penitential Sermons he had read with so much edification, that he confided to him the state of his mind, and asked for advice. Francke encouraged him in the good fight, which, by God's grace, he had begun, and advised him to continue his studies at Berlin, in the Frederic-Gymnasium, which was then managed by Joachim Lange, who was afterwards a Professor at Halle. In *Lange* and *Spener* he found faithful teachers, was much assisted by *Canstein*, and was beginning to attain thorough profoundness in his studies, when sickness obliged him to return home to his sister, whose care he enjoyed for a year. While at home he repeated every thing which he had been learning, and tried in every way to make use of his gifts for the good of his neighbours; "for", he writes, "my constant thought was that my life would be very short, wherefore I hastened so much the more towards my goal, and though I was often reminded both in letters and by word of mouth, to spare my body, yet I thought it was better to have lived a short and a good life, than a long and a bad one."

When he had regained a little strength, he visited various Universities, but in no place was he better pleased than at Halle with Francke. He found there students of a like mind with himself, and faithful instruction from the Professors; but the thought of the responsibility of the clerical profession and his bodily weakness so depressed him, that he began to think that it would be better to give up theology and occupy himself with agriculture, in order thus to live in peace for the salvation of his own soul, without loading himself with the guilt of others. "I was," he writes, "something like Jonas, who wished to be freed from a like heavy burden, but was at last obliged to listen to the commands of God; for though I was not thrown into the sea like Jonas, yet I had to undergo severe punishments from the hand of God, which obliged me at last to become captive to his will." In this undecided state, he turned to his academical teacher (probably Francke) who tried to encourage him and to induce him to give up the idea of abandoning theology, by representing to him how much both churches and schools stood in need of active workers in the Lord's service. In this conversation they spoke of sending preachers of the Gospel into heathen countries, and Ziegenbalg heard his teacher make a remark which not only struck him at the time, but of which he retained a lively recollection when he was in the East Indies. "If one can truly lead a soul to God from amongst that people," said the worthy man, "it is as much as winning a hundred in Europe, for these latter have each day means and opportunity sufficient for their conversion, while the former are entirely without them." Ziegenbalg now determined not to give up theology, but he was soon obliged to leave Halle on account of his health, and occupied himself in teaching, first at Merseburg and then at Erfurt, but in both places for a short time only. He then spent a year with his sister in Pulsnitz, and went from thence to Berlin and whilst he was there Lütkens' letter, asking for Missionaries to be employed by the King of Denmark arrived.

It was proposed to him whether he would like to take up this calling. Ziegenbalg without refusing tried to excuse himself at first on account of his youth and delicate health; but the men, in whom he placed the most confidence, combated his scruples, and he soon felt himself bound in conscience to go whithersoever the Lord should call him. It was a great pleasure to him that his school-and university-friend *Heinrich Plütschau*, decided to go with him. The cause was taken up so zealously at Copenhagen that they did not even receive permission to take a personal adieu of their friends. In October 1705 they went from Berlin to Copenhagen, were kindly received by the King and Lütkens, and were ordained by *Dr. Bornemann*, Bishop of Zealand.* However their short stay in Copenhagen was not without trials. The world in general was quite indifferent to the undertaking, or else declared it chimerical and useless, and laughed at their zeal and their hopes of blessed fruits from the Mission. The two young men were considered as well meaning enthusiasts, and their undertaking as adventurous and aimless. Remain in the country and support yourselves honestly, was the cry.

Perhaps, my reader, though not altogether of this opinion you may after what you have heard hitherto, not yet feel much confidence in Ziegenbalg as a Missionary. You look to his youth and inexperience, to his delicate health and low spirits, and you ask: " Is it such an one who should be sent to the heathen"? Delay your judgement for a while and follow him into the scene of his labours. You will find him both capable and faithful.

* The King's Instruction given to the Missionaries, we shall give to the Public in an Appendix.

CHAPTER III.

THE FIRST MESSENGERS ARE DESPATCHED AND ARRIVE IN INDIA.—THE PEOPLE OF TRANQUEBAR.—THE MISSIONARIES LEARN THE LANGUAGES, MAKE PROSELYTES, BUILD A CHURCH, FOUND SCHOOLS AND ARE PERSECUTED.

"On the 29th of November 1705, we, Heinrich Plütschau and Bartholomäus Ziegenbalg, under the good Providence of God and upon the gracious command of His Royal Majesty of Denmark and Norway King Frederick IV. left Copenhagen for the East Indies, as the first Missionaries to make known the Gospel of Christ to the heathen on the Coromandel Coast. Many gave us but small hopes for a good and blessed issue to our undertaking, but faith in an all-powerful God and confidence in the promises of his holy Word comforted us and gave us courage under all trials, and helped us by degrees to change the difficult and dangerous voyage into a blessing."

It is thus that the Missionaries begin their communication on the events of the first year. The ship in which their passage was taken was the *Sophia Hedewig*, and her voyage was considered on the whole a good one, as she reached the Cape of Good Hope in April 1706, where they made their first acquaintance with heathens amongst the Hottentots. They grieved much over their degraded bodily and spiritual condition, and thought that by God's help it would not be impossible to learn their language and form it into a written tongue; but their field of work had already been appointed in another place. When the ship sailed from the Cape they determined each to choose a subject for his meditations during the remainder of the voyage, so as to use the time to edification. Plütschau chose Truth, and Ziegenbalg Wisdom, "for," says he, "our ship was called the Sophia, which means Wisdom, and our employment was of that nature that we ought to know where true Wisdom was to be found. When I had meditated daily on this subject for a month, and my heart had rejoiced in it through the testimony of the Holy Scriptures, it seemed to me useful and edifying that such good thoughts should be put into writing and communicated to my dear friends in my Fatherland as a standing testimony of the grace of God, who by his heavenly wisdom had carried me over the great Ocean in a ship which had become a school to me." Thus began the tolerably detailed sketch of Ziegenbalg's treatise on true Wisdom, which he finished after his arrival in Tranquebar when he was ill and could not occupy himself for some weeks with the regular work of the Mission. "I wished," said he, "not to let this time pass over uselessly, but to occupy myself with such things as should keep me constantly ready for death. I remembered how the meditation on true wisdom had given me great peace of mind while at sea, so that neither the roaring of the wind, the rushing of the mighty waves, nor the cries and noise of the crew could disturb my thoughts, but that by God's assistance I was able to keep myself in such a condition as to feel always prepared either for life or death;—with these recollections I took up my meditations again, and though very weak, I finished them in a very short time." The preface to the treatise, from which these remarks are taken, is dated Tranquebar July 18th 1707.

It was dedicated to Princess Sophia Hedewig, and was printed at Leipzig in 1710.

On *the 9th July* 1706 the two first Missionaries arrived at their desired haven, Tranquebar, and landed with their hearts deeply moved by the sight of the crowds of pagans for whose salvation they had come to work. They found however amongst the Danish Merchants and Officials not only no sympathy for their undertaking, but a cold and almost inimical reception. At first they would not even receive the Missionaries, though they could show the King's hand and seal, but left them till the evening in the burning heat, first outside the gates and then in the market place, when finally the Secretary, Herr Attrup, dared to take them in and secured a lodging for them in the house of his father-in-law. "We must acknowledge," say the Missionaries, "that *Prayer* was our all-important assistance to begin our high and weighty employment with courage, without fear of trouble and danger. For as we had no human being near us of whom we could ask advice as to how this or that should be begun, we went always to our dear Father in Heaven and laid every thing before him in prayer, and we were heard and supported by him both in advice and in deed. If we asked advice of any one here in India we were even more dissuaded from our undertaking than we had been in Europe, for the impossibility of succeeding in our aim was always held up to us. And indeed we found many and great difficulties, and when we considered them could not promise ourselves any entrance amongst the heathen; yet we did not let our courage sink, but read the Acts of the Apostles to strengthen our faith and would not neglect any means which we thought might be useful for beginning our employment with a blessing."

We will now consider the people amongst whom the Missionaries were to live and commence their sphere of usefulness. "The inhabitants," says Ziegenbalg, a consist partly of white Europeans, partly of half-white Portuguese, partly of yellow Moors, but principally of black-brown Malabarians. I do not exactly know the number of these various inhabitants, but I must say that Tranquebar is a well-peopled town, swarming with old and young, especially as its trade attracts men of all nations both by sea and land." Ziegenbalg mentions here 4 classes in the Danish dominions in the East Indies, and amongst these we will first notice the larger portion of the population, "the black-brown Malabarians." This is the name by which the Hindûs, the heathen portion of the population, are generally mentioned in the Missionary Reports. Their language is Tamil, which has long been formed into a written language;—they write their books and letters with an iron style on palm-leaves. They possess authors on almost all sciences, and are expert in many trades and handicrafts. "Most Christians in Europe," says Ziegenbalg, "suppose the Malabarians to be a very barbarous people, but this arises from the Europeans who have been amongst them not understanding their language, so that they have not been able to read their books, but have drawn their conclusions from outward appearances. I must acknowledge that when I first came amongst them I could not imagine that their language had proper rules, or that their life had the laws of civil order, and took up all sorts of false ideas on their actions as if they had neither a civil nor a moral law,—but as soon as I had gained a little acquaintance with their language and could talk to them on various subjects, I began to have a much better opinion of them and when at last I was able to read their own books I found that the Malabarians discussed the same philosophical subjects as the Savans of Europe, and that they had a regular written law, wherein all theological subjects were treated of and demonstrated. This surprised me extremely, and I was delighted to be thoroughly instructed in their heathenism from their own writings." Ziegenbalg relates that the Malabarians were well aware that there was only one Supreme Being, and that he had heard a Native learned man discourse so well on this highest Being that he could not refrain from asking him why they worshipped many gods, when they knew so well that there was but One. He received the following answer: "A schoolmaster would prove himself very perverted, who should begin teaching his scholars to read by giving them a difficult poem;—he must begin with the A B C. So it is with the knowledge of God; one must begin with the little gods and rise up step by step, till one reaches the highest Being. This Being does not trouble himself about this earth, but has created other great gods, who in their turn have smaller gods under them, by whom everything is governed. As one has been created by the gods, and received many benefits from them, it is quite right and suitable to pray to them, especially as in the end the whole of the honour flows to the highest God. So think the wise, but the people accept the whole crowd of gods without further thought, and show equal reverence to any of the 330 Million gods who come to their knowledge." There is no unity amongst the heathen about their gods, in fact there are almost as many opinions as there are heads. The gods who have the most worshippers are Brahma, Vishnu and Siva.

The *Malabarians* are, as is well known, divided into castes, of which they number 96. Every Native belongs to a caste from the time of his birth; even their Kings have not the power to change a man's caste. If any one marries out of his own caste, or does not observe its manners and customs, he is thrust out, and not even his nearest relation will have any thing to do with him. Of the principal castes we may mention: the *Brahmins*, of whom consist the nobles and priests, but who sometimes occupy themselves with agriculture and keeping cattle;—the *Sudras* who form the grade of merchants and peasants, and carry on many trades; -and the *Pariahs*, who support themselves with difficulty by hard daily labour, and by those occupations which are considered disgraceful by other castes. Whosoever is converted to Christianity loses his caste. At the time of the arrival of the Missionaries there were 5 great Pagodas or heathen Temples in the town of Tranquebar.

Next to the Malabarians we will mention the *Portuguese*, the children of European fathers and Native mothers. These people have been called Portuguese, because from the Portuguese having once possessed the dominion of the East Indies, their language, half or perhaps altogether corrupted, was kept up amongst those Natives who were in the closest connection with Europeans, even when the latter were of a different nation. The Portuguese language was thus the medium of communication between the Europeans and the Natives, for few Europeans could speak Tamil, and many Natives, especially those who were born or brought up in the houses of Europeans spoke Portuguese from their childhood, and knew but little of their mother tongue. This class gave up the Indian and adopted the European style of dress. They were heathens, unless the Europeans on whom they were dependant, cared to have them baptized. Before the arrival of our Missionaries many hundreds had joined the Roman

Catholic communion, but many became members of the Portuguese congregation, which the Missionaries founded. Those who were not in the service of Europeans often enlisted as soldiers or sailors. Their colour varied according to their degree of distance from European blood. Those Natives who had adopted the European dress and Portuguese language because many generations before they may have descended from an European were called black Portuguese.

The Missionary Reports speak of the Mohammedans as *Moors*, because the Spanish and Portuguese called all Mohammedans *os Muoros*. They had spread themselves from Arabia over the whole of India, where they were very numerous and well off in the world. Their religion was not only paramount in the dominions of the Great Mogul, but was tolerated also in the countries round about. The Moors filled the most important political and military posts at the Courts of the heathen Kings, while others devoted themselves to trade and commerce and became rich merchants. Ziegenbalg declares that all the Mohammedans were originally foreigners, and that he did not know a single Malabar Mohammedan. Other Missionaries on the contrary make a distinction, and say that there are two Mohammedan sects, who both believe themselves to belong to the Sunnites or Orthodox; the one, the Tuluckens, consisting of foreigners and the other, the Sonagens or native Malabarians. The first understand Tamil, but make use of Hindostanee in speaking, and of Persian in writing; the latter, like other Malabarians, speak Tamil and Portuguese, but in their schools and mosques, they, as well as the Tuluckens, use Arabic. The Moors were more favoured by nature than the Malabarians, but were more inimical to the Christian religion than the heathen. Ziegenbalg often visited them and they him; but they were not very willing to listen to arguments, as they rested on the fact that their religion was the most widely spread and had subdued three parts of the earth, on which account when they wrote a letter they cut off three corners and left only one remaining, as a type of possessing three parts of the world, while the Christians had but one. On the arrival of the Missionaries the Moors had a large mosque in Tranquebar, and several in the village of Poreiar.

In speaking at last of the *Christians*, we must begin with the *Roman Catholic* Native Congregation; but unfortunately there is no detailed account of its rise and progress. It was probably founded in the 17th Century, but the exact year and the attendant circumstances cannot be given. In 1763 when the Jesuits who had left Pondichery on its being taken by the English in 1761, tried to establish themselves in Tranquebar, fruitless enquiries were made on this subject; after which the Evangelical Missionaries say that some time before the beginning of the Danish Mission, the Roman Catholics had a Church close to the principal gate of the Fort of Tranquebar, within the town-wall. The exact time of its erection they could not ascertain. A free exercise of their religion is said to have been granted to the Roman Catholics by the Company on account of the Portuguese having once defended the town; but the Missionaries could not gain any accurate information on this point, nor learn that this privilege had ever received the Royal confirmation. At the time when Attrup was the Commandant (about 1726) the Roman Catholics received permission to build a Chapel dedicated to St. Xavier in the suburb of Sattankudi, probably because Attrup's wife was a Roman Catholic. I cannot find any mention of the number of the Roman Catholics at the time of Ziegenbalg's arrival, but only that they were governed by a Padre Vicarius, who was subordinate to the Bishop of St. Thomè or Mailapur, whose diocese extended over the whole Coromandel Coast and Bengal. The Missionaries make constant complaints of the ignorance of the Roman Catholics, their opposition to the Gospel, and unjustifiable methods of making proselytes.

Tranquebar, with the district thereto belonging, in which Ziegenbalg mentions 15 villages, belonged originally to 'the Kingdom of Tanjore, which, as he says, extended 24 German miles in length, and 17 in breadth. The King of Tanjore, who was himself tributary to the Great Mogul, received an annual tribute from the Danes, but had nothing to do with the Government of Tranquebar, which was entirely managed from Denmark. Consequently there were some Danish Officials and Employès of the Company who formed a congregation amongst themselves, and had built a Church, called Zion, to which two Pastors were appointed, of whom Ziegenbalg says that they preached twice a week, but that they seldom remained in Tranquebar more than two or three years, for as there was a clergyman on board each ship that arrived, it was easy for them to make an exchange. But this was not the case with the Danish Pastor, *Jacob Clementin*, who came out the second time to Tranquebar with the Missionaries in 1706, and remained there to the day of his death in 1730. The Colony was governed by a Commandant, at that time *John Sigismund Hassius*, and by a Council, chosen by the Company.

Having thus made a slight acquaintance with the people amongst whom the Missionaries were to work, let us now consider how they began their work. Of course the language must from the beginning be an important point with them, and we see them not only attacking Portuguese, which from its resemblance to Latin must have been easy to them, but also Tamil, which was quite strange to them, and for many reasons must have been extremely difficult. Six days after their arrival they made a beginning with the Portuguese. They learnt to speak this language as it is spoken in Portugal from books, having obtained a Grammar and a New Testament, printed in Batavia. They learnt the Indo-Portuguese dialect by daily communication with the people about them, and used it for *viva voce* instruction, while the European Portuguese being employed as a written tongue and in the schools, the congregation by degrees became accustomed to, and learned to understand it.

It was much more difficult to them to make themselves masters of the Tamil language, as all printed and written means of assistance were wanting, and at first they could not find any one who by knowing Tamil as well as some language known to them, could become their teacher. They tried it in all ways, but could not succeed. At last after some months had passed away, they fell in with an old Malabar schoolmaster, whom they took into their service and agreed that they should pay him a certain sum for bringing his school into their houses. Both schoolmaster and school-children were heathens, but the Missionaries wished to observe closely how the Malabarians taught children, to make acquaintance with the young people, to learn what they could, and were not ashamed of becoming pupils of the heathen schoolmaster. The two Missionaries might be seen amongst the children, seated on the ground and like them, tracing out first letters, then syllables and finally words, in the sand. Thus they learned to read, to write and to pronounce a number of words, but the meaning of words was unknown to them, for the schoolmaster did not understand

Portuguese. It became therefore an important point to find an interpreter. They began with various people in various ways, but without success. At last they heard that in the country, not far from Tranquebar, there was a learned Malabarian of the name of Aleppa, 46 years of age, who not only knew different Indian languages, but also from daily communication with Europeans, understood Portuguese, Danish, German and Dutch. In October 1706, they persuaded him to take service with them in Tranquebar, where they kept him for two years at a considerable expense. Certainly he could not teach them the language grammatically, but he was equal to explaining the meanings of words and helping them to understand books written in Tamil. So by degrees they gained an insight into the Grammar. Not only did they read Tamil Manuscripts every day, but they translated from German into Tamil and from Tamil into German, and had a Native to read Tamil to them, that they might acquire a correct pronunciation. "For this purpose," says Ziegenbalg, "I choose such books as I should wish to imitate both in speaking and writing. I have had such authors read to me a hundred times, that there might not be a word or an expression which I did not know and could not imitate. Indeed in the three years that I have been in India, I have scarcely read a German or Latin book, but have given up all my time to reading Malabar books, have talked diligently with the heathen, and executed all my business in their tongue, so that now (1709) it is as easy to me as my mother-tongue, and in the last two years I have been enabled to write several books in Tamil."

One cannot but admire Ziegenbalg's zeal and diligence in mastering this foreign language. Two years after his arrival he was able to send Lütkens his Tamil library, which is still to be seen in manuscript at Halle. He describes therein a number of Tamil books which he divides into four classes. The first class contains a description of 14 books which he had himself written in Tamil. The next treats of 21 books, written by Papist authors, that is Roman Catholic Missionaries, who had been a long time before on that coast, and had studied the language. Amongst these he particularly notices one for the fluency he had acquired, whose equal had not since appeared amongst the Papist Missionaries, "for now," says he, "there are very few amongst them who trouble themselves much about the language, or could compose any thing in it." The third class treats of 119 books by Hindûs, mostly on the subject of their religion. The fourth class contains 11 books, written by Mohammedan authors, on their religion. It would have cost Ziegenbalg many hundred dollars to have all these copied out; but the greater number he had bought, for which purpose he used to send his Malabar writer many days' journey into the country. In this way he discovered how books were to be obtained, and found that the widows of Brahmins would sell them for a mere trifle. When Ziegenbalg first began to read Tamil books, he had three persons with him;—the above-named translator, Aleppa, whom he afterwards dispensed with and gave up to his colleagues; a native poet, who enlarged upon the histories which they read, and explained the difficulties in poetry, and finally, a Malabar writer, who was to write down all words and expressions which he had not met with in other books. Thus began Ziegenbalg's Malabar Dictionary, which in the course of two years contained 20,000 words and expressions; one column in Tamil characters, one in Roman type written according to the pronunciation, and a third with the meaning in German.

He not only read historical, theological and philosophical writings, but also medical and philological, in order to find words for his Dictionary. When 4 years later this Lexicon had grown to 40,000 words and expressions, it was arranged according to the Tamil alphabet, so that the derived and compound words might be found near their source. He collected moreover a poetical Dictionary of 17,000 words out of all kinds of poetical writings, under the guidance of experienced Tamil poets. "This Dictionary," says he, "will help me but little when I read and preach the word of God, but it is a key to all poetical books, and as I take great trouble to understand the worship of the heathen from their own books, and wish much to prove their errors therefrom, necessity obliges me to venture so far into the poet's domain. When, as often happens, the poets of the country visit me, or I them, one hears little but verses from their mouth in confirmation of their teaching. It is therefore necessary for me to understand them, so as to be able to oppose them thoroughly". Of the poetical language he says, that there is as much difference between it and that employed in daily life, as between Latin and German. Ziegenbalg considered his Dictionaries as great treasures not so much on account of the great care and trouble that he had spent on them, as in the consideration of the uses to which they might be put, uses, for which he hoped that with God's blessing, they would become invaluable.

But though it was thus necessary for the Missionaries to learn both Tamil and Portuguese, yet they did not so devote themselves to their acquisition as to forget the people who spoke them; neither were they of opinion that a thorough acquaintance with the language must necessarily precede all Missionary work. In November 1706, they began to catechise in Portuguese, and in Tamil in January of the following year. They taught the

Catechumens daily for two hours in the house where they lodged; using the New Testament and a Catechism printed in Portuguese by the Dutch in Batavia. They altered this Catechism, and were very soon able to write or translate the necessary books for themselves. They first translated the five principal heads of Luther's Catechism without explanation, and afterwards completed the whole. They also preached in the German language to Europeans both in their own house, and every Wednesday in Zion Church with the consent of the Commandant and the Danish pastors. By their faithful preaching of the word of God, a great movement arose amongst the Christians as well as amongst the Mohammedans and Pagans. The house of the Missionaries was always filled with listeners, but opposition arose both amongst Christians and Heathens. The Missionaries now divided the work, so that each should take one language; Ziegenbalg took Tamil, and Plütschau Portuguese; yet, as a subordinate occupation, each was to occupy himself with the language of the other. They translated many prayers and hymns into both languages; the hymns partly arranged according to European choral melodies, partly in such Tamil verses, that they might be sung after the native manner. The first baptism took place in May 1707, when five slaves who could speak Portuguese were baptized in Zion Church, after undergoing an examination.

The Missionaries now began to feel the want of some place where they could every week receive those on whom they might confer the rite of Christian baptism. At first they only thought of erecting a small school-house outside the town, but afterwards they thought it better to build a small church, for which the authorities pointed out a place to them in the town amongst the heathen. But the worst was, that they had very small means for building it, and they could not look for help to Denmark or Germany, for a ship which arrived about this time—the first after the arrival of the Missionaries—not only brought them no assistance, but not even an encouraging letter, so that it seemed the time for giving up what they had begun rather than for building churches, and indeed many advised them to do so. But Ziegenbalg was so confident in his cause, that though he might appear abandoned for a time he would not give up either the one or the other. "We began," he writes, "in great poverty, but in firm trust and confidence in God, to build in a great heathen street in the city, and though we did not know how we should bring the work to a conclusion, God so strengthened our faith amidst all obstacles, that we spent upon it all that we could save from our salaries" (the King had granted to each a yearly salary of 200 Rix-dollars) "and whatever we had laid up before. Many mocked us but some were moved to pity and to helping us. Thus this house of assembly was carried on with all speed, 30 persons, who were all heathens, working at it daily. On the 4th of August 1707 (exactly two months after laying the first stone) it was consecrated in both languages, in the presence of a great number of Christians, Mohammedans and Heathens, and the church received the name of "New Jerusalem." They now preached there twice every Sunday on the articles of faith, both in the Tamil and Portuguese tongues. On Fridays and Sundays, and afterwards on Wednesdays also, they catechised on Luther's Catechism, or on subjects in connection with it. The Epistles, Gospels and Collects were also brought into use, and almost at every service there were many heathens present who did not regularly belong to the congregation (which had grown to 35 persons by the end of the year) but stood to listen at the doors and windows. Simultaneously with the beginning of the church, the Danish Ritual was translated into Tamil and Portuguese, so that as soon as the church was finished, they had formularies for the sacraments and ecclesiastical ordinances. On the 5th September the sacrament of Baptism was administered for the first time in New Jerusalem Church, and the Holy Supper was partaken of on the same day. Before the end of the year schools were also erected, one Dano-Portuguese, with a master who understood Danish, German and Portuguese, under Plütschau's superintendence, and the other a Tamil school under Ziegenbalg with a baptised native teacher. In both they gave food, drink, clothes, and books to the children. "Though this, like every thing else," writes Ziegenbalg, "was begun with great want of funds, yet God has never put our faith and confidence in Him to shame; for we have never been obliged to give up any of these institutions, though we were often hard pressed, and many a time knew not in the evening how we should provide for the next day."

At last a ship arrived from Denmark in the middle of the summer of 1708. The Missionaries found that but half the promised 2000 Rix-dollars was on board; the other half with their letters had been put on board another ship, which had been wrecked, and though the money had been saved from it, it had been taken back to Denmark; still the 1000 Dollars would have been of the greatest use to them in their career of wide-spread activity;—but in landing part of the cargo from the ship, the Mission-money sunk to the bottom and was never seen again. At a time when a door seemed opened for the word in all directions, though the messengers were in great necessity and want, it must have been a hard trial to see the expected help from Denmark sink to the bottom of the sea;—but it seems to have caused no vexation to the Commandant and his attachés, who pointed out to Ziegenbalg that they had always been right in saying, that Heaven was very high above our heads and Copenhagen very far off. At the same time a messenger came to the Missionaries from the Roman Catholic Christians in Tanjore, requesting them to assist them, as they were suffering from a great persecution and had now neither churches nor priests, so that many of them wished to come and settle in Tranquebar:—but twice was Ziegenbalg obliged to let such messengers depart, without being able to arrange any thing for them. He was himself persecuted, and was glad to be able to begin the translation of the New Testament by the end of the year 1708, a work, which though it required the whole force of his mind, was begun very quietly and without observation. But he had scarcely reached the 23rd chapter of the Gospel according to St. Matthew, when on the 19th November 1708, he was arrested and passed four months in the Castle Prison.

CHAPTER IV.

ZIEGENBALG IN PRISON.—HELP IN NEED.—ZIEGENBALG IS ATTACKED AS A FALSE APOSTLE IN A GERMAN UNIVERSITY.— THE HISTORY OF GRUENDLER'S YOUTH.

It is not quite clear what excuse the Commandant could have brought forward for placing so quiet, modest and unassuming a man as Ziegenbalg in prison. We must be satisfied with some explanations of Ziegenbalg's in an unprinted Manuscript which are not quite so colourless and indefinite as those that were printed at Halle. "God gave his rich blessing to all that we began in his name," writes he, "and yet we had a determined opposition, not only from the heathen, but also from the European Christians; even the Commandant and the whole Privy Council were quite opposed to us, so that not only did they not assist us in any point, but tried in every way to impede the holy work. Our congregations were increased weekly, and Heathens, Mohammedans and Christians were constrained to acknowledge that such a work was from God, but the authorities here would not acknowledge it to be so, but acted in such a manner from their hatred and envy, that even the heathen were vexed. The more we spoke the truth the more were we persecuted, so that at last it seemed as if they wished to exterminate both us and our congregations."

Ziegenbalg found himself obliged at last to apply directly to the King for protection not only for himself, but also for his congregation, which in the space of two years and a half had increased to 100 persons, beside those who were being prepared for Baptism. Unassuming and modest as he was and well as he had learned patiently to bear mockery and persecution of all kinds, he was not afraid of speaking the truth freely and of defending his rights when he considered it to be his duty, especially when he was called upon by the helpless against the unjust decisions of men in power. Such a case occurred when a poor widow, to whose complicated difficulties the Commandant would not listen, begged Ziegenbalg for his assistance. The Commandant was so angry with him for this, that he broke out into open threats. Ziegenbalg feared the worst, but waited in full confidence in God and his good cause for the issue. He wrote to the Commandant offering to stand by the result of a fair trial, appealed to the King as his highest judge, declared himself quite willing to submit to the appointed authorities, but added an earnest warning. Upon this he was publicly carried off like a criminal by armed men, put in prison, and so closely guarded by soldiers, that no one was allowed to see him or speak to him. Before he left his room, he fell on his knees and prayed aloud with such fervour that it made a great impression even on his guards and their leader. Comforted and courageous he then accompained them, and consecrated his prison with hymns and prayers. It grieved him most to reflect that even if the Mission were not altogether stopped by this tyrannical manner of acting, it must be much injured, that many who were in the act of joining the Evangelical congregation would be frightened away, and that those who had announced themselves as candidates for Baptism, would draw back. "The tyrannical hearts," says Ziegenbalg "raged and roared till they had almost scattered our congregation; but there were many who pitied our situation even to hot tears, and prayed for us without ceasing." The anger and cruelty of the Commandant even went so far as to deny pen, ink, and paper to the innocent prisoner, and still more a writer, by whose help he most heartily desired to continue his translation of the New Testament. He therefore chose a subject from the word of God on which to meditate, namely, the ministry;—and he found great joy and comfort in considering how all the men of God both in the Old and New Testaments had been persecuted for their faithfulness and veracity, and imprisoned and killed as traitors and leaders of sedition. He wished much to write down some of these thoughts, but as that could not be, he sought by prayer and holy meditation to gather strength for the future. "When I had thus spent a month in delightful communion with God," he writes, "I was woken in the night by my guard, and asked whether I should like to have a lead pencil. I looked upon this as an extraordinary direction from God and said that it would be very useful to me, but that I had no paper to write on. Then the person standing near me gave me a black book of white paper, and told me that all the inhabitants of the town, Christians as well as Heathen, felt sincere sympathy with me." He accepted this fulfilment of his wishes as coming from the hand of God and immediately began to write out his meditations on the work of the ministry. The cruelty of man made him but the more anxious to write pure truth, as he found it both in the word of God by the enlightening influence of the Holy Ghost, and in his own experience. He finished this work which is now unprinted in the library at Halle, during seven weeks of his imprisonment. Beside the Preface, Introduction and Biography there are 717 closely written Quarto pages.

Unjustly and cruelly as he was treated, Ziegenbalg showed so little bitterness towards his persecutors that he wished them a happy New Year from his prison without reminding them of his position. The Commandant took this in good part and asked him whether he could serve him in any thing. Ziegenbalg only asked for his Malabar writer to enable him to continue his translation of the New Testament. Meanwhile without his intervention, a third party was arranging an agreement. On this he declared that he must send a true account of all to Copenhagen, as in duty bound by his instructions, but he added in a letter to the Commandant and the Council that he was very far from feeling any personal hatred, and was quite willing to knit together the bonds of peace and unity. He continues, "I declare before the omniscient God, before my most gracious King and the whole of evangelical Christendom, that I am pure and guiltless from the blood of those heathens, who may have been ruined by the withdrawal of my ministry. Ah, consider what you are doing, you are not fighting against me but against God and your King." He concludes thus, "From all this you may see that I harbour no ill feeling against you, but also that I have no fear of you, and that I can write the truth in godly joy in my prison as I used to do in freedom, and I hope that I shall continue in this happy courage so long as I am defending the truth, and not my own person. Meanwhile though you have forbidden me many things which I have requested of you, you have not been able to prevent me from praying for you, neither will you be able to forbid it for the future."

The natural result of so presumptuous a letter from a prisoner was that he remained where he was. He was rejoiced, however, by the news that his friend and colleague Plütschau was working with great courage in the congregation, and keeping every thing up as well as he could. As soon as he had finished his work on the Ministry, he began another on Christianity, which also lies unprinted at Halle. He had not yet finished this when he was informed that his opponents were ready to go to any extremes: then, thought he, I will go to extremes in love; and invited the Commandant and his wife to come to see him in prison, when he showed them so much friendliness and respect, that the Commandant could no longer keep up his ill feeling towards him. The first agreement was that they should talk over the truth with sincerity and without bitterness. This took place, they were reconciled, and separated with friendly words. Not long after Ziegenbalg was publicly released from confinement, and received with great joy by his congregation. He closes his detailed account of these events, which were indeed very disagreeable to himself and his friends, but which brought a blessing on himself and on the Mission, with an exhortation to the reader, and with a prayer in which he thanks God for all the mercy He has shown him, and vows to serve Him truly during the remainder of his life.

After this the Missionaries passed five very anxious months. Their school-children must be fed, their servants must be paid, and they themselves must live, and yet they received no money; even their salary was for some time withheld. Their only resource was to call upon God in prayer. This they did faithfully and the Lord helped them faithfully. A person, from whom they had least expected it, brought them 40 Rix-dollars on the condition that they should repay them as soon as the ship should arrive from Denmark, and some one else lent them 20 dollars on the same conditions. In this way they collected 200 dollars from different quarters, and did not suffer from actual want though it was close to their door;—but on the 20th of July they experienced how the Lord not only gives his people their daily bread, but abundance also, when they are able to bear it. A ship arrived from Denmark bringing them many friendly and comfortable letters, and 3000 Rix-dollars of money and 3 new fellow-labourers, of whom one, *Johann Ernst Gründler*, became one of the most active workers in the Tranquebar Mission and Ziegenbalg's right hand. The troubles which they had undergone, and the great assistance which thus reached them will be best pictured by Ziegenbalg's Preface to his book on Christianity, which was written on the 20th of August 1709.

"My dear Colleague and I were much comforted in our troubles in this heathen land, by learning on the arrival of a ship that there were many people in Europe who rejoiced that the light of the Gospel had risen upon the heathen, that they prayed to God for its blessed progress, and that they had set themselves with much zeal to give us a helping hand by external means towards the conversion of the heathen, for which aim many pious hearts both in Denmark and Germany had collected a rich provision and sent it to the care of us unworthy servants. May God be eternally praised and blessed for such unspeakable mercy, by which he has refreshed and comforted us in our hard trials and persecutions. It had seemed before as if we were forsaken by all men, and as if not a soul in Europe thought of us, for we had been expecting letters for three years and had not received any. But when we found by many letters that many thousand souls had thought of us, and exerted themselves for the progress of the holy Gospel amongst the heathen, and had sent us such a rich provision as a mark of their hearty love, our joy was so exuberant that we could not express it in words. As David says, "Unto the upright there ariseth light in the darkness: from him that is gracious, and full of compassion, and righteous." Things had come to such a pass with us, that it appeared to the eyes of all men as if all that we had undertaken must fall to the ground. For we were so hemmed in on all sides, every exterior means was so cut off from us, that very often we had not a farthing in the house for the support of our Malabar and Portuguese school-children or of ourselves. Instead of any pity being shown towards us, every opportunity for persecuting us was eagerly seized, until at last I was imprisoned for the sake of the truth for four months. The people who ought to have assisted my colleague in working in Tamil, were driven out of the town. Some of our congregation were forbidden under pain of punishment to attend our Church again. All the heathens were frightened away from us, so that though they perceived the injustice, and felt some pity for us, they did not dare to speak to, or hold any familiar communion with us. Even the greater part of the European Christians were forbidden under pain of punishment to come into our houses or churches, or hold any intercourse with us. Thus our congregation was entirely destroyed, and it was a work of time to re-assemble it. The name of God and Evangelical religion were blasphemed amongst Heathens and Christians. In fact—our sufferings and persecutions were so severe, that unless God had stood by us in a supernatural way and supported us by His consolation, we could not long have held out against such troubles. It would not so have cut us to the heart had we been persecuted by Heathens and Mohammedans as witnesses to the truth, but that those who laid their hands on us should have been Lutherans and sworn subjects of our King, who ought to have found pleasure in assisting us zealously in our work, this was very painful and cost us many tears. What then befell me in my zeal for the ministry, I now see to have been a beneficial trial from God, and have experienced, that God has turned it all to my advantage, while my imprisonment in the East Indies has been as a bell ringing far and wide throughout Europe to awaken many thousand souls to compassionate us and our young and growing Christian community. And as God allowed me to prepare two books in my prison without the knowledge of my enemies, namely, on the Ministry which is pleasing to God, and on the Christianity which is pleasing to God, I have thought it right to dedicate the first to all true Teachers and Witnesses of the truth in Denmark and Germany, but particularly to those highly-beloved Fathers who have contributed so much to the promotion of the holy work amongst the heathens: and the second to all true Christians and children of God in Denmark and Germany, but particularly to you, my beloved friends and brethren, who out of your hearty love have contributed so rich a sum towards the planting of the Christian religion amongst the heathen. May the Lord reward you for such love and mercy, may he bless your hearts and fill them with spiritual gifts. May he increase within you his knowledge, his grace, his love, and let you find mercy in the time of your need. Ah! my Brethren and Friends in the Lord; let us be closely bound together in the bonds of love. Do not tire in the further promotion of this work. Think of the overflowing mercy which God has shown to you, that he saved your fathers from a blind heathenism, and brought them to the saving knowledge of Jesus Christ, in which you now stand and enjoy so many of the gracious gifts of God. Think of this and consider what a suitable opportunity is now offered you for proving your gratitude. When you see us so happy in this work, that we are willing to suffer any troubles, yea even to lose our lives for the sake of the heathen, you must acknowledge that the finger of God is with us. Let your faith be active in love, and prove to us by your contributions that you take pleasure in magnifying the name of our God amongst strange nations in distant countries. Be our fellow-workers amongst the heathen, that we may together enjoy the blessings resulting therefrom throughout eternity. Seek with us to fight the good fight of faith, till we overcome all, and gain a crown of life. Your fellow-worker in Jesus Christ with much faith and love

Bartholomäus Ziegenbalg."

We have now seen how much the Missionaries suffered from the opposition of nominal Christians in India, but it will scarcely be believed that at the same time they did not get on much better in Europe. In the year 1708 when they were in the greatest trouble and Ziegenbalg in prison, there was a public disputation at Wittenberg *de Pseudo-Apostolis* under the presidency of Dr. Neumann, of which we will give an extract, so that the reader may compare what was said there of our Tranquebar Missionaries with the true state of affairs with which he has already been made acquainted.

"That the office of the Apostles ceased with the Apostles is well known; but *false Apostles* have not disappeared; on the contrary in our times they have broken into the Church in crowds. Almost all are of opinion that new Apostles are to be sent out before the last days, who are to make known the Gospel to the world, or more properly speaking shall trumpet forth their fictitious blessed kingdom. It was they who, not long ago, went through Belgium, England, France and Italy. Some have gone to Pensylvania, Russia, some to Constantinople, some to Smyrna and some to Corinth; but everywhere they are far remved from the footsteps of the Apostles, as they use their religion as a means of gain. Lately a pair of Brothers has sailed off to Malabar, whether from their own impulse, or as they aver, by the order of His Majesty the King of Denmark, I cannot say. But as they had opposed themselves to the Copenhagen theologians before their departure, and as they declared that they would not unite with the servants of the word, who had already assembled a church in Tranquebar, one cannot hope that they are inclined to spread the Church of Christ. On the contrary, one cannot but fear that they will rend and destroy the church which is already planted there amongst the heathen. Let any one look at the writings of these Missionaries which have lately been made public."

When the news of this disputation arrived in Copenhagen, it was very easy for Dr. Lütkens to overthrow these false and groundless accusations; but the Missionaries have only received their complete acquittal from posterity which has been in a position to see and judge their work.

Thus the enemies of the Mission were indeed at work, but its friends were no less active, and as we have remarked before, sent out most important help in the summer of 1709, one of the new brethren becoming a great blessing to it. *Johann Ernst Gründler*, who was six years older than Ziegenbalg was born at Weissensee in Thuringia, where his father was a *carder*. He was first sent to the school in his native town, then to Quedlinburg, and finally to the then celebrated Gymnasium at Weissenfels. At his earnest request his father allowed him to pursue academical studies. He then went to the university of Leipzig, then to Wittenberg, where he took the degree of Master of Arts, and at last in 1701 to Halle. Here he was much struck by a sermon on true and false humility, and felt that in spite of all outward appearance he had never been truly humble but full of vanity and pride. He wrote on this subject to the preacher whose sermon had made so deep an impression on his mind, "It is the great mercy of God, which I have never prized sufficiently before, not only to have brought me to this place but to have led me to true repentance and a thorough change of my thoroughly corrupted heart. From the deceptions of Satan it had flattered itself that it was an altar whereon an acceptable sacrifice might be offered to the living God, but the words of truth which proceeded from your blessed heart and eloquent mouth have most fully persuaded me that the Christianity in which I had lived for, alas! twenty-four years, was nothing more than a decent Paganism. Ah! how clearly I felt that till then I had been like a stream, the surface of which shines indeed like silver, but in the bottom of which toads and serpents breed. My only anxiety is to be united to God in the communion of the Holy Ghost through Christ, and the right way and means have now been pointed out to me. I have experienced the mercy of the Lord;—He has destroyed the old brood of sin and driven out the unclean beasts, I mean my ruling lusts and evil desires, and he has raised up a holy temple in my soul, and thus, founded on Christ the corner-stone, he has made of me a living stone fit for the Temple of God."

Gründler now became a teacher in the Pedagogium at Halle, and worked with zeal and diligence for the improvement both of himself and others, and the blessing on his work which he perceived, encouraged him so much, that he longed to become useful to a greater number. It then occurred to him to go to the East Indies; he talked it over with his relations, and assured them that his desire to take a share in the conversion of the heathen was so great, that he would willingly go at his own expense, if no other means could be found. A short time after he mentioned the affair to his superiors, and begged them to think of him if any one should be required for Missionary work in the East Indies. This was promised, and a year after when a letter arrived from Denmark asking for a Missionary, Gründler was recommended. A student, *Polycarpus Jordan*, followed him at his own expense, to be an unordained assistant to the Mission. In Copenhagen Gründler preached before King Frederick IV. taking for his text verses 1 to 6 of the 4th Chapter of St. Paul's Epistle to the Ephesians, and was ordained by the Bishop of Zealand, Dr. Bornemann, together with *Johann Georg Bövingh*, on the 31st October 1708. In the following month the three set sail, and arrived in Tranquebar in the summer of 1709.

We will let Gründler himself describe his arrival in a letter to his relations. "Many thousand miles from my Fatherland and from you, my dear friends," he writes, "my heart would be heavy, indeed almost unbearable, at the thought of living in a country and amongst a people whom I did not know before, were it not that in this my occupation amongst the heathen, God so fills me with his fatherly comfort and inward joy, that I can say with truth that I have a great desire to live in this country, and as an unworthy servant of God to make known the Gospel to the Heathen for their salvation and happiness, notwithstanding the many troubles, great opposition and bodily discomforts with which we meet. But oh! may a faithful God lead everything to conduce to his own glory; without his holy call and will it would be grievous to me to live here for one day; but with these, I am determined by his grace not merely to spend many years here, but to finish my poor, yet in God happy pilgrimage in this heathen country. For we see a great harvest before us, and the Lord of the harvest has shown us so much favour, that we ought not to be frightened or fatigued by any opposition, but should work on with comfort, endeavouring to prove ourselves faithful, as our Lord expects of us. Whether he has ordered that I should remain for a long or for a short time as a poor instrument for his service amongst the heathen, may his grace make me ever more fit for it, and may all go forward according to his holy will and counsel. On the 20th of July, about noon, we were joyful and thankful to reach the end of our voyage and anchor in Tranquebar. A boat soon came off to the ship. I was not able to land till the following day, and as I was on my way to the Missionaries' house, I met them coming to fetch me. We fell on each other's necks with great joy, and they took me into their dwelling. At the door stood many of their congregation, both great and small, of whom they said to me, "Here you see our plants from amongst the Heathen". They all made an oriental salutation; when I wished to say something to them, I was so deeply moved, that I could not restrain my tears, but was obliged to seek for a place where I could weep; partly at the thought of the troubles which these poor black sheep and lambs had undergone;—but partly with joy at the sight of them. Our first occupation was to fall on our knees together, and praise God: then we partook of dinner. The children, who are supported on what God sends from time to time to these two men, amounted then to 13 in the Malabar school and 5 in the Portuguese. Thus I saw a Malabar meal for the first time. The children sat on the ground with their feet crossed under them; (the old people sit in the same way.) Each one had an earthen bowl before him, filled with rice boiled in water, and on it lay a small baked fish. This was their first and last course, and is the daily noon and evening meal amongst the Malabarians. Instead of a knife or spoon, they made skilful use of their two first fingers, according to the custom of their country. Their bed takes but little preparation. They lie on a mat on the ground; and require neither coverlet nor pillow. The same piece of linen with which boys and men cover the lower parts of the body by day (the upper part of the body and legs are quite bare) serves them for a covering by night. The women and girls have also a piece of linen hanging down from the head which covers the upper part of the body, leaving only the face exposed. The dress of these women resembles that in which Mary is usually painted beneath the cross of Christ, and these Malabarians do not change their fashions as we do."

Gründler fell very seriously ill soon after his arrival, but happily recovered. At first he applied himself to Portuguese as the superintendence of the Portuguese school was confided to him; but the Tamil language and intercourse with the Hindûs soon became his principal occupation. When help arrived from Europe, the elder Missionaries gave account of their housekeeping. The debts were paid, and 1000 Rix-dollars were spent in the purchase of a suitable dwelling for the four Missionaries with their servants and scholars; as hitherto they had been obliged to hire a house. The new dwelling was consecrated with prayer and hymns.

CHAPTER V.

ZIEGENBALG'S JOURNIES, CORRESPONDENCE AND CONVERSATIONS WITH THE NATIVES.—CATECHUMENS.

It is a noticeable fact that in Ziegenbalg's first activity in the East Indies, he did not remain stationary in one place, but often undertook journies into the country in order to become acquainted with the natives, and to seize on any opportunity for making the Gospel known. His journies were not confined to the Danish domain, but embraced a wide range. In 1708 he went to Negapatam, and afterwards extended his journey to Madras: but before entering on a description of this long journey, it may be well here to describe one of the shorter ones which he undertook soon after the arrival of the new Missionaries. It is remarkable both on account of the lively description which he himself gives of it, and because a way was thus opened for the Mission into the kingdom of Tanjore.

On the 2nd of September 1709 Ziegenbalg started from Tranquebar, intending to penetrate into the domains of the King of Tanjore wherever it was possible. When he informed his servants after they had started, whither their journey tended, they were quite startled and assured him that he was running into great danger. He answered, "If God is with us, no one can hurt us. If my undertaking is impossible, or if the time has not yet come for making known the Gospel in this country,

God will declare his will to us. Meanwhile, if any one of you has a timid heart, let him return." Not one of his people would consent to this. They journeyed on till they came to a village where he exchanged his black clothes for white, put a white turban on his head, a red-striped piece of linen over his shoulders, and red slippers on his feet. He required of his people that they should always speak the truth on their journey; for example, if any one asked them, whence they came, they were to say, From Tranquebar; Where are you going? To any place to which we can penetrate; Who is your master? A teacher from Tranquebar; What have you come for? To seek out people who wish to hear the truth and to have the word of God made known to them. This rule was scrupulously followed. As the whole country was under water, they were obliged to travel along the banks. They met many heathens who passed them without speaking to them. A Mohammedan who met him cried out to Ziegenbalg, "Pattani, Pattani!" "I am not a Pattani" (that is, white Mohammedan) answered he and went on. They travelled from six o' clock in the morning till about noon without touching any villages in order that they might not be at once known;—but as the people were growing tired and hungry, they turned towards the little town of Perumalei, where they met a number of Hindûs, Brahmins, taxgatherers, writers, and overseers of the revenue of the province, making in all a large and important assembly. Ziegenbalg would willingly have passed on, but that they might not think he was afraid, he went up to them courageously and asked what they were doing. "We are writing down the accounts of the province," said they, and then asked whence he came, where he was going, who he was, and what he wanted. He answered that he came from Tranquebar, that he was going to the next town and thence further into Tanjore, that he was a Priest and sought those people who wished to be instructed in the word of God. "Oh," said the people, "you must certainly be that young Priest from Tranquebar who can preach in Tamil." Yes, said Ziegenbalg, I am he, do you know me? Yes, answered the head-Brahmin, I talked to you for a long time at Anandamangalam; and I, said the overseer, was in Tranquebar 14 days ago, and heard you preach. I am very glad to hear it, answered Ziegenbalg. But, said the others, we are much surprised that you venture so far into the country; such a journey may bring you into great danger, and we advise you, as good friends, to return, else some misfortune may befall you even this very day. Ziegenbalg answered, God, in whose name I have set forth, and whose Gospel I try to make known, will be able to protect me. We do not doubt that, said the people, and we know that you preach true and holy things; but the world is wicked, and no one cares for truth. Neither justice nor oaths are of any consequence amongst the Hindûs, so that they would not scruple to do you harm. Yet they would scruple to kill a fly, said Ziegenbalg, and why should they wish to kill me, who will show them the way to eternal happiness. They will not kill you, answered the people, we can assure you of that, but they will certainly take you prisoner at the first place where you stop. We are servants of the King of Tanjore, and must not let any white man enter his dominions unless he has a pass from the King or from those next in power to him. As you have no pass, we ought to detain you ourselves till we have sent a messenger to the King, but we will not do that, because we know your good intentions. We let you pass, but we advise you to return. Ziegenbalg thanked them, but asked them at the same time why so much fuss was made about him. The report has been spread throughout the country, said the people, that you are making Christians in Tranquebar, and writing Tamil books on your doctrine:— moreover they say that this year you have received tuns of gold from Europe; so that when the Hindûs see you, they will say, "Ha ha, this is the man who rejects our religion in Tranquebar, and wishes to make every one Christians, and who receives so much money. At all events he must have some thousand dollars about him. We will keep him prisoner till we have got all his ready money from him, and then we will send him on to the King of Tanjore who will keep him prisoner till he pays a high ransom." We therefore advise you to return, for the report that you are here will soon spread. But, said Ziegenbalg, how can they know so immediately that I have left Tranquebar. If a cow, answered they, strays from Tranquebar into our country, no one pays any attention to it, because such cows are to be seen everywhere in crowds; but if an elephant were to stray, all would hasten to look at such a wonder, because elephants are novelties in our country. So if a plain man, one of our equals, comes here from Tranquebar, no one asks, Where do you come from? and, Whither do you go? because he is like us and belongs to our people. But when you come, it is like an elephant, because you are a white priest, and always talk about religion: therefore you cannot remain hidden. Then Ziegenbalg said: "As God has raised up such a commotion amongst you heathen on account of the Gospel being made known, it ought to be a pleasure to you to talk with me, and to be able to ask all particulars of the truth which leads to salvation." Wise and inquisitive people, said they, would consider it a pleasure to talk to you every day, but there are few such in thi country, and they cannot save you from the hands of those who love money. Ziegenbalg then inquired in what manner he should obtain a pass from the King, and was advised first to ask permission to build a house in his territories, as when he had been there for some time with his scholars, he would then be considered as an inhabitant and as the King's subject, and would be free to travel wherever he liked. He thanked them for their advice, and especially for the sake of his congregation, determined not to expose himself to the danger of the journey. He was hospitably treated, returned by another road and arrived the same evening in Tranquebar, where his colleagues were much surprised by his hasty return, but rejoiced in the news which he brought them.

Another means by which Ziegenbalg brought himself into contact with the Natives, was by entering into correspondence with them. Wherever learned and experienced men were living, he sent letters and laid such questions before them as he thought each one could best answer. Answers were not wanting. In 3 months he received 55 letters, which he put together and dedicated to the Crown-Prince Christian (afterwards Christian VI.) and he afterwards sent another collection of 44 letters. We will give extracts from some of these letters as samples, not selecting those which treat of the political or social life of the Natives, but of religion. Some defend their Heathenism, others are shaking in it, and others again are evidently in the act of giving themselves up to the truth.

"All that you write and say proves that you despise religion and worship; for you declare that all that is written in our holy books is false and deceitful, and that we in reading such books are confused and led away from God, indeed that every thing that is written in them is contrary to the holiness of God, and to the reason of man. The adventures which have happened to our gods in various parts of this earth and in other worlds you hold to be poetical fables, and say that they are altogether a deception of the devil. The very gods which we worship and from whom we expect salvation, you consider as devils, and say that under their forms we are only worshipping devils. It seems absurd to you when we say that there are 14 worlds, 330 millions of gods, 48,000 prophets and many musicians:—moreover that we attribute bodily forms, wives, children, playthings and the like to our gods, seems to you pure folly. Our sacrifices, our feasts, our whole Pagoda-worship seem sinful to you. You consider it sinful folly when we adorn ourselves with strings of pearls" (the Rosaries of the Heathen which they use when they pray, and with the use of which much superstition is bound up) "when we smear ourselves with ashes and cow-dung, that we honour cows so highly, reverence the sun, think much of unlucky days, and carry on fortune-telling: moreover our pilgrimages to holy places you consider as nonsense only fit for fools. You blame our carefulness in purification, our reading many prayers for the forgiveness of sins and the obtaining of salvation, you even blame our manifold penitences, our caste-regulations, our manner of eating, our fasts, our manner of living, even our good works, and our alms, for you declare that we are all Heathens,* standing under a curse, that our hearts are not converted, that we are unpleasing to God with all our good works, and that we can never be saved in spite of all our worship, because the ways in which we walk are not God's ways but those which we have chosen for ourselves."

"Now it is very true that much amongst us is to be blamed. All sorts of sin and injustice have full sway over us, which ought not to be; but at the same time you need not despise every-

*The Malabarians do not like to be called Heathens (Anyani, i. e. Unwise.)

thing. If we were heathens and our religion were quite false, you would find neither virtue nor good works amongst us;—but now you meet with many virtues and people active in good works; yea even some who live so holy a life that no sin can be imputed to them. Is it possible then that a law which disclaims all sin, and leads to good, can be a false law? Every nation has its own fashions, manners and laws which appear absurd to other nations. It is the same with religions. God is manifold in all his creations and in all his works, and therefore he will be worshipped in different ways. Our law and our religion are good in themselves, and it is our own fault that they are thus blamed, partly because we do not live up to them, and partly because we have not such a knowledge of them as to refute all objections by true arguments and to be able to defend our precepts circumstantially."

"Moreover we find much to blame in the Christians who have come from Europe into this country, and if religion is to be judged by its fruits, we cannot think very well of your religion when we see how little justice and modesty there is amongst Christians. They perform very few good works, give very few alms, have no penitences, willingly accept presents, drink strong drinks, illtreat animals and use them for food, care very little about bodily cleanliness, look down upon all others as inferiors and are very avaricious, proud and passionate. Indeed our Brahmins say that the white people are descended from the giants, that they do not know the difference between good and evil, but sin continuously. Any one who has read and understood their law, think good of their religion, though it seems to be not very reasonable that they believe in a God who was tortured and put to death by his own people. But who are we that we should write about such things. However long we may dispute about religion, we may all finally say:—we are all God's creatures, and have a like entrance into and exit from this world. In so far as God shows mercy towards us we are blessed; as he rules us and reigns over us, we must live under him and can neither add to nor take away from any thing which he has ordained concerning us."

The author of this letter was very far from Christianity, we will now give another whose writer was a little nearer. "You wish to know the reasons why the Hindûs delay joining the Christian religion, but particularly why we, who have read your religious books and know your precepts, do not unite ourselves to your Church. Now we have seen what dogmas are contained in your law and we cannot say but that they are good and agree with the truth: but the reasons why we do not join your Church are these. We have a great many good friends, who would be much displeased by it; if we did it alone, we should be persecuted to death, and not find security nor protection anywhere. It is very difficult for us to give up doing what our fathers and grandfathers have done, for all like to honour their ancestors, and to go along the same road which all their people have gone and are still going. Moreover we must seek our livelihood in the country where we live: we are married, we have wives and children who would cause us great difficulty. We are sunk too deep in the vanities of this world, and look more at the present than at the future, and we believe moreover that God will bless us if we direct our lives according to what we acknowledge as truth in your law, even if we do not give the external sign of joining your Church. You know moreover that we place little confidence in the outward forms of our religion. In short, the fear of man has withheld us till now, and does so still, for one likes to remain with those people amongst whom he is born, be they good or evil."

"Others delay from the following causes. They do not properly understand the excellence of your law and your religion, but see and hear only something here and there. They know that there are sects amongst Christians and can see how the one persecutes the other. The differences of caste are not observed amongst Christians, they do not wash when they sit to meals, they do not attend to cleanliness and modesty, they make no difference amongst meats, but even eat great living animals which are larger than a man and cry out when their life is taken from them, they drink strong drinks. These are the principal reasons which prevent the Hindûs from joining the Christians. The judgments which they pass on your religion are various. Some say: this religion is well ordered;—the law is open to all and contains truth; their whole law points to the one true God, to whom they keep firm; no other religion has such good institutions as this; their churches, schools and houses are much better arranged than ours. Others say on the contrary: the Christians have a holy law, but their life is quite different from their law, and they have no advantage over us. Finally there are some who jest and say; these Christians are complete Heathens, are not afraid of the greatest sins; there is nothing good either in them or their law. That this is all true you will find from other quarters. May God give us all a better understanding that we may acknowledge our faults and live so as you live and teach every one to live."

Now follows the letter of one who seems to be very near to the kingdom of God: "I send my greeting to the Priests in Tranquebar, who by their holy teaching try to drive out Heathenism and to set up truth and wisdom, and I write them this letter as they ask me to inform them in what I believe and how

I hope to be saved. My belief is this:—I have firmly laid hold on the truth that there is but one God and Lord, who has created the world and all the living creatures that are therein. When I see wise and holy Priests, I honour them as much as possible, listen to their teachings and warnings, and pay great attention to them in my heart. All other things, as Pagodas, Idols, Sacrifices, Feasts, Ceremonies and which are considered as belonging to religion, I consider as some thing which may be performed according to the fancy and fashion of the world, without being of importance in themselves. My whole religious service consists in this:—morning and evening I consider that there is a God who has created me, I ponder this truth in my heart and say, "Lord! all that I do is sinful!" I meditate on this truth with grief, and at last I cry out, "Lord! remit and forgive our sins!" Then I consider what learned people say and do, and consider which is good and evil. The idolatrous fashion of one worshipping one god and one worshipping another and the various ceremonies which are carried on in the Pagodas are fancy and confusion, to which men are attached, because they make an appearance in the eyes of the world. Moreover I am quite convinced that our learned men are not right in saying that every thing must go on as it has done in the time of our fathers. This is a vain fancy of the world; I consider that what you write and speak and teach on the remission of sins and the practice of good is the truth. The best learning amongst us is dark and incomprehensible; no one except the Brahmins knows what is in the books of our law. How can we receive salvation from a law which we neither know nor understand? I hold firmly to the belief that one God has created every thing, and say continually, "Lord! forgive me my sins, those which I know and those which I do not know!" Then I reflect upon what it may be his will for me to do. It is your books which have helped me to do this, without them I should have been like a beast. I do not know what God will do with me further. I often say to myself, "you do not deserve to be saved, for you think, do, speak, see and hear unnumbered sins every day." Then the thought occurs to me "How is it possible that you should be saved with so many sins." For you Missionaries indeed, this may not seem so difficult, for you have given up all, excepting such things as lead to salvation. It is possible that by your prayers I may become fit for salvation. This is all that I have to tell you."

Finally we may add a letter from one who wished to join the Missionaries. "I fall at the feet of the teachers of truth, the Tranquebar Priests who are ready to help every one, and I bring my entreaties in all humility before them. As I have learned that you are endowed with wisdom, learning and holiness, and live according to the commands of your God, daily fighting the three enemies, the world, sin and the flesh, trying to spread the truth of your law in all parts, willing to suffer for the cause of truth, never tiring of doing good to all and kind services to every one, so I do not doubt, but firmly believe that in a future world you shall receive the reward, the crown and the sceptre from the throne of God. But as when a beautiful flower is picked, the stalk, and even the thorns on its stalk are picked with it, and become participators of its happiness, so I, a useless stalk and thorn, hope to be raised to that world with such sweet-smelling flowers as yourselves; and I pray that Jesus Christ will help me to see your faces daily, to serve you and ever to hear the law which God has given. That is my wish and my humble request."

We have another witness of the manner in which Ziegenbalg conducted his intercourse with the Heathens and Mohammedans and made Christ known to them, in the conversations which he had with them and which he afterwards wrote down. There are three collections of such conversations, one containing 16, another 18, and a third 20. Of these I will give two from the first collection, one with a Hindû, only in abstract, the other with a Mohammedan, at full.

"On the 6th of March 1707 a Brahmin who was considered very wise and learned came to me, Ziegenbalg. I asked him with what intentions he came, on which he answered, "I have come to have a good talk with you." I then asked him to choose whether I should ask him questions, or he me, and as he chose the former I asked him whether he acknowledged One divine Being, to which he answered, "yes."

Ziegenbalg. "How is that possible, when you Malabarians worship so many gods?"

Brahmin. "We believe in one divine Being, in whom everything has its origin; but we say also that from him have sprung three great gods, Brahma, Vishnu and Siva, and from these again have sprung many others, of whom we read in the books of our law. As these three great, as well as all the smaller gods, have all sprung from the Being above all beings, and are his deputies over all animate and inanimate things, in them we honour the Being above all beings, the highest God, who takes this worship as if it were offered to himself."

Z. "God has given a good understanding to you Malabarians, so that you can talk very sensibly of natural things, and yet you are so blind and unwise when you come to spiritual things that without thought you stiffly and firmly believe what your poets fabricated long ago, and which has come down to you in pretty verses. For is it not a very foolish opinion that the Being of all beings should have multiplied himself into many gods? This error originates in your not possessing or understanding the revealed word of the Eternal God; for as your fathers would not follow the truth unto salvation, God gave them up unto a righteous judgement that they should believe a lie; and because you believe such lies up to this day you talk so corruptly of God and prove thereby that you do not truly honour any God."

B. "Our religion is the oldest of all religions. Many pious kings have reigned over us, and we have had many holy prophets and learned men. These have all believed what we now believe. If our religion were false, would there not have been one amongst them who would have discovered it, and taught us a better way? Would God have allowed our religion to spread so far and to stand for so long, had it been false?"

Z. "The truth of a religion does not depend on its antiquity or on the number of its adherents. The devil and sin are both old, and govern a large part of the world: but it would be wrong therefore to say that the devil is pious and that sin is pleasing to God." He then goes on to prove that the truth or falsehood of a religion must be tested by the word of God. "As the heathen have not the word of God, they cannot test their religion by it; still if they would use their reason, they would see the incongruity of many things in which they believe. This has happened to many heathens, who have cast away their Polytheism, and seen that the tales of the gods which are related in their sacred books, are lies. Yet as the greater number withstand the truth, God allows them to be ruined in their blindness; but he has no pleasure in false religions, and is not the cause of the condemnation of the heathen. He has sought your fathers, and he seeks you now, but he compels no one."

B. "God has created both the good and the evil; he is the author of virtue and vice, as well as of salvation and destruction;

without him nothing can take place in the world. If some are good, pious and holy, they are so according to the will of God: and again if some are wicked, sinful and unholy, they are sinners according to the will of God. If we are mistaken in our religion and our worship, it happens with the consent of God. What can we do? What is to happen to us on this earth, and how God has willed that we are to live and conduct ourselves, is all written on our heads. How can we alter what God has determined?"

Z. "It is true that God has created all, but all good and holy, instead of wicked and sinful. You blaspheme God when you say that he is the origin of all the sin and evil in the world. If men only do good and evil according to the will of God, of what use are you Brahmins? Wherefore has God ordained teachers in the world to instruct disobedient men? Wherefore has he revealed his word to the world? Wherefore has he instituted kings and magistrates, who are to punish the evil, and reward the good? If God had willed us to sin, this would all be useless; and it would be wrong to punish sinners, if God had formed them for sinning and was pleased with their sins. Many incongruities would follow from this, as: that God himself was a sinner and that evil not being displeasing to him, he could not be that righteous Judge who rewards virtue and punishes vice. This opinion opens the way to all sin, and keeps you back from conversion; but it arises from your not having a right knowledge of the creation of man."

B. "We say that Brahma in the beginning created men, that some became devils, who have increased in infinity, and that others remained men, and that from them have sprung all the men who are now on the earth."

Ziegenbalg now showed him that not Brahma, but the one

true God was the creator of everything, and instructed him in the creation of man, the fall as a consequence of the temptations of the devil, and of the evil use made by our first parents of their free-will. The fault was not God's any more than it would be the king's fault if his palace on which he had expended great care and money were burned down. The devil and man alone were guilty, but "if you will listen with attention, I will show you how you can be saved from the consequences of the fall."

B. "We are both men, and live upon one earth. One God has created us. How then should we not listen willingly to one another? each remains free to believe what he likes?"

Ziegenbalg then made Christ known to him, spoke with him on the extension of the kingdom of Christ, showed him that it had been announced to them before, and that it had now come to him, and exhorted him to be obedient to the voice of God and to believe in his only begotten.

B. "God has made himself known in your country and amongst you white Christians in a different way from what he has done here amongst us black Malabarians. You believe in what he has declared to you and we believe in what he has declared to us. With you in Europe Christ became a man, here in India Vishnu became a man. You expect to be saved through Christ, we through Vishnu. It is God's pleasure to reveal himself in different ways in different countries."

Z. "Vishnu's many changes of which you talk and write so much are so absurd and incongruous that instead of considering them as pleasing to the holy God, they rather appear as a delusion of the devil. You even say that he came upon earth as a pig, as a fish, as a turtle and half as a lion and half as a man. How can you believe that such a monster can be your saviour and sanctifier? And who was able to speak to this animal to know that it was God who was thus transformed? Did Vishnu come in these forms to save pigs, fish and turtles? If he had wished to save men, he would certainly have come as a man, that he might be able to talk with men. Truly you say that he also came as a man upon earth under various names; but in these histories I only find that he deceived others by his cunning, and by his wars and cruel blood-sheddings brought ruin rather than salvation into the world. Truly I wonder that you Brahmins can believe such things and teach them to others as being holy."

B. "Every man can be saved by his own religion if he does that which is good and avoids that which is evil."

Ziegenbalg remarked that it was only through Christ that this could be done and pointed to faith and baptism for those who wished to do right.

B. "I do not find fault with anything you have said, yet I think that when one believes in God and leads a quiet virtuous and holy life, it is unnecessary to believe in Christ and to be baptized."

Z. "I have represented the necessity of this faith to you by my words; but I cannot give you that faith in Christ. Go and humble yourself before the God of heaven and earth, and pray to him to enlighten you by the word you have now heard, and then you will acknowledge how necessary it is for a sinner to believe in Christ, and to recognize him as his Saviour."

The Brahmin thanked him and departed.

"On the 5th of July 1707, a Mohammedan priest with several of his followers came to see me. He was an overseer over several other priests, and living in the interior had heard that we were introducing a new religion into India. As he had never spoken with an European priest, he wished to communicate with us and hear what we were teaching. Almost as soon as we began to speak, he said "I am very much surprised that you have learned Tamil so quickly, as it is generally a very difficult language to Europeans."

Z. "You Moors and Malabarians should take that as a sign that God will cause something extraordinary to happen amongst you at this time. You may guess therefrom how great is my love towards you that it has led me to such diligence in learning the language."

He now asked me to show him the Holy Scriptures, and I showed him the Old Testament in Hebrew, and the New Testament in Greek. He asked me to read something out of the Old Testament, on which I read to him the 3rd Chapter of the 1st book of Moses; but as he did not understand Hebrew, he asked me to explain it in Tamil. I then began to go through the Chapter verse by verse, and explained to him the creation, the fall and the renewal of man. This pleased him very much, he said that much of it agreed with their teaching, and asked me to read and explain something from the New Testament. I then read to him the 3rd Chapter of the Gospel according to St. John and gave a short explanation of each verse. They all listened with great attention and said often "that agrees with our religion, only that we apply to Mohammed what you say of Christ."

Z. "The cause that so much of the Old and New Testaments agrees with your religion is that Mohammed had a Jew and a Christian with him who helped him to form his precepts. The Jew gave him the histories out of the Old Testament, the Christian the histories and ideas of the New Testament, but both debased and corrupted. What your religion contains of good and true, is taken from our Holy Scriptures; but what is false and wicked originates in Mohammed."

M. "How can you judge of Mohammed in that way when you have no correct history of him?"

Z. "We Christians have far more reliable accounts of the life and person of Mohammed than you have: for when the Moors wished to make all men accept their religion by force, many Christians escaped from their hands, who have left to us unprejudiced accounts of his person, his scandalous life, and unjust manner of spreading his religion. The accounts of him on the contrary, which you have, are written by people who carefully concealed his vices and invented false miracles for him, either because they were in his power, or that, as adherents to his religion, they chose to adorn it by writing a good account of him. These histories are not unknown to us in Europe; some are printed, others exist in manuscript, and they are read and understood by many learned men who know your language; indeed we have your Koran in Arabic, Latin, French, German, and Dutch, which enables us to pass a correct judgment on it. The reason that you Moors are so attached to the untruths of your Mohammed is that you have never beheld the truth of our Christian religion; for a man who has never seen or heard of any bird but a black raven, thinks that it sings beautifully and that it is the best of birds; but let him hear the lovely song of a nightingale, and he becomes aware that the cry of a raven is disagreeable to the ears and has nothing pleasant in it. So, as long as you Mohammedans have only heard Mohammed's writings, you may think that no religion can be better than yours, but if you would take the trouble of examining into the truth of our religion, you would change your ideas entirely."

M. "You Christians believe in three Gods, we believe in one. Now who shoots most wide of the mark?"

Z. "We do not distinguish three Gods, but three persons in one divine Being, namely, Father, Son, and Holy Spirit, so that it may be truly said of each person that he is very God and yet there are not three Gods but one God."

M. "How can you prove this?"

Z. "I will give you a simile. We see but one sun in heaven, and yet we are aware of three things in it;—there is the body of the sun, the lustre which it throws out, and the warmth from the lustre. These three things are so connected that we could not have the warmth without the light, nor the light if there were no body of the sun there. Now though these three things are produced by the sun, no one would say that the sun is threefold; but all would agree that there is but one sun. So the Divine Being is but one, yet it consists of three persons, who are so united, that any one who despises the Holy Ghost, cannot acknowledge the Son, and whoever does not believe in and acknowledge the Son, cannot believe in or acknowledge the Father. Therefore though you profess to believe in one God, the Creator of heaven and earth, you cannot be saved unless you also believe in his Son Jesus Christ, the Saviour of the world; for without Christ is no salvation either for time or eternity; but you cannot believe in Jesus Christ, if you will not allow yourselves to be enlightened by the Holy Ghost. I could explain the mystery of the Trinity to you at great length, both by reasons from the Scriptures, and by similes from nature, but for this time I will content myself with giving you some advice:—go and reflect upon your sinful life, let it bring you to true penitence, begin to doubt your security, and think of the justice of God who will only accept of holy souls for eternal salvation. Then you will acknowledge how necessary a Saviour is to you. Go further; consider the teaching, life, sufferings and merits of Christ; oppose to this the teaching and life of Mohammed from your Koran, and pray heartily to God that he will teach you to know which of these two has saved the human race, and through whose merits you can receive forgiveness of sins and justification; if you do this with sincerity, God will certainly teach you that not Mohammed, but Christ alone is your Redeemer and Sanctifier. When you have reached this point, the Holy Ghost will give you light and understanding to comprehend the other mysteries of God; for before a man has really repented and experienced a change of heart, he may hear much of divine things without being able to understand them."

M. "We have a great deal about Christ in our law, and call him Isa Rabi, the Prophet Isa, and always speak well of him; but we cannot consider him as the actual Son of God, nor respect him more than Mohammed, for it seems to us very incongruous that God should actually have a Son."

Z. "It appears so to you because you try to measure these divine mysteries by your reason, and do not understand the truth of God's word, and have not that care for your souls which would lead you to think "What path shall we take to free ourselves from the misery of sin, and to attain true justification and sanctification." But if you think that what we believe of Christ is strange, how can you believe such much stranger things of Mohammed? You say that Mohammed is next to God and his best friend; and yet you must acknowledge that he was given up to polygamy and fleshly lusts, that he carried on war against many nations, and that whoever would not receive his religion was put to death in the most merciless manner.

How does that agree with the holiness and justice of God. Would God have chosen such an one for his most intimate friend, and for the salvation of all men, one who was full of unclean lusts, who allowed a plurality of wives, and shed so much innocent blood?"

M. "We know well that he had many wives, but we cannot blame that, for the pious kings David and Solomon had many wives, and they are considered to be men of God in your law as well as ours. As for Mohammed's wars he had a command from God to cleanse the world of all those who would not accept his religion."

Z. "It is true that we read that both Solomon and David had many wives, but this was not by God's command, but of their own wills and the customs which had crept in amongst the Jews. As you agree that Christ was a great Prophet, you ought in justice to reflect on what he said to the Jews in the days of his flesh (Matth. 19. 4.) "Have ye not read that he which made them at the beginning made them male and female, and said, for this cause shall a man leave father and mother and shall cleave to his wife; and they twain shall be one flesh?" As for what you say of Mohammed's wars being undertaken by God's command, it is quite contrary to the justice and love of God; for God will that all men should be saved and brought to a knowledge of the truth, yet he forces none, and leaves all to the exercise of their own free will, whether they will accept it to their salvation or reject it to their condemnation; it is enough that God has thus offered them his grace, which they may accept if they will and be saved. Now as Mohammed used force to bring men to his views we may suppose that his was a false religion, because it is not one of the properties of truth to constrain men to accept it."

M. "What can I say against it? There is certainly something in our law, against which I have doubts myself, yet we will talk of this another time; we have said enough for this time."

Z. "If you only meditate over this little, and are really anxious about the things which belong to your salvation, it will do you much good. May the Lord Jesus give you wisdom and a new heart, both to know him rightly and to believe firmly in him so that you may participate in his merits to your salvation both for time and eternity." Thereupon I said adieu to him and begged him to keep up a correspondence with me.

Let us now hear Ziegenbalg's account of what he had learned in his conversations with the heathen; — he says "Though they are in great error and thick darkness both with regard to their lives and teaching, yet I must declare that my conversations with them have often led me to deeper consideration of many subjects, and that both in theology and in philosophy I have learned much of which neither I nor other students had thought before. I remember that many learned people in Europe have written on the manner in which the heathen ought to be converted: but there was no difficulty in this, as there was no one but themselves to contradict them. If these men were to come here, they would find that for one reason which they brought forward, the heathen would have ten to oppose them. It requires great wisdom to converse with such people, and to bring them to a conviction that their heathenism is false and our christianity true. Neither Logic, nor Metaphysics, but God alone can give this wisdom;— therefore those to whom wisdom is necessary in their intercourse with the heathen must give their most diligent endeavours to live in such a way that the Triune God may hold communion with them, and give them whatsoever they should speak in that hour."

That the life of many nominal christians is a great hindrance to the conversion of the heathen, has been already mentioned, and will be often in future by the Missionaries. "The heathen," says Ziegenbalg, "often declare that they would rather be with their fathers and their own people in hell, than without them in heaven. The cause of these hard words is, that they feel great bitterness and ill-will against the christians, because they often treat them cruelly, look upon them as a set of black dogs and lead a scandalous life amongst them. When I was once talking to them, and seemed to have reached their consciences, they answered me: — "If you christians with your eating and drinking, your fornication and adultery, your dancing and music, your cursing and swearing, and your wicked lives, expect to be saved, surely we with our quiet orderly lives may hope for it also, even if our religion be false and altogether a fabrication." I was very much surprised at this, and asked them what they really thought of us christians. They would not answer till I had promised that no harm should result to them from what they might say: and then they declared that they considered christians to be a most stupid and ignorant people who never thought of God or of eternity. I asked them how they could think so when they saw that we had a church in which preaching and singing were carried on three times in the week at which all the Europeans were present. They answered that they heard and saw us certainly, but that they believed that the priests taught nothing in church but how to eat and drink, to game and illtreat the Blacks. They did not understand the Danish language in which the service was conducted, but seeing the actions of the congregation immediately after it, never doubted but these were the lessons they had learned. This conversation was held before Jerusalem Church was built; when they heard christianity preached there in their mother-tongue, they altered their opinion, but still they continued to be scandalized by the lives and examples of many christians; especially when they found that they were too proud and haughty to recognise converted and baptized heathen as brethren, that generally they were ashamed to stand godfather for them, and if they consented, did it with an ill-grace, and did not assist them in any manner."

The good cause however made progress in spite of all obstacles, and before we close this chapter we shall see what the first Missionaries have to tell of their converts, and what they think of the whole work of conversion amongst the heathen.

"We give the name of catechumens," say they, "to those natives who wish to become christians, who are therefore instructed in christianity by means of questions and answers till they have come to the knowledge of the truth, who are led by this truth to a God-fearing walk and to give up their heathenish customs, until finally in true conversion and faith in the Lord, they desire to be baptized. When they have received this rite they cease to be catechumens and are called christians. We also call our converts from Papacy catechumens, until their knowledge and conduct fit them for the reception of the Lord's Supper.—When a heathen declared that he wished to become a christian, the Missionaries examined, as far as they could, into the motives which led him to such a step; represented to him, that he who would follow Christ must deny himself and take up his cross, they pointed out to him the mocking and persecution which would await him on the part of his countrymen and former friends. Many drew back at this; but those who remained firm were regularly instructed by the Missionaries. They learned the Catechism, which the catechist made them repeat after him, explaining it from time to time. When they had learned the Catechism, there was no hurry in baptizing them, but they were exercised in the Scriptures. Many remained catechumens for many months, others for more than a year, before the Missionaries could satisfy their consciences that they might not be incurring the guilt of bringing weeds into the garden of the Lord. In this time of preparation persecution often attacked them; sometimes their relations and friends, sometimes those who belonged to their caste, tried to dissuade them from their purpose both by fear and love, by threats and entreaties. When they came and complained of this to the Missionaries, they reminded them that they had warned them of it and of the Lord's words in the 10th chapter of the Gospel according to St. Matthew. A few stood firm, the greater number fell away. It often happened that those who had come for instruction showed themselves unworthy even after several months had elapsed. Some would not go to school like little children, and others showed no emotion, no fruits of conversion. The catechumens were all obliged to work at their trades, whether painting cotton, weaving, or any similar occupation, for the Missionaries would only contribute that which was absolutely necessary for their support. Those who remained firm and in whom the word of God seemed to have found a good soil, were at last baptized, after which their heathen friends gave them up entirely, so that persecution almost ceased. The Missionaries testify of their black congregation, that they often make the white christians ashamed; still they complain, that their progress in piety was in the whole but slow and yet there were some in whom God's grace evidently proved its power. With special pleasure and hope they looked upon the rising generation. "If one is to make any lasting change amongst the heathen," says Ziegenbalg, "one must turn one's attention particularly to the young; for with adults, though they can learn and believe the articles of faith, and even conform to the rules of our christian church, yet one sees that it is very difficult for them to give up their hearts to the working of the Holy Spirit; and though many are very zealous in trying to bring others to christianity, yet there are many faults in their conduct, which in mature age are not easily laid aside. It is very different with the young; they can be brought to christianity with much more ease and more thoroughly than the old. Therefore from the very beginning we have taken great trouble to work diligently with the young. I and my colleague are so fond of the children, that we have determined to bring up those children at our own expense, whose parents shall join the congregation; for then we can bring them up in our own way, and hope to find people amongst them who will be suited to spread the christian religion." And in another place, "experience has taught us, that if we wish for good christians, we must work diligently with God's word on the young; for though the old people who are very seldom able to read and write, often make a good beginning in christianity, yet it is very difficult, as they cannot read and inquire into God's word for themselves, to keep them to a lively knowledge of divine truth by verbal instruction." Gründler says, "more especially, we have great pleasure in our children; for what a benefit it is to the coming race, yea to all eternity, that so many heathen children should grow up in the fear and discipline of the Lord. It is the seed of God, will by degrees grow up, and spread throughout these heathen lands."

These hopes failed, and here as in other places it was proved that christian instruction at school can do little when the children do not see a christian life in the houses of their parents. If the Tranquebar Mission has been changed in our time into a mere school-institution, one cannot say but that the first Missionaries contributed to it, as they raised school-teaching to an undue eminence, and the free publication and preaching of the word seem to have fallen more and more into the shade. It must not be said however that the preaching of the Gospel was neglected; what has been already said proves to the contrary; yet it is too true that especially in later times the Evangelists became school-masters, and continually waited to see a strong christian race arise out of their schools, and waited-alas! in vain. The very first boy who was baptized by Gründler with great expectations at Poreiar, degenerated as he grew older; but neither many such sad experiences, nor a consideration of the conduct of the Apostles could awake the later Missionaries out of their school-dream, and convince them that a Missionary should preach to the heathen, not keep school for their children, and that a christian school-life will be quickly produced by a christian home-life. I will conclude with Gründler's remarkable words, which will prove that this very excellent man did not over-rate his own usefulness, but spoke of it in expressions, to which the truth-loving historian can fully subscribe. "With regard to present conversions," he says, "one cannot hope that we should see the blessed time when the righteous God shall gather the fulness of the heathen together, and cause them to enter into his fold. But it is doubtless true that of our poor unworthy work God will make a small specimen of that time of grace, for which it prepares the way. By the grace of God we are made harbingers of his grace, until the Lord shall open wide the kingdom of his mercy to the heathen. The witness and mark of the living God, which has shown itself in this work, says clearly to us, that *his* hand has begun it and that it will support and carry it on."

The labour both amongst catechumens and christians was very much increased by their being divided into two congregations. The Missionaries considered this to be necessary. "It is true that in the whole world there is one communion in the Lord, which is the Christian Church," said they, "but as in this Church there are many different congregations, so on account of their different languages, it has been necessary to divide even the little flock which the Lord has here called into his Church, into the Portuguese and Tamil congregations."

CHAPTER VI.

TAMIL TRANSLATION OF THE NEW TESTAMENT.—PRINTING IN TRANQUEBAR.—THE ENGLISH, GERMAN AND DANISH FRIENDS OF THE MISSION.—THE MISSIONARY-COLLEGE IS FOUNDED.

It has been already remarked that about the end of the year (17. Oct.) 1708 Ziegenbalg began to translate the New Testament into the Tamil language. Though this work was interrupted (19 Nov.) by his imprisonment, he took it up again as soon as he was liberated, and continued the translation of book after book till on the 21st of March 1711, he was able to say "All the books of the New Testament are now translated; this is a treasure in India, which surpasses all other Indian treasures." He translated it from the Greek, but he had Latin, German, Danish, Portuguese, and Dutch Bibles at hand, as well as various Commentaries; to which he referred in the most difficult places. But besides the learned apparatus which Ziegenbalg thus brought to his work, he himself mentions other aids, which must not be thought lightly of.

1. Hearty prayer to God; Psalm. 119. 18. "Open thou mine eyes, that I may behold wondrous things out of thy law."

2. A hearty obedience to the word, so that the divine truths which one wishes to translate, may first become truth, life and spirit to the heart. St. John 7. 17. "If any man will do his will, he shall know of the doctrine, whether it be of God, or whether I speak of myself."

3. A knowledge of the manner in which the Holy Ghost speaks to us in the Scriptures. 1 Cor. 14. 11. "Therefore, if I know not the meaning of the voice, I shall be unto him that speaketh a barbarian; and he that speaketh shall be a barbarian unto me."

4. A diligent comparison with other explanatory authors; this I call "comparing spiritual things with spiritual." 1 Cor. 2. 13.

5. A careful attention to the context. 2 Pet. 1. 20 "No prophecy of the Scripture is of any private interpretation."

6. A conscientious consideration of the *Analogia fidei*, so that nothing may be set down which shall be contrary to those articles of faith which have been clearly proved to be founded on the Holy Scriptures. Rom. 12. 6.

When the translation had been carefully revised, and a printing press with Tamil letters received in Tranquebar, (we shall give the history of this soon) they proceeded to print it. The first part which embraced the Gospels and the Acts of the Apostles was printed at the Mission-press in 1714. The other part, which embraced the remaining books, was printed in smaller letters on account of the want of paper and was ready in 1715.

The Missionaries obtained a Portuguese translation of the New Testament in a much easier way, for the work had been already done by a Roman Catholic priest, John Ferreira d'Almeida, who had joined the evangelical church in Batavia. His translation, which follows the Dutch very closely, had been twice printed by the Dutch in quarto and when the English (of whose assistance to the Mission we shall so frequently have occasion to speak) heard of this, they caused it to be reprinted in Octavo at Amsterdam at great expense, and sent many hundred bound copies to the Missionaries in Tranquebar.

There was also a Portuguese translation of the books of the Old Testament. A Dutch merchant at Paliacate (Pulicat) lent the 5 books of Moses in Portuguese to the Missionaries, who had them copied; and in a manuscript belonging to the church at Negapatam, they found a translation of nearly all the other books, which they also obtained permission to copy. It is not known who made this translation; but it was probably done in Batavia. Gründler went carefully through it and prepared it for the press.

As soon as Ziegenbalg had finished the Tamil translation of the New Testament, he began with the books of the Old Testament, for which he had a sort of pattern; as in the year 1711 when on a journey, he had found a very old Tamil book amongst some Roman Catholic Missionaries, in which the histories of the Old Testament were given in question and answer. He received permission to copy it, on the condition that he would send them a copy of his translation of the New Testament, which was not then printed. He therefore went through this old book, improved the language and meaning, cleansed it from the papistical leaven which was to be found here and there, and used it in the congregation and schools until a translation of the complete books of the Old Testament was ready. This was but a slow work, for Ziegenbalg's voyage to Europe and his death interrupted the work, so that he got no further than the book of Ruth. He followed the system of division into chapters, but thought it better to give up that into verses, as, owing to the different construction of the languages, what would come first in Greek or Hebrew would come last in Tamil, and thus cause confusion. Moreover he said that God's word might be translated as clearly into Tamil as into any European language, and that he did not begin the translation of the Bible until he felt himself at home in the language, and had acquired a clear and flowing style. In the year 1740 his translation was put to a severe test when a linguistic dispute broke out between the Missionaries of Cuddalore and those of Tranquebar. The Tranquebar Missionaries, Pressier, Walther and Worm, had undertaken to revise it and had brought out the Gospel according to St. Matthew in 1739; but their work was attacked by the Cuddalore Missionary Geister, and by Benjamin Schultze, who was Ziegenbalg's successor in the work of translating the Old Testament, and who declared the revised edition to be a failure. Because the Roman Catholic Beschi had laughed at the language of the Tranquebar Missionaries, they had now introduced poetical expressions quite incomprehensible to the mass of the people: but Schultze declares "that Ziegenbalg's translation is distinct and clear, has been understood by Sudras and Pariahs, by high and low, and that many impartial Brahmins had admired it, had praised its distinctness, and added that they would not take upon themselves to do it equally well." He therefore advised "that the old translation of Ziegenbalg should be retained, and that no one should trouble themselves about the sneers of the Roman Catholic, who would of course be better pleased if the Bible were quite incomprehensible; he said that the Missionaries might as well read from a Latin or German as from a high Tamil Bible, as it could not be comprehended by the common people." The result was that the new revised translation was given up, and that the Missionary College ordered Ziegenbalg's to be reprinted. His success is the more remarkable, as he carried on his work without assistance from any native. In a letter written in 1708 he says that he intends to be quite alone in his translation, merely employing a Malabar writer to put down what he shall dictate; "for I require no help from others, and even if I wished for it, I could not get it. Neither amongst the Christians nor the Malabarians can I find one person who could translate a sentence without mistakes. It is true that our interpreter knows several European languages, but he has only been able to help me in the meaning of words, in which he has also been very useful to my dear colleague:—the grammatical rules I had to find out for myself by a diligent study of Tamil books." Schultze's attack on the revised translation of St. Matthew was answered by a sharp contradiction from the Tranquebar Missionaries: still even they agreed that he was right as to the clearness of the translations by Ziegenbalg and Gründler.

We have seen reason to admire the quickness with which Ziegenbalg completed so skilful a translation of the New Testament, and we may also wonder to see the Missionaries so early supplied with the means of printing and distributing it. But the reason was that Missionary work in the East Indies had awakened the sympathy of Christians in Denmark, Germany and England, so that what was perhaps not thought of in one place for the furthering of the cause, was sent out by another. The English were the first to send a printing-press to the Mission, and that leads us now to speak of the English friends of the cause.

As the publication of the first letter from the Missionaries had caused great excitement in Germany, it was thought well to make it known in England, and the German chaplain of Prince George of Denmark, A. W. Böhme, translated it into English and published it in the year 1709 with a preface and a dedication to the great society *de propaganda fide in partibus transmarinis*, inviting it to assist the Tranquebar Mission. Many of the members of the society, and particularly the president, the Archbishop of Canterbury, were much interested in the Mission, and yet they considered that the society would be going beyond its charter, if it interfered with the East Indies, as the West Indies were so clearly pointed out as its field for work: but another society took up the request most jealously, "the Society for promoting christian knowledge" which has since become so important to the Tranquebar Mission, supporting it for many years both by actions and advice. Some members of this society met several times during the week to deliberate on the Mission to the Hindûs, and what they determined on, was then laid before the whole society. A short account of the aims of the Mission was printed, and circulated not only in London, but throughout England, with a request for subscriptions. This request met with so favourable a reception that the society was not only enabled, as has been stated before, to have the New Testament printed in Portuguese, but hearing how much money the Missionaries had been obliged to spend on the copying of books, it despatched a printing-press with Roman letters and all the necessary apparatus. But as it was of no use to send a printing-press if no one in Tranquebar understood the use of it, the society took a pious man of the name of Jonas Fincke (who had been for some time teacher at the German school in London) into its service, caused him to be taught printing, and having obtained a free passage from the East India Company both for press and printer, despatched both in the spring of 1711. But the Hon. Company's ship was taken by the French on the coast of Brazil, Fincke was plundered and made a prisoner of war. The ship was afterwards released, and allowed to continue her voyage; but Fincke was attacked by a violent fever and died off the Cape of Good Hope. All that was in the ship's hold had escaped the French plunderers, and thus the printing-press, together with books and paper reached India almost unhurt in August 1712. It fortunately happened that amongst the Company's soldiers who were in Tranquebar, there was one who understood printing. The Missionaries were enabled to engage him, to pay him wages, and began to print Portuguese books. In the year 1712 they brought out a translation of Prof. Francke's five questions on the order of grace and an A. B. C. and in 1713 they printed the small Catechism, an extract from Spener's catechism, the history of the passion, a hymn-book, and a report of the Tranquebar schools.

The Tamil printing-press, which quickly followed the Portuguese, was due to the German friends of the Mission. They not only collected gifts for the Mission from the whole of Germany at Halle, but considered over in what manner they could be of use to it. The people there, though unacquainted with the Tamil language, succeeded in making some Tamil letters, which they hastily tried and sent out to Tranquebar; where the first part of the New Testament, as well as other things, was printed with them. This sample, the very first thing ever printed in Tamil characters, was the Apostle's Creed, and the friends in Halle, when they despatched it with the printing-press, requested soon to be requited by a copy of the New Testament in Tamil. Three people went with the press, Johann Berlin, Johann Gottlieb Adler and his brother aged 14 years who reached India after an uncommonly quick voyage. As the Missionaries had a printer already, Berlin was placed in the Portuguese school. Adler was a great assistance to the Mission during many years both as a letter-founder and a mechanic, for as the letters sent from Europe were rather large he immediately set to work on the preparation of smaller type; and it being very expensive to get paper from Europe, he set up a paper-mill at Poreiar: this was afterwards given up.

While Germany and England were thus emulous in assisting the Mission, its founder, King Frederick IV, was by no means inactive; but both he and the whole royal family were anxious to prove their love to the cause. The king, who always had the Missionary reports read to him, rejoiced in the progress of the work, but was soon grieved to hear of the opposition to them, then of a sad quarrel, and then of the gravest accusations against the Missionaries. He often expressed himself to their advantage, and declared that he would support them in the position in which he had placed them. In order to secure the necessary income to the Mission in future years, the king decreed in the year 1711 that 2000 Rix-dollars should be yearly set aside from the treasury for the East Indian Mission, partly to pay four Missionaries, partly to keep up the schools and other institutions. This arrangement is entered in the Fundatsen for Postkassen of the 19th of July 1712, and in § 3 of the same it is said "Under pain of God's punishment no change is to take place in this; but this donation shall remain as a perpetual gift and alimentation for the Missionaries, and those connected with the schools." Certainly one knows what is generally the fate of these eternal gifts, but this one has lasted till now, and to the honour of the successors of Frederick IV be it spoken, they have rather added to than decreased the sum, even in the most pressing times, and when the spirit of the Mission had so nearly evaporated that it was unable to keep up the respect which had formerly been its due.

The Court-preacher Lütkens received the news of this donation on his dying bed, and was filled with the most living joy: "now I shall die willingly" said he "after having lived to feel this joy. God bless the King." A Royal Rescript was sent to the Direction of the East India Company, enjoining them to make known to the Commandant and Council in Tranquebar that they were not to use force or severity towards the Missionaries, but were to help them in every way in the prosecution of their work, until the differences which had arisen between the Commandant and the Missionaries, should be settled by a Royal rosolution. When the Tamil printing-press was sent out, the King gave a Latin Protectorium to Berlin and Adler, and two years later he gave the Missionaries permission to print in Tranquebar without being subject to the Censor. How the king supported the Mission by money, and did not allow himself to be disheartened by untoward events will be best seen by the following Royal letter to the Missionaries:—

"Venerable, Beloved, Faithful!

From the most gracious letter which we sent to you on the 19th of January you will learn our most gracious pleasure in your faithfulness and activity. On the 10th of February we sent on board the East Indiaman Dansborg 2000 Rix-dollars which we graciously sent to assist you in your work which is so pleasing to God, besides the yearly sum which is appointed for you from our treasury. But as by the permission of God, the ship Dansborg was wrecked not far from Skagen in Jutland, we have thought fit that you should not suffer by this misfortune, but have renewed our former gift, so that you will receive 2000 Rix-dollars by the first ship from England; and we shall further take care that the sum destined for you from the treasury shall leave England in May, or soon after. When we read your letters to the late Dr. Lütkens, and Bishop Ocksen, especially that of the 5th January 1712, we were not a little rejoiced to see that in spite of the opposition which contrary to our most gracious will and intention, has befallen you, you have shown yourselves immovable and courageous. The plague, war, and other disturbances have prevented the fulfilment of your wishes as to a final decision being given about these long disagreements. But we have already given such orders, and even now are sending such commands to the Commandant, that we have no doubt of his fulfilling them with the most submissive obedience. We shall in future make such arrangements that our subjects shall not be any obstacle to you in the prosecution of your work. More especially, that there should not be any hinderance to the advantage which you expect from the Tamil and Portuguese printing-press, we herewith send you a most gracious privilege allowing you to print without supervision from the Censor, feeling confident that you will use it with such circumspection, that no one will have any reason to complain of you. Go bravely forward with the work of your profession, promote the conversion of the heathen to whom you have been sent, and know that you may feel assured of our constant favour, and that you may freely lay your just complaints before us; as it is our most gracious pleasure to receive your dutiful accounts of your progress in the work of conversion, and to make arrangements for the removal of any obstacles and hinderances thereto. We remain favourably disposed to you with all grace.

Frederick R."

Copenhagen, 26th February 1714.

The Crown-Prince also (afterwards Christian VI.) to whom the Missionaries had dedicated their correspondence with the natives, wrote to them in the following terms:—

"We have seen with much pleasure, both by your letter dated January 3rd 1713, and by the correspondence dedicated to us, that you still keep up your laudable zeal, and take all measures, both by speaking and writing, to destroy the kingdom of Satan and to raise the kingdom of Christ in the souls of men. Now we can well imagine, and we see some signs in your dedication, that heavy difficulties and various oppositions have met you in your christian efforts, for the enemy of the human race is very ready to lay first one and then the other in your way in order to hinder the progress of the Gospel amongst the blind heathen, and to make your occupation useless. But you are well aware that it has always been the custom of the evil spirit to oppose all that is good, and to hinder the extension of Christ's kingdom. Therefore do not let this discourage you, for if it were not so, you might doubt whether your work were pleasing to the Lord: indeed you must be so far from allowing this opposition to frighten you from your undertaking which is so pleasing to God, that you must rather gain a more cheerful courage therefrom, and continue with comfort the work which you have begun, ever remembering that he, whose honour you sincerely seek to advance, and who will work in you powerfully by his spirit, is far stronger and more powerful than all your adversaries. And next to God, you may expect particular protection and active help from the king, our most gracious Sovereign and father, if you continue to show, as you have hitherto done, that you have nothing so much at heart as the honour of God and the eternal welfare of his wandering sheep. Neither will we fail, so far as in us lies, to recognize your faithfulness and earnest work with much favour, and to assist the progress of this beneficial work to the utmost of our power. May the Lord give you the spirit of wisdom, courage, gentleness and patience, that you may walk uprightly in his eyes and in the eyes of all men, and enlarge his flock by your discreet zeal and untiring diligence. Further, as we are convinced of your humble obedience and gratitude by your dedication and your christian wishes, we assure you that we have graciously accepted both, and we remain favourably disposed to you with all grace.

Christian."

Copenhagen, 26th January 1714.

Lütkens had retained the superintendence of the Tranquebar Mission as long as he lived, and when he died and the Bishop of Zeeland would have nothing to do with it, the king put it into the hands of Professors Trellund and Lodberg, but towards the close of the year 1714 he founded a regular College for this purpose, called *Collegium de cursu evangelii promovendo*, but generally called the Mission College which consisted of the following members:—Privy Counsellor J. G. von Holsten (who was President for many years,) the Lord Steward to the Queen W. M. von Buseck; the theological Professor Johann Steenbuch, Provost and Profr. Jakob Lodberg, and the Chamberlain to the Princes Chr. Wendt (Secretary.) This College received (10th Dec. 1714) its instructions from the king, concluding thus:—"This is our most gracious will, which we desire to be submissively followed, as you will answer for it in time and eternity, before us and the Lord and Judge of all. Keep yourselves faithful servants to God and your king, that our zeal and care, and your work may not be in vain." In January 1715 the Mission-College published a Prospectus and invited others to participate in the work.

The Mission now had a strong, one might almost say a too-decided protection from royalty, which did not escape the attention of the English. Already in December 1714 the English society wrote thus to Tranquebar:—"It seems to us, dear

Brethren, that in carrying on your work you place a little too much hope on the help, power, and command of His Majesty the King of Denmark (which however, we heartily wish you should obtain) and that you nourish the thought, that all the difficulties which have stood in your way hitherto will give way, and that your work will go on easy if but the king will protect and help you. But you know that the spread of the gospel does not depend on human power, but on the spirit of God, and that the Lord alone gives blessing and prosperity. He is powerful enough to carry on the work, not only without human help, but even when human power is opposed to it. The Christian religion has always blossomed most beautifully under crosses and tribulations, and will always so blossom. Raise your eyes therefore to the hills from whence cometh help, and let your trust be in the Lord who has made heaven and earth."

I cannot refrain from quoting another part of the same letter where English friends say:—"We do not doubt that your work has been made much easier to you by the printing-press which you are now arranging; but take care that you are not inconsiderately led into so much translating and printing that you do not find sufficient time for constant intercourse with the heathen."

Such counsel must certainly be called a word at the right time.

CHAPTER VII.

PLUETSCHAU GOES HOME.—ZIEGENBALG'S VISIT TO EUROPE AND RETURN TO TRANQUEBAR.—THE NEW JERUSALEM-CHURCH IS BUILT.—ZIEGENBALG'S ADDRESS WHEN THE FIRST STONE IS LAID.

In the year 1711 Plütschau went home, in order to give a viva voce report of the progress of the Mission, and to make active efforts for the removal of the obstacles which the Commandant still continued to throw in the way of the Missionaries. Plütschau received the highest testimonials from Ziegenbalg "We are actuated by the same spirit," said he, "and are quite of one mind in every thing, which has facilitated and helped our employment not a little." After some years of faithful work in Tranquebar he longed to return, and before his departure it was arranged that he should not come back, but should remain in Europe to further the cause of the Mission there; not a trace however remains of his having done anything there for the good of Tranquebar. He became Pastor of Beyenflieth in Holstein.

The Missionaries being still fettered by obstacles occupied the time which remained free from the care of the congregations in translating the Bible and in other christian works; sometimes they went on journies, and at the time of Plütschau's departure, Ziegenbalg was on the point of starting on a journey to Madras which had very nearly cost him his life. He heard in Madras that a great heathen feast was to take place at Tirupadi, at which great numbers of the worshippers of

Vishnu were accustomed to assemble; he therefore determined to go there and take the opportunity of publishing the word of God to the heathen. He travelled five days into the interior, making known the Gospel wherever he went, to the pleasure of the Hindûs but to the great dissatisfaction of the Brahmins. As the country was overflowed, and he was generally obliged to walk bare-foot, he got swellings and boils on his feet. On the fifth day he was obliged to rest till the swelling and pain should pass off a little. Some Brahmins came and had a conversation with him, but went away very angry. The next morning before 4 o'clock, while he was still asleep, a school-boy named David, (who afterwards became a Catechist) who was with him, heard the Brahmins coming up very softly; "He sleeps" said they, in the Telugu language, which David understood "come let us kill him." The boy immediately awoke Ziegenbalg who called up his people, and the murderers fled.

The congregation in Tranquebar increased in spite of all hinderances, and in the year 1712, when Ziegenbalg and Gründler concluded their first historical account of the Mission, it consisted of more than 200 persons, while more than 50 children were taught in the school for the natives; these numbers increased proportionably in the following years, but more slowly than the Missionaries thought it might and ought to have been. They felt themselves hindered in their usefulness in many way, and thought that the Danish Government might remove the obstacles by stringent rules. When no result appeared from Plütschau's return to Denmark—he seems to have been one of those quiet men, who follow their path and do their work faithfully, but are unable to come forward with any power—Ziegenbalg saw more and more clearly that he himself ought to undertake a voyage to Europe. The Commandant and the

Council had let Plütschau go very peaceably, being probably persuaded that he would not be dangerous to them in Denmark; but when, in the year 1714 Ziegenbalg prepared to return, they became very uneasy and thought it best to make peace with him before he started. When this peace, or amnesty, was offered, he accepted it willingly, for he was far from feeling any bitterness towards his enemies, and was very glad that the Mission should be freed from the persecution of its opposers during his absence. A regular document was therefore drawn up which ran thus:—

"I Johann Sigismund Hassius, Commandant of Dansborg in Tranquebar, and Chief of the states of the chartered India Company, and we Missionaries Ziegenbalg and Gründler, have several times consulted together, whether the differences which took place between us several years ago, might not be arranged to the satisfaction of both parties and to the requirements of our employments, so that the past might be forgotten and forgiven; but this has never come to pass, because each wished to show his zeal in the exercise of his profession and was determined to stand by his rights to the uttermost. But as we learn from the letters we have lately received from Copenhagen that an amnesty is much desired there, and do not doubt that his Royal Majesty of Denmark and Norway would confirm it, we the undersigned, in the name of God and in consideration of our christian obligations, as also for the furtherance of the work of conversion amongst the heathen and for the general good, have taken the christian and firm determination to forget and forgive for ever all those quarrels which have taken place between us, by whatsoever name they may be called; and on account of this christian compact they are to be abrogated for all time and we give each other the assurance that we at all times and on all occasions will seek the advantage of each other. On both sides we feel assured that when his Royal Majesty of Denmark and Norway shall receive this amnesty by the hands of Bartholomäus Ziegenbalg, the Missionary, who is now about to start for Denmark, he will give his most gracious consent thereto, and will allow both sides to continue to enjoy his royal favour. For the greater security of both parties, two similar copies of this have been prepared, to which correct signatures have been signed, and of which each party retains one.

J. S. Hassius. Bartholomäus Ziegenbalg.
Andreas Krahe. Johannes Ernestus Gründler.
C. Brun.
Jacob Panck.

Tranquebar, 15th October 1714."

It was a great grief to Ziegenbalg to leave his congregation and colleagues. The black christians came to him in tears, begging him to alter his resolution; when he answered that the voyage was undertaken for their advantage and that he should soon return, they appeared satisfied, but when he preached his farewell sermon a cry of grief arose from young and old. The day before his departure all his congregation gathered round him; he exhorted, comforted and blessed them, after which they accompanied him to the shore entreating him not to deceive their hopes by remaining away very long. Even the heathen asked him to remain, some wrote to him on the subject. Ziegenbalg answered that they could not be in earnest as they would not pay any attention to the gospel which had now been preached amongst them for so many years: on this they remarked that though they had not accepted the christian religion, yet they liked to have persons amongst them who stood near to God and by whom both they and their country profited: many of them accompanied him to the sea-shore and begged him to return. It was a great comfort to him to be able to leave Gründler in Tranquebar;—"I could", says he, "confide everything with the greatest confidence to Gründler, who has now been with me for seven years, and who is so completely of the same opinion with myself and shows such skill, activity and uprightness in the prosecution of this important work, that I could not have found a better and more faithful assistant, if I had thousands to choose from." Jordan went home with Ziegenbalg, but Berlin remained as an assistant for the Portuguese congregation, Gründler taking the superintendence of the whole. On the last day of October 1714 Ziegenbalg sailed in the ship *Frederick IV.* and undertook the occupation of chaplain on board. He took with him also a boy from the Tamil school, in order to practise the language; and during the voyage translated the book of Joshua into Tamil and worked at a Tamil Grammar, which was afterwards printed during his stay in Halle. The ship remained for a month at the Cape of Good Hope, during which time Ziegenbalg renewed his acquaintance with the Hottentots. He communicated with one of their headman in the Dutch language, and asked him whether he believed in a God. Sir, answered he, who can avoid believing in a God? Whoever does not believe it, has only to look up or to look down, and he must perceive that there is a God. Do you then serve this God? asked Ziegenbalg, to which he replied that God had better servants than they were. From his further conversation it appeared that he had some idea of good and evil, of heaven and hell, but that he knew not where he and his country-men would go after death, the merciful God alone knew that, and that they were very willing to be taught if a priest were sent to them. On this Ziegenbalg remarked: "If you accept the christian religion, you must dress a little more like human beings, you must learn handicrafts, and build little houses or huts into which we can come to make known the word of God to you and to begin something for your advantage:"—(their huts are like baker's ovens, into which an European can scarcely enter) to which the Hottentot answered "the Europeans are to a great extent, fools. They build great houses, though their bodies only occupy a small space. They require so much to fill their bodies inside and to clothe them outside, that they have not enough at home, but are obliged to come into this and other countries to seek for food and clothing. We do not wish for money or merchandise, and as we do not dress or live like Europeans, so we do not need to work and plague ourselves as they do."

On the 1st of June 1715 Ziegenbalg landed at Bergen in Norway, whence on account of the Swedish war he went in a Hamburg ship to Hamburg, and thence to Stralsund, where Frederick IV. was encamped. He was very graciously received, was desired to preach before the king, and to prepare a report on the state of the Mission;—he then went to Copenhagen, where he conferred with the Mission-college, and received most favourable decisions from the Director of the Asiatic Company. He then returned to Germany and spend most of his time at Halle, where he married *Maria Dorothea Salzmann*, who had formerly been his pupil at Merseburg, where her father was Government Secretary. During his stay at Halle the Danish king appointed him Provost to the Tranquebar Mission, after which during a very severe winter he travelled through Holland to England, where he received great attention both from the society for the promotion of christian knowledge, and from many eminent divines; he had an audience with the king and Royal family, preached many times in the Savoy and royal Chapels, and received many contributions for the Mission. In the month of March 1716 he left England and reached Madras in August. The news of his arrival was joyfully received, and everywhere on his journey from Madras to Tranquebar he received marks of love and confidence both from Natives and Europeans. The Commandant Hassius was recalled by the Company in the year that Ziegenbalg returned. His successor Brun showed great good feeling towards the Missionaries, especially in their church-building.

The church build in 1707 had now become too small for the congregations, and they had for some years been thinking of building another, but it was not until Ziegenbalg returned from Europe that they set about it in earnest. On the 9th February 1717 the foundation stone was laid by the new Commandant, and Ziegenbalg preached on the 11th verse of the 3rd Chapter of St. Paul's first Epistle to the Corinthians. The sermon is given here to give the reader an idea of his style. His sermons were generally very long, according to the fashion of the time, so that this one is called a short discourse:—

"As we are assembled here in the name of the tri-une God to lay the first stone of a new Church, we have great cause to remember these words of the Apostle:— "For other foundation can no man lay than that is laid, which is Jesus Christ." The apostle does not speak here of the foundations of a Church of brick or stone, but of the foundation of the Christian Church itself, which is the community of the saints on earth, and he proves very forcibly that Jesus Christ is alone its rudiment and foundation. Both as prophet, high-priest, and king, he is the foundation of the Christian Church. As prophet he is the foundation of the Church, in that he, as the greatest of all prophets, whose coming had been fortold long before, made known to us for our salvation the will of his heavenly Father and the great council of God and by his holy teaching pointed out the way to salvation simply and clearly; on this teaching, the whole Christian Church is built up as on a firm rock, the holy Prophets of the Old Testament together with the holy Apostles of the New, and all their followers, having contributed to raise it. As high-priest he is the foundation of the Church, in that he, as a true high-priest, reconciled the whole world to God, and on the Cross offered himself up as a perfect sacrifice to his heavenly Father for our sins, and by this sacrifice obtained eternal redemption for the whole human race, and sits now as a High-Priest at the right hand of God, causing all spiritual benefits to be richly poured out on his faithful people, interceding for them daily, and giving them his priestly blessing. On this priestly reconciliation, sacrifice, redemption, intercession and blessing the whole Christian Church is founded, and thereby receives through faith the forgiveness of sins, and God's grace, power, life, redemption and salvation. Finally our Lord and Saviour Jesus Christ is the foundation of his Church in his kingly office and in that he, as Lord of Lords and King of Kings, has saved us men from the power of sin and the devil, has collected his Church together on earth where he rules and reigns over it and is powerful in extending it amongst all people and languages, in protecting it against all enemies, in supporting it in all troubles, yea, even in making it blessed to all eternity; and God's church on earth is so firmly founded on this kingly power and dominion of our Lord Jesus Christ that the gates of hell shall not prevail against it."

"This Christian Church, which is built on Jesus Christ alone, and which we see spread throughout the world, requires visible church buildings, in which its members may assemble to unite in prayer and praise to God, to hear the doctrine of Jesus for their edification and growth in grace, and to partake of the holy Sacraments to their salvation; so that we see that in every place where christians can excercise their religion freely, such buildings rise up amongst them. It is true that God has no pleasure in great temples nor magnificent churches. As the Prophet says, the most high dwelleth not in temples made with hands, "Heaven is my throne, and earth is my footstool: what house will ye build me? saith the Lord; or what is the place of my rest? Has not my hand made all?" We must not therefore put a fleshly trust in temples and churches, as if we were good christians and a people well-pleasing to God when we have churches amongst us in which the true word of God is preached and the sacraments faithfully administered, even though our lives do not conform thereto;—the Prophet Jeremiah warns the Jews against this, when he says "Trust ye not in lying words, saying, the temple of the Lord, the temple of the Lord, the temple of the Lord, are these. But thoroughly amend your ways and your doings, and thoroughly execute judgment between a man and his neighbour." Therefore we must not think that the proclamation of the word of God and the power of the sacraments, are in any way affected by the absence or presence of an external church; for our Lord himself, the foundation of the church, did not confine himself to the temple, but preached to the people in the high-ways, in the market-places, in the deserts, on mountains, from a ship and other places; and the holy Apostles followed his example, and generally baptized in rivers, and partook of the Lord's Supper in private houses, a custom which the primitive church retained for many years on account of the persecution of heathen emperors. And yet we must acknowledge that the Church was then in its best condition and that such teaching produced much fruit."

"All faithful teachers and preachers, who labour in the planting and spreading of the Christian religion, must use their utmost endeavours to lead those to whom they publish the sanctifying doctrines of Jesus, to become living temple fit for the habitation of the tri-une God, in which he may perfect his divine image. And yet it is to be considered as one of the good gifts of God when we possess such Church buildings as enable us to hold regular assemblies and to be edified by the preaching of the Word of God. More especially we Europeans, who are dwelling in a heathen land, so far from our own christian Europe, should consider that God has sent us a peculiar benefit in allowing us to hear the Gospel of Christ preached in its full richness and to have such buildings amongst us in which we may weekly assemble, and use the means of grace to the salvation of our souls. As in the times of the Old Testament God often allowed his people Israel, who then formed the church to dwell amongst heathen nations, in order to give the latter an opportunity of being converted, so now, we may consider that God has allowed us to come into this heathen land, that by our teaching, our life and our conduct we should give these heathens an opportunity of being converted. It was particularly with this intention that his Royal Majesty of Denmark and Norway, our most gracious king and ruler, Frederick IV. sent us Missionaries into this country, that we should publish the saving gospel of Christ to the heathen, and by God's power work for their conversion with his word. From our first arrival until this day it has been our constant effort richly to preach Jesus Christ and him crucified to the heathen of these eastern countries, and to help them to such faith in him that they might be freed from their blindness, converted and saved. Though we grieve much over the unfruitfulness of our attempts, and see that our aim is gained with very few, yet we have reason to praise God highly in that he has not left us quite without fruit and blessing, but has so favoured our unworthy service that a small congregation has been gathered to Christ Jesus from amongst the heathen, which has hitherto been richly nourished with the word of God. By its constant growth, this congregation has become too large for our present church, and as we have a lively faith that God will save more souls from year to year, we have thought it right to build a new church, and are now assembled to lay the first stone in the name of the tri-une God."

"May our Saviour Jesus Christ, who is the foundation of this Church, give his grace and blessing to our undertaking, and not only cause this building to be finished without hinderances, but permit us to attain our desire of converting many heathen souls throughout this country, till heathenism shall be driven out, and true christianity make progress. May he graciously take pity on all these heathen, remove the curse which has rested on this country, drive away heathen blindness by the light of the Gospel, and make all here bright in the East. As his word has come so near to this people, may he also give them grace that it may reach their hearts, and enlighten, convert, regenerate, justify, sanctify and save them. May he bring the glory of the false gods to shame and make his name great and glorious amongst them. May he send down his help from above on us, who are teachers, and give his heavenly blessing to our work. Whenever we shall open our mouths in the new Church to glorify his holy name, may he give divine power to his word, and cause it to bring forth much fruit. May he bring forward none but faithful teachers, who shall be able and willing to work for the conversion of the heathen. May he bring all who shall assemble in this new church to a sanctifying knowledge of the truth, and to the obedience of the faith. May he accept of all those who shall be baptized in the tri-une God, and keep them constantly in the covenant of his grace. May he strengthen the love, faith and hope of those who approach his holy table, and arm them with divine power to conquer the world, the flesh and the devil. May he graciously listen to the prayers and grant the requests of those who shall come into this house to pour out their hearts before him and to ask for various gifts. May he cause his word to go forth from this Jerusalem throughout this heathen country, and open a wider path for the progress of the gospel that the fulness of the gentiles may enter."

After the first stone had been laid, the building made rapid progress, and on the 11th of October 1717, the new church was consecrated, and named Jerusalem like the old one; Ziegenbalg preached on the occasion from the 6th chapter of Jeremiah, the 19th to the 21st verses. The old church was given up to the Catechists, and used also for funerals. The work of church-building did not interrupt the work of conversion; in the year 1717, more than thirty natives were admitted by baptism into the christian community, and in 1718 upwards of fifty. In the beginning of the year 1718, Ziegenbalg undertook a journey to Cuddalore in order to make all arrangements necessary for a school for native children, which the English wished to establish there, and he occupied himself with his usual zeal on the way, in discoursing of the things which belong to the kingdom of God, both with Hindûs and Mohammedans. It was after this journey that he prepared the third collection of his conversations with the natives, the last book which he sent to the press, for the time drew near when this good and faithful servant was to be called from his work amongst the heathen to the rest of his Lord.

CHAPTER VIII.

ZIEGENBALG'S DEATH.—THE ARRIVAL OF NEW MISSIONARIES.—GRUENDLER'S DEATH.—LETTER OF THE ARCHBISHOP OF CANTERBURY.—CONTROVERSIES RESPECTING THE MISSION.—JENS SIVERTSEN.

Ziegenbalg was the first who preached in the new church; he was also the first who was buried there. His health had been but indifferent during the last months of the year 1718, and he was then seized with pains in the stomach and a severe cough. He still continued to superintend nearly all his affairs, but was confined for a whole month to a sick bed. About Christmas he partially recovered, so that though his voice was very weak, he was able to preach both on that festival and on New Year's day. These sermons were his last. He began to take steel by the advice of a Dutch physician, but could not keep it up. When he became aware that his strength was failing more and more, he called Gründler to him on the 10th of February 1719, gave up the superintendence of the Mission to him, handed over the accounts and other documents, and placed in his hands his last will and testament, both with regard to his family and to the Mission. He wished much to receive the Lord's Supper the next day, but when he grew worse in the night, he began to long for Gründler, yet waited till 5 o'clock in the morning, before he would allow him to be called. Meanwhile his wife read to him the 14th to the 17th chapters of St. John's Gospel, the 8th Chapter of St. Paul's Epistle to the Romans, and the 5th

9 *

chapter of the 2nd Epistle to the Corinthians. When Gründler came he begged him to administer the Sacrament immediately, which he did with hearty prayers and many tears. In the afternoon he called the whole congregation before him, exhorted them and bade them adieu. He then seemed to rally, and his family began to entertain hope, but his strength did not return. "On the 23rd," says his wife, "he rose in the morning, and himself conducted morning prayers with me. From this I did not expect that this would be the day of his death, but about 9 o'clock the truth became too evident, and I therefore sent for Herr Gründler and his wife. As soon as he saw Gründler he asked him to pray with him, which he did. After the prayer, one who was present said to him: "The apostle of the gentiles, St. Paul, desired to depart and to be with Christ," to which he answered with a weak voice "O, most willing! May Christ cleanse me from my sins by his blood, and clothed in his righteousness, allow me to leave the earth to enter into his kingdom." When he was in the pains of death, and laboured painfully, one said to him "This is the last contest; hold out courageously by the strength of Christ, and think with Paul:— I have fought a good fight, I have finished my course, I have kept the faith. Now is there laid up for me a crown of righteousness, which the Lord, even the righteous judge, shall give me in that day." To this he answered "Ah yes, through Christ I shall endure in this contest, that I may receive a like glorious crown." Some what later he said, "I can say no more. May God bless that which I have spoken." Gründler answered, "The Lord will cause what you have spoken to be an eternal blessing," on which Ziegenbalg said, "Christ says, Father I will that where I am, there my servant may be also," he then put his hand hastily to his eyes and exclaimed "How is it all so clear; it seems as if the sun were shining in my eyes." He then asked that the hymn "Jesus, meine Zuversicht" ("He in whom I put my trust") should be played on the Piano and sung, which was done; the hymn was sung all through. At last he asked to be lifted from his bed and placed in his arm-chair, where he died almost immediately, aged 36 years. "But," says his wife, "the patience, peace and complete resignation to the will of God with which he bore all his sufferings and his whole illness will be indelibly impressed on my heart as long as I live." The next day he was buried in Jerusalem church; Gründler preached the funeral sermon on the 29 and 30th verses of the 3rd chapter of St. John, and showed 1st, how Ziegenbalg had rejoiced in the knowledge of Christ and wished to make him known to the heathen, 2nd, how he had led the members of the congregation to Christ, and finally how he had given his life to the cause.

Ziegenbalg's death caused universal grief both amongst Europeans and Natives, even including heathens. But no one suffered more severely than Gründler, who had been united to him by the closest brotherly love, and who had now to support the whole burden of the work of the Mission. But there were two things in which his loss was most severely felt; viz:—the intercourse with the heathen and the translation of the Bible. In these he had been a master, and his loss was for the time irreparable. Gründler was suffering both in mind and body, but it was not the time to give way to sickness. For some months he was so weak that he was obliged to sit while he was preaching. On one such occasion, he, in the presence of the congregation, begged God with many tears not to chastise his poor flock so severely and not deprive them of both their shepherds at once, but according to his mercy and love to prolong his life until the arrival of the new Missionaries who were then on their way, and until he should have instructed them in their work. The Lord heard his prayer.

His three new colleagues arrived in September. These were, *Benjamin Schultze* of Sonnenburg in the province of Neumark, *Nikolaus Dal* from the village of Anslet in the district of Hadersleben, and *J. Heinrich Kistenmacher* from Burg in the Duchy of Magdeburg, of whom the two first worked many years for the East India Mission, but the latter was called away by death in 1722. It is easy to understand that the managers of the Mission in Halle and Denmark made all possible haste to send off these men as soon as they had offered their services, because Ziegenbalg and Gründler had repeatedly sent earnest entreaties for help; but to be in such a hurry for their departure as not to ordain them was almost inexcusable, and had very nearly caused the young congregation in Tranquebar to be left without any ordained teacher. When Schultze and his companions arrived, they heard of Ziegenbalg's death and Gründler's severe illness. It is true that Gründler was rather better, and began immediately to instruct the new comers in the language, to make them acquainted with the congregation and to introduce them to the heathen; but this was only a beginning which was soon interrupted by Gründler's illness and death. This faithful servant of the Lord had for many years accustomed himself to the idea of living and dying in India, as his letters to his relations prove. In a letter dated 1712, he writes to them "Do not think that I shall return to Europe. It is true that the appointed three years have passed, but I do not think that in spite of all our wishes, we have yet begun to work properly at the conversion of the heathen. In the strength of God we will make a good beginning this year, and go bravely forward in years to come, so that the prince of darkness and his idol-worshippers shall give way to Jesus, who is king over the heathen also. Pray for me your son and brother, for it is God who must strengthen, support and protect us. The help of man is of no avail, and we have it not, but only their enmity." In another letter he expresses himself thus: — "Do not entertain any hopes of my return, for my dear colleague, Provost Ziegenbalg and I have quite determined to show our love to God and to the wishes of our most gracious king by sacrificing our lives to the service of the heathen here in the East Indies, and to appear before the throne of the Lamb with our black brethren."

Ziegenbalg had now gone to his home, and Gründler who had seen the fulfilment of his wish with regard to his successors, was soon to follow him. In the beginning of the year 1720 he was attacked with diarrhœa to which he paid little attention at first, but as it lasted, he took precautions against it. He was thinking on taking a journey into the dominions of the great Mogul, and as an opportunity offered of going to Cuddalore in an English ship, he wished to take advantage of it; but before starting he ordained Schultze and appointed him as his substitute; Schultze preached on this occasion from 1. Cor. 9, 27. His friends wished much to dissuade him from the journey, but he was determined, saying that this was an opportunity which scarcely offered itself once a year. With five persons, amongst whom were two experienced catechists, he began his journey on the 10th of February, but becoming worse, he returned to Tranquebar in a very exhausted state on the 27th of the same month. "On the 15th of March," says Schultze, "I was frightened to see him come to church, and I asked him what he wished." "To read the Liturgy from the altar," said he. "But," said I, "you can scarcely walk, and you suffer so from thirst, that you can scarcely speak; why do you wish to do this?" "I must," answered he. "He sat a little time in the vestry and drank some cold tea, to quiet his burning thirst. This was his last walk;—he wished to pronounce the blessing over the congregation he was about to leave, and thus to say his final adieu."

On the 19th of March Schultze was with him early in the morning to talk over affairs connected with the Mission; he was fatigued and hot, but no one thought that it would be his last day. When Schultze was obliged to leave him, he wished him every blessing, and lay quietly praying till in the afternoon he gave up the ghost, aged 43 years. "Who can feel greater grief than I," says Schultze, "whose heart can weep more than mine? here lay the last support of the Mission. I was inexperienced both in the strange language and in the extensive business of the Mission. For half a year my soul refused to be comforted and could not submit to the severe blow which God had given me, and this lasted until it pleased the Most High to rejoice and comfort me by his help. Help and counsel were difficult to be obtained, but I have found every thing in God." Gründler was buried the next day in Jerusalem Church near to Ziegenbalg and Schultze preached from Revelations 14, 13. These two men of God lie buried, the one on the right, the other on the left side of the altar, and the places are marked by copper plates, with Latin inscriptions, composed by Schultze.

We will here give an encouraging letter from the Archbishop of Canterbury to Ziegenbalg and Gründler, (which, being dated from the 1st January 1719, arrived in Tranquebar after Ziegenbalg's death) as a witness of the opinion which the Primate of England entertained of the Tranquebar Mission. "It is very long, Reverend Sirs, since I had the pleasure of receiving your letter. During this time I have often sought a good opportunity for sending you my best thanks for your kind feeling towards me, and as such an opportunity is now offered by our common friend, Mr. Newman, I send you, my Brothers and Fellow-workers in the Lord, my hearty New-Year's wishes for all good, and pray that by God's grace, you may bring many from darkness to light, from idolatry to the worship of the true God, from the shades of death and the power of Satan to the hope of eternal life and the freedom of the children of God through the merits and mediation of our dear Lord and Saviour! Amen. Reverend Sirs, As often as I read your letter to the Society for the propagation of the Gospel (whose chief ornament you are,) and turn my attention to the fact of the light of the Gospel now rising to the people of India, shining again upon them after the lapse of so many centuries, I can but praise the unspeakable goodness of God, who has visited so many and such distant nations, and esteem you very happy in that God has called you to this excellent work to the honour of his name and to the salvation of so many thousand souls. Let others gain titles and honours, for which they have neither gone through trouble or danger, but lived perhaps in idleness, or in the common round of their profession amongst christians, but you will gain both lasting fame in time and a great reward in eternity, for you have laboured in the vineyard which you yourselves planted in faith, you have made known the name of Christ amidst innumerable dangers and difficulties, you have assembled a congregation where his name was before unknown, and you have faithfully remained by it to support it. I consider that your lot is far higher than all church-dignities. Let others be prelates, patriarchs and popes, let them be adorned with purple and scarlet, let them desire bowings and genuflections; you have won a greater honour than all these, and when that day comes when the great Shepherd shall reward his sheep each one according to his work, a far more magnificent recompense will be given to you, for you shall be taken into the holy company of the Prophets, Evangelists and Apostles, and shall, with them, shine like suns amongst the stars for ever.

Judging of you from all impartial accounts, such a reward will certainly be given you, and as such a glorious recompense awaits you in heaven for all your labours and dangers, continue indefatigable in the work to which the Holy Ghost has called you. God has already given you a pledge of his grace in the progress you have made, which could not have been accomplished without his powerful aid. You have begun successfully, go on courageously. He, who has conducted you in safety over so many seas to those distant coasts, and who has given you such favour in the eyes of those whose protection was important for your work; he, who will give you rich support in that work, far surpassing your expectations, leading new members into your flock to their eternal salvation, he will also continue to favour your efforts, and by your means bring India into his service.

How happy you will be when standing before the throne of Christ and presenting those heathen who have been converted by your preaching, you shall say "Here are we, Lord, and those whom thou hast given us," and then, justified in that day, you shall not only receive from your Redeemer the blessed reward of your work but shall hear that noble praise "Well done, good and faithful servants, enter ye into the joy of your Lord."

May the good and great God favour you in every part of your work! May he give you colleagues, as numerous and as useful as you can desire; may he extend your church; may he open the hearts of those to whom you preach the Gospel of Christ, that they may receive saving faith, and may he protect you and yours from all evils and from all dangers. And when you have finished your course, may he who has called you to, and supported you in this work, give you an unfading crown of glory.

So wishes and prays Venerable Men,

Your faithful fellow-labourer in Christ

William Cantuar.

At our residence of Lambeth, 1st January 1719."

I should have liked to have closed the account of Ziegenbalg's and Gründler's labours with this testimony to their usefulness, but it seems right to bring those forward also who speak of the Mission and the Missionaries in a very different tone; more especially as the friends to the work were free in Denmark to praise that which the king and the court favoured and encouraged, while its opposers expressed their feelings either anonymously or under assumed names, sometimes in manuscript, or by books printed abroad, in order to escape the Censor.*

The contest between the stiff upholders of orthodoxy and the so-called Pietists, whose head quarters were at Halle, was carried on with great acrimony in Germany in the beginning of the 18th century, and as the first Missionaries came from Halle, this was quite enough to make them suspicious. We have already described that in 1708 when they were suffering from great distress and poverty, they were attacked with shameful accusations in a disputation held at Wittenberg. In the same

*A long note follows here giving the titles of all the writings against the Mission, and in an Appendix a manuscript is given at length entitled "A short and true relation of the rise and progress of the Dano-Malabarian Mission;—written from pure love to truth, by Christian Aletophilos A. D. 1715;" but it was thought that these very rare and obscure books would be of little interest to the English reader.—*Trans.*

year one of the combatants, V. E. Löscher, Superintendent at Dresden, began to speak of the Mission to the East Indies in his periodical called "Unschuldige Nachrichten," praising the thing itself and blessing king Frederick IV for his undertaking, but raising doubts about the calling of Missionaries in general and about the orthodoxy of the Missionaries of Halle. The same tone was taken up both in Denmark and Germany, by all who were opposed to the Halle school, and they received fresh strength, when in 1711 J. G. Bövingh returned to Europe, much discontented with the other Missionaries.

This Westphalian, *J. G. Bövingh*, and his book have troubled me a great deal; for on the one side, he is an eye-witness, who was in the closest relation with the Missionaries, as their colleague, for some years; so that his report on the East India Mission of which he took quite a different view than Ziegenbalg and Gründler cannot be entirely disregarded;—on the other side he shows himself to have had a personal feeling against these men, by whom he felt himself left in the back-ground; he shows himself moreover to have been the instrument of a secret but bitter party who wished to overthrow the Mission, and therefore I cannot but place his work on a level with the others which proceeded from the same source.

Bövingh did not bring out his book himself; but a friend of his made use of the journal which he kept on his voyage to India in 1708—9, of his remarks on the Hottentots during a three week's stay at the Cape, of an account of Tranquebar and the Malabarians, and of some letters which he wrote with a great deal of warmth to a friend in Holstein while there was a disagreement between himself and his colleagues.

The anonymous compiler published these all in the lump, though Bövingh himself says in one of his letters, that owing to sickness and his ignorance of Tamil his accounts are very insufficient, adding that he should be very sorry if any one asked for his writings in order to print them. "It might happen" adds he, "that many things might be taken in a sense entirely wrong: and then one could but say *relata refero.*" After such a declaration one cannot pass a very severe judgement on Bövingh for the contents of his book, but must reserve our indignation for the man who printed his imperfect statements, but he being anonymous, escapes likewise.

According to Bövingh, his colleagues began to overlook him even before they left Copenhagen. Gründler alone took charge of the money, and kept the key of the box in his pocket. Disunion and quarrels arose on the voyage. The others thought that his prayers and expositions of Scripture were spiritless, and would not acknowledge him as a good Christian, so that, says he, I advise every true Israelite not to undertake such a troublesome voyage with people from Halle. As soon as they landed, Gründler and Jordan prejudiced the first Missionaries against him, and as he did not approve of all that Ziegenbalg did, more especially his severe letters to the Council, his situation became still worse, and when he was seized with illness not long after, the rest looked upon it as the judgement of God: instead of receiving consolation from them, Plütschau who was his Confessor treated him very harshly. When Plütschau not long after was taken with the same illness, he was treated by the others in the same way.*

*However much this may be overdrawn in Bövingh's account, yet there seems to have been really some disagreement between Ziegenbalg and Plütschau, which accounts for the return of the latter in 1711 and for his inactivity afterwards for the Mission. In spite of this, Bövingh could not draw over Plütschau to his side, for he complains of his Nicodemus-like fear, and that he would not break with the people at Halle.

Though Bövingh is obliged to allow Ziegenbalg's diligence and magnificent command of languages, and though his account in many respects strengthens what we have hitherto said in his favour, yet he raises many complaints against the conduct of the first Missionaries; some unimportant, but others important. He accuses them of wasting the money belonging to the Mission. The large sum which arrived in 1709, was soon gone; had they followed his, Bövingh's, advice, there would have been 2000 Rthlr. remaining, and the interest would have been almost enough for them to live on. The Commandant Hassius had declared that the Missionaries were enough to consume a whole kingdom. The state of the congregation was bad. It was only the poorest and most miserable people who became proselytes;—slaves, who came to church perhaps twice a year and who were soon sold again by their masters; papists, who made fools of the Missionaries, in order to gain some worldly advantage from them and then went their way;—and shilling-christians, who kept to the congregation as long as money was distributed weekly (which greatly encouraged idleness) but remained away as soon as the supplies were stopped; so that the Roman-Catholics were not wrong in saying that the Missionaries bought people. Ziegenbalg had put an end to the Missionary - Conference in a very arbitrary way, and had taken entire possession of the money which came from Halle, keeping it in a separate chest, which might be called a hellish, instead of Hallish chest, for it became a regular apple of discord. He had made an evil use of the power of the keys in excluding Plütschau's writer from the congregation; he had also abrogated the reading of the Collect, Gospel and Epistle at the early, and afternoon service, and had preached very little of faith and salvation, but suspiciously of works and other doctrines &c.

I have now laid Bövingh's complaints before the reader, and will proceed to add some remarks. He is united in his views to the bitterest enemies of the Mission, Commandant Hassius and the Papists; much of what he adduces is mere talk and much is clearly untrue. The sequel of the Mission has fully given the lie to his prophecy of future misfortunes. His often repeated wish was that an orthodox Theologian, well versed in dogmatic and casuistic theology should be sent to take the superintendence of the Mission: if this were not done, he feared that the whole work would fall to the ground. Now this was not done, and when some time after a Provost *(Probst)* was appointed, it was that very Ziegenbalg whom he had calumniated, and yet the work stood and increased. But what became of Bövingh who was so wise in his own conceit, that he wished to begin to work amongst the heathen on his own account, and in October 1710 bought a native dress in which he intended to preach the gospel?—In 1711 he had done, and went—home to get a parish, while Ziegenbalg and Gründler sacrificed their lives in the service of the Mission. Meanwhile he did great harm to these far-away living men, who had by his thoughtless judgement to wait for their justification from a future generation, for the controversial writers of that day ever again repeated, that Bövingh had altered his opinion of the Tranquebar Mission.

" It is alas! but too certain, " says the *Apologia et Apologeticum secundum pro sententia Anonymi Hauniensis*, " that the Missionaries are pietists and heterodox. Any one who wishes to be convinced of this need only turn to the Halle reports, 2 Contin. p. 85 and 101 where Millenarian hopes are expressed. Instead of relating other errors, it will be enough to say that they are saturated with the Halle theology, with the exception of one, J. G. Bövingh from Kiel. Herr Johann Sigismund Hassius, Commandant of Dansborg, particularly accuses them of pietistic heterodoxy in a letter which he wrote on the 20th of October 1707 to the Reverend Mr. Ivar Brinch (then afternoon-preacher and provost of Holmens Church) and of which I have a copy before me. In the account of the quarrel amongst the Missionaries, which was printed in 1712, Bövingh, who was then a Missionary, describes their heterodox notions and proves that it is highly important that an orthodox theologian should be sent out as their Inspector. If it is advanced that they cannot be heterodox because they were examined and approved by the Bishop, who afterwards ordained them, I should answer that they could very easily conceal their pietistic errors during an hour's examination; but how unwillingly Bishop Bornemann was to receive them, and what approbation they reaped, is known to all, and need not be repeated here."

Now that suspicions had thus been thrown on the orthodoxy of the Missionaries, and that Bövingh was ready to say so much against them, it will readily be believed that great discontent arose when the king continued to protect them. "When a royal letter" Pontoppidan relates, "was sent through Denmark, ordering a petition for the India and Finmark Mission to be introduced into the Church prayers, a spirit of distrust arose which showed itself in a Latin pamphlet by an anonymous author (Dr. Joh. B.) which had a large circulation. How rational this was may be judged from the fact that the principal reasoning was that as the law was only once given from Mount Sinai, the Gospel should only once be given from Mount Zion or Jerusalem &c.—but the conversion of the northern nations in the 9th century is of itself sufficient to prove the falsity of this. Another anonymous author (Wendt, a member and

Secretary of the Missionary College) answered this very forcibly. Yet he did not bring his opponent to reason, for the latter brought out a rejoinder, which was as bad as his first production."

As Pontoppidan's decision is not quite impartial, I must quote something more of the anonymous pamphlet, and then show who that Dr. Joh. B. is, who is mentioned by Pontoppidan as its author. Leaving out what is quite incongruous and unimportant, the following train of thought may be quoted: — "The conversion of the Jews took place in the first Christian times. The fulness of the Gentiles has been gathered in. If the work of conversion is to recommence, it must be with the Jews. But as the solemn announcement of the law only took place once, so must it be with the gospel. In any case there must be a particular call to it, like that of Jonah when he was sent to Nineveh. The prophets did not travel about the world, and Christ blames the Pharisees who did so. After Christ's Church had been founded, the Apostles commanded their successors not to go forth, but rather to watch over the flocks which had already been gathered together. If any one is to be sent out, he should be orthodox, in possession of the gift of tongues, of learning and of wisdom; but the Tranquebar Missionaries are pietists; their converts are slaves, who have been attracted by the love of money or freedom; they have not converted a single Mohammedan. Whether we should pray for the conversion of the heathen (with the exception of Jews, Turks and Heretics) without a particular reason constraining us thereto, I leave to wiser people to decide." It is true that remarks are to be found in this pamphlet which may be useful to Missionary work; but it is not concealed that it is hatred to the Halle-School which brings them forth, and it is still more clearly shown in the two Apologies which followed it. The tone of these is passionate and coarse throughout, and may be taken as a proof of the bitter feeling against the Mission in one section of the Danish Church.

Pontoppidan tells us that Dr. Joh. B. was the author of the above pamphlet, and by these letters can only be meant the then Professor of Theology, Johannes Bartholin, as I shall proceed to show. In that same year, 1715, there appeared a manuscript in the German language entitled "A short and true account of the rise and progress of the Dano-Malabar Mission; by Christian Alethophilus." In this the theological Professor Trellund is attacked, partly on account of his share in the management of the Mission, partly on account of some declarations he had made about it in a disputation. That Trellund laid this attack to the account of his colleague, Bartholin, is to be seen from the comic dedication of his "Vindication of Truth" which he put forth against this attack. He dedicates his book to the Bishop and the other members of the theological faculty, Bartholin, Steenbuch, and Lintrup, and desires them to judge between him and his anonymous assailant; but, he adds, "Bishop Worm, having approved my disputation which is herein attacked, has in a way made it his own, and therefore cannot judge his own cause; Steenbuch, who is a member of the Missionary College cannot do so either, neither indeed can Lintrup who has acted as Censor to the book. Therefore I must beg you, my dear colleague, Johann Bartholin, to take the office of judge upon yourself, you who are fortunately left to me when I am robbed of the others. Only give your usual care, and do what—I will not say, a friend (for I do not wish to mention our friendship here) but an impartial judge and the first theological Professor of our Faculty must do. I do not desire you to give me the name of my assailant, though probably it would be known to you sooner than to me, but only if, as it may chance, you are acquainted with his obscure name, that you will speak to the conscience of that man, and as a judge and a theologian, lay the business of his conduct before him, that he may secretly strive to do away with the wicked and public insult which he has thrown on an innocent theologian, who never did him any harm."

Bartholin's party, very naturally could not bear to see him thus placed in the pillory, and in the year 1718 an answer appeared at Amsterdam, entitled "Truth justifies itself" in which the personal attack on Bartholin was not left unnoticed. The author warns Trellund to beware of the fate of Asahel (2. Sam. 2.) who pursued Abner, and would not be moved by his warnings to leave him, and was in consequence struck through by Abner's spear. "Trellund," it says, "calls out, strikes and hurts by his pointed dedication, an old experienced and learned theologian, who is also his innocent colleague, and who could not possibly know anything of Alethophilus and his writings sooner than Trellund himself." Thus we see that Pontoppidan's opinion of Bartholin's authorship was not founded on any thing that he or his party had acknowledged, but that he was pointed out as the leader of the cabal against the Mission by those who defended it.

It is easy to imagine that Trellund and the cause which he advocated meet with no gentle treatment in the Amsterdam publication. The mode of operation is the same as in the attacks which had preceded it. The Mission is praised, but the orthodoxy of the Missionaries is suspected, without their having been convicted of departing from sound teaching in any particular. How far these personalities are carried, may be judged from the account given of the noble and active Ziegenbalg, who, without even a pretence at proofs, is called "a Pietist and an impions Idiot, who behaves in Tranquebar more like an innkeeper and a merchant, than a Missionary, and who cares much less about conversion than about his base gains." I think that the reader who has learned to know Ziegenbalg better, will be satisfied to close the whole affair with this specimen, and yet will not be sorry that all these attacks have been thus brought to light. I cannot but remark what a powerful light they throw on the position of theological parties at that time, though this is not the place for considering them at length.

Of all that was written in defence of the Mission, Hornung's disputation "On the conversion of the heathen" is the largest. He divides it into four chapters; the first treats of the call of the heathen in general; the second of the different ways and means of spreading the faith; the third of the Roman Catholic Missions, and the fourth of that founded by Frederic IV. Hornung passes in review the objections which have been brought against the Mission, and speaks of the mistrust which has been publicly expressed of the orthodoxy of the Missionaries, "I will not mix in the new quarrels which have now lasted for some years on this subject, for others have already answered these complaints. The Missionaries have been accused of holding Halle principles (of which it has not yet been proved that they are opposed to the analogy of faith,) but no reasonable person has any cause to doubt their orthodoxy. I am certain that the late Lütkens and other excellent and far-sighted men would not have recommended these men to the King for so great a work, had they not been sound in the faith. Moreover they went through a double examination before such a theologian as Bishop Bornemann, of whose orthodoxy no one can doubt, and received from him a written and most complete testimonial." Hornung's book is dedicated to king Frederic IV.

Before I leave the first period of the Tranquebar Mission, and begin to relate how Schultze and his colleagues carried on the work which Ziegenbalg and Gründler had begun, I am induced to mention a Dane who from the first took part in the work with perseverance and faithfulness, though in a subordinate position. His name was *Jens Sivertsen.* In the year 1738 he had occasion to write to the Mission-College to introduce his son, whom he was then sending to Europe. As he gives his autobiography there, I will quote it:—

"I was born at Copenhagen in the year 1690 of honest and Christian parents: they truly loved and feared God, and brought up me and my brothers and sisters to do the same, more especially my mother who had the principal care of our education, as my father was very little at home, for he went as a workman to Iceland. For some years before her death God visited her with a severe consumption, and finally took her from this sinful earth when I was but ten years old, (the eldest of her four children.) She had a very christian and edifying end, and in her last moments she gave me most powerful aud noble exhortations to the fear of God and to piety, together with her maternal blessing, which, thanks to God, has not remained without fruit. When I was fourteen years old I entered the service of Prof. Sören Linterup, who was then Provost of the Convent, and as from my very childhood I had felt an extraordinary desire to see the East Indies (praying to God for it morning and evening) I embarked in 1705 with the first Missionaries on board the ship Sophia Hedwig, and arrived in the roads here on the 9th of July, 1706. I remained in the service of the Company for two years, and went to Bengal, Acheen, and Malacca. Sometimes when I was on shore, I attended the service which the Missionaries performed several afternoons in the week for the edification of the Europeans, and wished that God would graciously give me the opportunity of often enjoying such edification and leading a christian and quiet life, for a sea-life and the habits of most sailors did not suit me. When I understood that on the request of the Missionaries the Company was about to part with one of its young men in order that he might serve them, I requested to be chosen, and in 1708 I entered the service of the Mission in God's name;—the agreement was that I was to be satisfied with my board and clothing. Separately I received 5 *fano* p. m. for my breakfast, and when the late Ziegenbalg was out of his prison in the spring of 1709, one Rix-dollar was given to me without my asking for it, and from the October of that year I received in all 2 Rix-dollars. As meanwhile I had made tolerable progress in Portuguese, the Missionaries appointed me to various services in the school. I was very much grieved at this, and excused myself both on account of my youth and my want of knowledge; but I was obliged to conform myself to it, and set to work tearfully yet courageously, teaching not only Danish, but also Portuguese children. In July 1710, I received 4 Rix-dollars monthly, with which I clothed and fed myself. As I found that I was in the way of another Mission-servant of the name of Otto Friedrich Radevitz*, I began to think of the sea again, and that with all my experience I might become a rich pilot or commander; so I asked for my discharge, which was favourably given, and signed by the first four Missionaries, and then in September I sailed for Bengal. As soon as I arrived there I received the appointment of steersman in a Danish vessel, but after being out four months I had suffered much from hunger and thirst and my life had been in danger."

*Radevitz was a Dane who served the Mission for many years and died as its Portuguese school-master in Madras in 1732.

Sivertsen goes on to relate how he returned to Tranquebar, and finally determined in March 1711 to take service with the Mission again, as the Missionaries were not pleased with Radevitz. From that time he continued to serve the Mission, on which he says, "thus for 30 years I have had my full work in church, in school, and in economy, and whatever the Missionaries ordered I have carried out in singleness of heart with faithfulness and diligence. During almost all the time I have been Precentor of the Portuguese congregation, and also at those times when the service was performed in German. For some years I used to catechise on Sunday afternoons, and repeat the Portuguese sermon which had been delivered in the morning. For some years I was steward, and kept the daily accounts, which is now done by the native Canacopoly (Accountant.) Now for some years I have performed the Church service, and have spent weekly in the school two hours for catechising, three hours for arithmetic, four hours for writing and one hour for singing. Every month the Canacopolies give me their accounts of money and rice, which I register in a book of which a duplicate is annually sent to Copenhagen, and an abstract to Halle. Moreover I write a duplicate of the Missionaries' journal, and translate and write all Dutch letters, so that I have no idle time throughout the year. I have in my charge and give out everything connected with the foundry, with the printing-press and with the book-binding, and these I am obliged to give out with my own hands as I cannot trust the natives. I read through the first proof-sheets of the Old Testament in Portuguese, and I have written a Portuguese ciphering book for the school, which is kept in the Mission-library, while a copy of it is used in the school. I will not say what I have employed my leisure hours in, lest I should be suspected of being one who praises himself.

What I write is for the honour and glory of God, who has helped me and stood by me for so many years with his Spirit and grace, preserving my life longer than that of any other European connected with the Mission, so that I can truly say "the Lord has been my helper," and he has preserved me for the great joy of seeing the Mission succeed in spite of the opposition, persecution, and obstacles with which Satan and wicked men have tried to ruin it, showing it to be his work, so that it has now spread far and wide to his honour; for which may his name be praised to all eternity."

"I cannot deny that many situations have been offered to me by the Danish and Dutch companies, as well as by private individuals, which would have given me double the income which I derived from the Mission, and which would have led me to wealth and dignity; but I thought of my proper calling, and considered how vain and transitory is this world with all its riches and honours, and also remembered the words of Christ: "What shall it profit a man if he shall gain the whole world and lose his own soul?" and therefore I have never wished that God should give more than daily bread and the necessaries of life to me and mine. He has given it like a gracious Father, even though sparingly at times, but he as an Omniscient God, knows what is best for his children. I wish thus to trust in the help of the Lord. May he give me enough in this world to leave an honourable name and calling to my family, but I shall leave them to a gracious God and trust that he will care for them if it should be his pleasure to call me away the first." Sivertsen concludes his letter by apologising for his bad composition and illegible writing (which however in 1838, a hundred years after, is very legible) "but as the writer who only has the use of his right eye" (he had lost the other from small-pox when only five years old) "can make it out, he hopes that others who have the use of two eyes, will be able to read it also."

In 1739 Jens Sivertsen hoped that after his long and faithful service he might be recalled, but he was persuaded to remain by the wish of the College "till God shall release me, and graciously call me into the heavenly Father-land, there to serve him for ever." He died on the 1st of June, 1741, and the Missionaries say that in all that he undertook he showed such an unselfish mind that they could perfectly rely on his fidelity. His sincere fear of God was clearly shown even in his last hours; when those who stood round him saw that he began to talk confusedly, they asked him whether he was thinking of his Saviour and what was his name, to which he answered "Jesus Christ; he liveth."

CHAPTER IX.

BENJAMIN SCHULTZE AND HIS COLLEAGUES. BRANCH MISSIONS IN MADRAS AND CUDDALORE. THE MISSIONARIES IN TRANQUEBAR UNTIL 1740.

At Gründler's death in 1720, the work of the Mission fell upon Schultze. If he did not possess the depth and solidity of Ziegenbalg and Gründler, he was yet a man of much power to whom it was easy to learn foreign languages and who also had the wish to do so. In talent he was far above his colleagues, the sickly Kistenmacher and the dilatory Dal, and he therefore became the head of the Mission and behaved very nobly in the difficult circumstances under which he was called to independent action.

The day after Gründler's death Schultze assembled his colleagues in the Mission-library, and exhorted them not to allow their courage to sink, but to continue the work they had begun, for which the Lord would give strength and blessing, if they trusted entirely to him. When they had strengthened themselves by a hearty prayer, pronounced by Schultze, they vowed to give him assistance in carrying out the work which had been begun, and gave him their hands in assurance thereof. Schultze also assembled the native congregation and spoke to them through an interpreter, as he was not yet at home in the language. Notwithstanding this, the congregation begged him to administer the sacrament of the Lord's Supper. Schultze did it as well as he could, but not without difficulty and hesitation;

when he afterwards apologized for this he was met with the assurance that no one had taken any offence, but that they were much rejoiced to see how far the Lord had helped him. In that very month (April, 1720) Schultze preached in Tamil for the first time, and he made such progress that he was soon quite familiar with it. In the summer he was seized with a severe fever, which left him a swelling in the feet. As he could not walk to church, he was carried there, and as he could not stand in the church, he sat in a chair.

The Portuguese Congregation had for a long time had their hymn-book, in which the most beautiful and powerful German hymns were collected and translated; but the natives had since Ziegenbalg's time only a very small collection of hymns, translated from the German, so that it was often difficult to find suitable hymns on the occasion of church-festivals. If any one had said to Schultze, you must, like the late Ziegenbalg, set to work to trans late more hymns, he would have answered that it was impossible for he was quite unequal to it; but he relates in his Diary for May 1722 that "one evening, when my colleagues had left me, the day's business being over and I left alone, I refreshed myself after the fatigues of the day by singing the beautiful song from the Halle hymn-book "Liebe, die du mich zum Bilde." When I had sung it through, I felt cheerful and happy. Then it occurred to me; see, you can sing that, but what can the poor Malabar school-children do? Oh, thought I, if one could but make this known to them! Then I felt a desire to make the attempt; I sat down, began to write, and went on so smoothly that I had soon finished several verses. I was so delighted that I could not stop till I had finished it. It was then 2 o'clock in the morning. Oh, thought I, this is charming, with God's help we can do much, with God nothing is impossible. He will continue to help." The next day Schultze translated the hymns "Nun bitten wir den Heil'gen Geist" "Allein Gott in der Höh' sei Ehr" and "Nun danket alle Gott," and in the following month many more.* When he had taught the native children how to sing them, he used to take them with him when he went to preach in the country, and would stop in the road when he reached a village, and begin a hymn with the children in the European style. The sound of 40 voices can be heard to a considerable distance; young and old, men and women hastened to see what was going on and in this way he often collected between 2 and 3 hundred people. When the song was finished, he prayed and then addressed the assemblage. After this he talked with individuals to see whether his speech had been understood, and though he could not himself talk with all, his catechists mingled with the crowd and talked to the people of what they had heard. He always spent one day in the week on these excursions, and sometimes preached four or five times a day.

In the year 1723 Schultze began the continuation of Ziegenbalg's translation of the Bible, which had only reached as far as the book of Ruth. This little book was the first part of the Bible which he translated, and he carried it out in this way. He took the Hebrew Bible and read a verse through; when he was certain that he understood it thoroughly, he repeated it to his writer in Tamil, when he and other natives thought that it was well expressed, Schultze dictated the verse for writing down: then the writer read it aloud to see whether anything had been left out, or whether perhaps some error had been made in writing it &c. There was also a learned Brahmin present, whom he had taken into his service in order to ask his advice

*Schultze's *Hymnologia Tamulica* containing 112 hymns was printed in 1723.

in difficult passages: and if a verse or text were difficult in the original, he had a Polyglot Bible and other good aids at hand. So he continued, translating one Biblical book after another till in the year 1725, he had completed the whole, including the Apocrypha. The Psalms of David were printed in 1724, and they made such good progress with the remaining books that in 1728 the whole Bible was printed in Tamil.

As I have narrated that Schultze, as well as the first Missionaries, liked to go out amongst the natives to publish the word of God, the reader may naturally wish to know what fruit was produced by their preaching. In general it may be said that there were some who embraced Christianity, were baptized, and showed the fruits of faith in their lives:—but if they did not belong to that little band who became teachers of their countrymen and of whom I shall give full particulars at a future time, there is no more to be said of them than of many sincere Christians of our own times, whose lives flow on quietly and unremarked by men though very precious in the sight of God: and yet I am tempted to tell the history of a heathen potter of Anandamangalam, who recived the name of Wedappen when he was baptized.

On the 25th of April 1725 Schultze went out as usual accompanied by the native school-children, teachers, catechists and writers as far as Anandamangalam, a place about half a (german) mile from Tranquebar, in the dominions of the king of Tanjore. At a cross-road they all began to sing, so that the people who had not seen them, might hear of their arrival. A crowd gathered round them, he preached to them and then explained to them what they had heard: in the midst of this, a messenger came from one of the principal men of the place, asking Schultze to visit him as he wished to hear something about

Christianity. He therefore went into this man's garden, whither the whole crowd followed him. The questions which the rich man wished to ask, were these:—How can the soul be united to God? and how can a man be certain of the truth of the Christian religion? Schultze answered that if he accepted the divine truth which was offered him, both would become clear, for if he opened his heart and prayed for help from God, he would assuredly find that his doubts were cleared up and that he would, as David says "see light in the light of the Lord." (Ps. 36, 10). It now became extremely hot, and Schultze, having recommended him to the mercy of God, said adieu, and was going to leave the garden, when a native who had been present the whole time and had paid great attention to what was said, came up saying that he wished to be saved, and asking what he should do: he had read the Tranquebar books and knew that Jesus Christ was the Saviour of men. Schultze talked with him as they walked along the road, and when they came to the last house of the place, the Native stood still and said, "This is my house, come in to us!" Schultze had wished to have gone on further, but thought that he ought not to refuse this man's invitation. When he went in, they wished him to sit down, and as there were neither benches, chairs nor stools, they turned over a large mortar used for punching rice for him to sit upon, while the rest squatted on the ground. The man then brought the Tranquebar books which he declared he had received from Schultze himself: the latter could not remember him, but asked him whether he had read them, and found that he not only read with ease, but understood what he read: and he then heard from him the following history:—

He was a potter, as his father and grand-father had been before him, but before he settled in Anandamangalam, he had wandered about the country for ten years without any settled occupation; his inducement was that he owed the priest 10 Rix-dollars, and as he considered it a great sin not to pay him, and had no chance of earning it, he determined to beg through the country in which he was so successful that he returned in ten years time and paid his debt. But he was now so accustomed to idleness that he had lost all taste for work, and he had on his wanderings become so well acquainted with the devotees who willingly submit to all sorts of bodily torture and are richly supported by alms, that he determined to choose this mode of life, and for two years he wandered naked through the country as a penitent; he attracted several disciples who took him as their priest, and gained a certain celebrity. At the end of this time he returned to his work, but built a little mud chapel close to his house to the goddess Mariamme, before whose image he performed idolatrous worship. As a large serpent appeared about this time in his house, he imagined that it was the goddess herself, and set milk for it whenever it came. He became famous throughout the neighbourhood, and the natives applied to him to heal the sick, to drive out devils, and to foretell the future; on which occasions he made use of a drum at the tones of which he seemed to become beside himself, twisted his head about and gave his answer. Moreover he had a pair of slippers made which were set with sharp spikes, which he wore when he went as a devotee from city to city and from house to house, collecting alms. When he was asked how he could bear to walk with them, he answered that he felt nothing, for he felt as if he were drunk and stupified; that at midday he used to take his slippers off and wash the blood from his feet, and that he never suffered from it. So deeply was this man sunk in the darkness of heathenism, and yet God had willed that he should be saved. During one of his wanderings he met with a Roman Catholic priest who had praised the Christian religion as the only one which could confer salvation. He had known Ziegenbalg but had no conversation with him; but he seemed to feel confidence in Schultze, who soon perceived that his heart was open to receive the truth, which appeared to make a great impression on him; he therefore exhorted him earnestly to leave the hard service of the devil, and accept of faith in Christ: he taught him to pray and advised him when he next saw the serpent to kill it instead of giving it milk. Schultze then prepared to return, the potter accompanied him part of the way, and promised that he would never again walk in his penitential slippers. "Then they are of no more use to you," said Schultze, "give them to me." He assented with joy, and gave them in charge to a boy to carry into Tranquebar. They were sent to Halle, where they long remained at the Orphanage.

He now sent his two sons to the Mission-school, but was soon persuaded by his friends to take them away again. The Missionaries however did not give him up, but often visited him in Anandamangalam, till in December 1726, he came with his old father and three children to beg admittance into the Church of Christ. His wife could not yet determine to follow him, but he hoped that she would do so ere long. To escape persecution, he took refuge in a neighbouring village in the Company's territories; the Brahmins meanwhile threatened his wife and represented to her that he had sold their children as slaves to the European priests, so that the woman became anxious and unhappy and would not follow her husband. He, however remained firm; he learned the short Catechism, and in January 1727 he visited the Missionaries with his father, and gave up all his heathen relics, though he evidently did it with fear.

The Missionaries made him a proposal which sounds a little extraordinary considering that he was still unbaptized and his wife quite a heathen; viz. that his youngest child which was but a few months old, should be baptized. After some scruples he agreed, and desired that the ceremony should take place at his own house that the Hindûs might see what was said and done on the occasion. For the people believed that beef (the greatest abomination to them) was put into the mouth of a baptized person, that brandy was given him to drink and that the water used at Baptism was brought from Europe. In order to disabuse them of this error the water was drawn from the potter's own spring;—the child was baptized in a Pandel which was erected in the garden and received the name of Eva. Besides the Christian sponsors, the father of the child was present, and answered all the questions, particularly that of renouncing the devil; many Hindûs were there, the mother was absent as she disapproved of the whole affair and the grandfather was persuaded to remain away by his youngest son. Poor Wedappen had a most painful night after this important day, tormented by cruel dreams: he hastened to the Missionaries who tried to console him and he strove more and more earnestly to free himself from the bonds of idolatry. His wife left him and returned to Anandamangalam with their youngest child; his old father was nowhere to be found but was hidden somewhere in the interior of the country. Meanwhile he studied diligently, comprehended christian truth thoroughly and begged for baptism. A few days later his wife sent to him to say that if he would come and fetch her she would return with him; to which he answered that as he had not asked her to go away, he should not fetch her, yet he wished her to return. She came, gave up her heathen relics, and began a course of christian instruction. On the 2nd of February, Wedappen was baptized, returned to his home and his work and employed his spare time in teaching his wife the Catechism. He remained steadfast in the faith, would not listen to his countrymen when they offered him money to induce him to practise his old arts, was zealous in leading others to Christ, had the joy of seeing his father and even his brother, who had been so opposed to it, open their hearts to the truth, died happily on the 21st of October 1729, and was buried in the Mission-yard at Poreiar.

It had long been Schultze's wish to undertake a Missionary-journey amongst the heathen. For more than six years he had been obliged to confine his zeal to Tranquebar and its immediate neighbourhood; he had only been able to do anything at a distance by means of books which were printed at the Tranquebar press, "but" says he, "*viva voce* preaching, the testimony of a living man, has a great advantage over the private reading of books everywhere, but more particularly amongst these heathen of the East Indies. Amongst thousands there may be perhaps one that can read, and many of those who can read are so stupid and indifferent that they will not take the trouble of understanding and applying to themselves what they read; which proves satisfactorily, that when God gives an opportunity, it is of the greatest importance for a Missionary to go out himself amongst the heathen, and make known the gospel to them by word of mouth. The first Missionaries, Ziegenbalg and Gründler, have left us a good example in this. It is true that the proverb says "*vox scripta manet*" and that what has been written can be read again and often repeated; but this is only to be understood of things which have already been put before us in a lively way by speech, and which we like to reconsider, in order to bring back the pleasure which we felt on first hearing them. The living voice always has something particularly enlivening and awakening, but more especially in those words which have proceeded from the holy mouth of God, and which have still the same power as when he first pronounced them. When our Lord Jesus Christ, and after him his disciples, began to seek and to save that which was lost, they spoke to the people, for the Eternal Wisdom, Jesus Christ, knew well which is the nearest way to the hearts of men. I would therefore dwell upon this—not that I consider the distribution of books as unimportant and unnecessary, for I have distributed books myself and continue so to do—but I consider that the *viva voce* publication of the Gospel is to be magnified above all other means. I therefore hold, that, when it is possible, it is one's duty to go forth oneself, to preach the gospel by *word of mouth.* If from distance, or any other cause, one cannot reach a place, it is all well enough to send books to those who wish for them. But as necessary and useful the verbal preaching of the gospel is, so *difficult* is it also." Meanwhile Schultze was obliged to remain where he was; for it was only he who could keep the native congregation together, and the completion of Ziegenbalg's translation of the Bible thoroughly occupied all his time. When he had nearly finished it, three new Missionaries, *Bosse*, *Pressier*, and *Walther* arrived in Tranquebar on the 19th of June 1725, and he became then very busy in helping them to learn tho languages; but when they had made a little progress he was very happy to leave them, more especially as there was not perfect unanimity between him and his colleagues.

On Sexagesima Sunday, 1726 Schultze bade adieu to the native congregation. The words of the gospel "A sower went forth to sow" sank deep into his mind, and for many years after they always reminded him of the day on which he had taken them for his text in Tranquebar. The next day he went as far as Cuddalore in a small vessel in order to escape the shameless custom-house officers, who forced money from all travellers journeying through the Tanjore territories; but from Cuddalore he continued his journey on foot. He travelled along the coast, but often turned aside to preach Christ in the dominions of the great Mogul. A few years before, the officials of the Mogul had been just as bad as those of the King of Tanjore, always taking more than their due, and even stripping poor travellers of their clothes to satisfy their extortion;—a rich Hindû in Madras was moved to pity, he went to the Mogul and offered him a large sum of money if he would altogether remit the tax on travellers;—the offer was accepted and two years before Schultze's journey the sea-coast as far as Madras was declared to be entirely free. The work of love of the compassionate heathen was now rewarded, for the messenger of the gospel was thus able to give his message without obstacles. At Madras he received a very friendly reception from an English clergyman, Mr. Leake, but he went on from there to Pulicat and further into the country. This journey was extremely difficult and dangerous; he was obliged at last to go barefoot, and sprained one foot in jumping over a ditch. He returned to Madras in the month of July, after preaching the gospel in one hundred places, and having recalled the Danish Mission to the recollection of many who had known it in Ziegenbalg's time: here he was taken seriously ill, but recovered in 14 days, and determined to fix his residence in Madras, having obtained the consent of the other Missionaries during a hasty journey to Tranquebar.

The English Society now took Schultze into its service, and determined to found a Mission in Madras; but until the consent of the Society was received, he had to pass some time inactive. He asked the Governor to allow him to renew a school for heathen children which had formerly existed in the town but which had fallen into decay. He not only received permission but help, whereon he hired a house amongst the natives in Black Town, and made known by a placard on his door that he would teach any children who were brought to him. The school began with twelve children, but soon increased. He moreover received visits from so many adults that he had not time to speak with each separately, but was obliged to fix an hour daily for making known the word of God to all who wished to listen. Between 9 and 10 o'clock every day he placed himself at his house-door, where all passers by might see and hear him and spoke to them of the things pertaining to the kingdom of God. He soon perceived that in Madras it would be necessary for him to learn Telugu;—this language, which is also called Gentoo, is connected with Tamil, but is yet so different from it that a knowledge of one does not enable a man to understand the other. Schultze compares them to German and Danish, and says that Telugu is not difficult to any one who is at home in Tamil. With the help of a Telugu Brahmin he soon made such progress in the language, that he began to translate the short Catechism, and between the years 1727 and 1732, he had translated first the New Testament and then the whole Bible. He afterwards translated Arnd's "True Christianity" and his "Garden of Paradise" and wrote a Telugu Grammar. His great opponents were the Roman Catholics, who had a numerous native congregation, and were much displeased at his settling in Madras. They tried to spread suspicions about his school, assuring the natives that all children who were sent there, would be baptized, which so frightened them, that the school was empty for three days:—they next reported that he had run away from Tranquebar with the money belonging to the Mission, and then, that from want of funds he would soon be obliged to go somewhere else. Even the English became impatient when he had been in Madras for two years without making a single convert, and began to ask whether it was of any use to maintain him there any longer: Schultze begged them to be patient, to consider that what he had hitherto done was but a preparation, that he was waiting for news from the Mission College and from the Society in England to know whether they approved of his settling in Madras. When he received permission in 1728, he made such rapid progress that from 1728—30 he had collected a congregation of above 200 persons. In 1730 he received a fellow-labourer in *Johann Anton Sartorius*, and two years later in *Johann Ernst Geister*, which would have led us to expect great results, but none followed. Schultze could not agree any better with his colleagues in one place than in another. One knows how great a temptation zealous and active men have to become arbitrary, self-satisfied and wilful; he had his full share of these temptations, and it seems but too clear that he sometimes forgot christian moderation, and allowed himself to be carried away by his lively temperament; in fact he was rather spirited and diligent than substantial; but in mind he was far above his colleagues, who could not enter into his peculiarities and were so discontented with him that there was nothing to do but to part. This was what happened in Tranquebar and then again in Madras, and it is curious to see how much Schultze was enlivened and relieved when Sartorius and Geister left him in 1737 to found a new Mission at Cuddalore. In 1736 when they were all together, the congregation only increased 13 persons in the course of the year, but from the middle to the end of 1737 Schultze alone baptized 117, and in the following year 63 adults and one child. And as if he had not enough to do with the charge of so large a flock to whom he already preached in two languages, he set earnestly to work in 1739 on the third Indian language, the Hindustàni, commonly called Moorish, because it is used by the Mohammedans. Schultze at first thought that it was an Arabic or Persian dialect, but he found out that he was mistaken and that it belonged to the same stock as the Tamil and Telugu (!?). Though the Mohammedans of the interior use this language, they write it in Persian characters. He was induced to learn it by receiving visits from many people who wished for Christian instruction and to whom he could not give it, from being unacquainted with their mother-tongue. He applied himself with his usual zeal and soon began translating the Bible: before he left India he had finished the New Testament, the Psalms, the Prophecy of Daniel and some chapters of Genesis;—moreover he wrote a Hindustàni Grammar and a refutation of the Koran, which together with a specimen of his translation of the Bible were printed at Halle, under his superintendence, when he returned to Europe.

Sartorius and *Geister* went in 1737 to Cuddalore as has been mentioned above, where the English Society wished to found a new Mission. Ziegenbalg had preached in that neighbourhood in 1710, in 1717 Gründler had begun a Tamil and Portuguese school there, which Ziegenbalg visited in 1718, preached in the neighbouring villages, and appointed Johann Beck from Würtemberg as superintendent of the school, but it did not succeed. Beck died in 1734 and the English Society then determined to send Sartorius and Geister to found a regular Mission there. They were received in a very friendly way by the English there, and began their work, but Sartorius died in 1738. Geister was now left alone for some years, when he received a Swedish colleague in *Johann Zacharias Kiernander*. The sequel of the Cuddalore Mission will be given at a future time.

Schultze's health was now very much broken, and in 1743 he obtained permission to return to Europe after remaining in India for twenty four years, and left the Madras Mission in the charge of Missionary *Johann Philipp Fabricius*:—the Christians baptized by him in Madras, besides converted Roman Catholics and christian children, amounted to 700. He went first to Copenhagen and thence to Halle, where he continued his linguistic studies with unabated energy though with failing health:—there Schwarz, who afterwards became so famous as a Missionary, and who like him came from Sonnenburg in the province of Neumark, received from him his first lessons in Tamil. He had his Tamil translations of Arnd's works printed during his stay in Halle; and also had some Telugu type cast, with which he printed his translations of the large and the small Catechisms and of other small works. He died at Halle in November 1760, aged 72.

We will now turn to those men in Tranquebar who were working contemporaneously with Schultze. Their activity amongst the natives will be best understood by what is said in the next chapter of the Priest Aaron and the Catechist Rayanaiken. We will first mention a native of Schleswig *Nicolaus Dal*, who came to India with Schultze in 1719. He was an upright, unselfish, hard-working and methodical man, but somewhat slow, hot-tempered and strange. He was not ordained when he arrived in Tranquebar, and though at first he applied himself both to Tamil and Portuguese, he soon confined himself almost exclusively to the latter language in which he became a great proficient. He considered the revision of the Portuguese translation of the Bible and of the Psalms as his great work, and though he was ordained in 1730 he says "I undertook baptisms and marriages for Herr Bosse and was therefore obliged to neglect the work on the Bible and Psalms, which sometimes makes me think whether I have done right in being ordained." The misunderstanding between him and Schultze of which he says that it had brought him into bad odour in Copenhagen, London and Halle, did not bring on daily bickerings between them. "I cannot," says he, "live in anger and bitterness with any one, so that it is quite wrong to suppose that Schultze and I lived in disunion with each other. By a note in 1722 and verbally in 1723 I told him the truth. This is the whole of our quarrel. Another thing is, to report his blunders by letters to Europe, and perhaps sometimes in words that sound harsh; this I did, but I very much doubt whether Sartorius and Geister made use of milder expressions." If Dal was too impatient with Schultze's weaknesses, and did not sufficiently recognise his zeal and ability, he was severely punished when the drunkard Bosse came in Schultze's place, for he was his special colleague amongst the Portuguese, and plagued him till the day of his death.

Dal was a Dane by birth, and knew no other but the Danish language until he was 13, and though he afterwards studied in Germany, he never forgot his fatherland and its language. I have been surprised to see that, though like the rest he wrote his letters in German, he was able to express himself in Danish so well in 1741, that it proves that a 22 years residence amongst German Missionaries in the East Indies had in no way injured his fluency in it. He was then writing for the press, wishing that what he said should be attached to certain copies of Pontoppidan's Explanation of the catechism which he intended sending to every parish in "Haderslevhuus Amt." "My reason," says he, "is, that though by God's will, my own dwelling is in a strange and distant land, I cannot forget my own dear country and my beloved countrymen, together with my relations and connections who are more than a hundred in number. I send you this beautiful Explanation of the Catechism composed by Herr Erik Pontoppidan, Court-preacher to his Majesty and Theological Professor and Assessor at the most excellent Mission College. Two causes have moved me to the choice of this book: — the first is its very edifying nature; the second is that at the end there is a notice of many good books which those who have the means and the desire can buy, and I wish that every Danish christian were provided with a New Testament and with Jersin's "Road of Life." "I can easily understand, my dear countrymen, that as God has given you a King who is always thinking of advancing the spiritual and temporal welfare of his people, it were heartily to be wished that, according to the first question in this Catechism, you should be happy on earth and finally blessed in heaven. Think only how delightful it would be, if, as Moses says, you were blessed in your going out and in your coming in, that the blessing of the Lord might rest on all that you have, in the house and in the field, that you might become a chosen people to the Lord (1 Pet. II. 10), blessed of the Lord which made heaven and earth (Ps. CXV. 15), and children of the living God." (Rom. IX. 26.) The letter is signed "Tranquebar in the East Indies, in the 22nd year of my residence in foreign parts, 16th September 1741. Your true friend and country-man from Anslet, in the parish Aller, *Nicolaus Dal*, Missionary and Servant of the word of God in the Portuguese congregation." Dal particularly sought to put such books as were directed against drunkenness, cursing and swearing, into the hands of his countrymen, and exerted himself both to distribute such books in his native place and to support his poor relations. Yet even in his benevolence his eccentricity appears; in writing to Jens Jacobsen, who was his Almoner to his family, he says "The unkind conduct of my family is becoming unbearable, and I do not feel myself in any way obliged to contract debts on their account, which would certainly remain unpaid were I to die this year:"—he then proceeds to give a list of those relations amongst whom 142 Rix-dollars were to be distributed, particularizing some of them thus:—"To old Jens Dal, though he has not deserved it, 10 Rix-dollars; to Karen, who has deserved it still less, 10 Rix-dollars; to Catharine, wife of Michael Jensen, who has deserved it least of all, 42 Rix-dollars; and 10 Rix-dollars to that wicked Hans Nielsen Dal in Anslet, who does not think 50 Rix-dollars worth a word." Out of his poverty he also helped to support the Mission. A certain Madame van Cloon in Batavia sent him a present of money for his support from time to time, which he deposited in the Mission, and as he did not think it proper to keep the money for himself, he presented to the Mission 500 dollars at once. He died in 1747, and was much beloved by the younger Missionaries.

Three young men, *Bosse*, *Pressier* and *Walther*, joined the Mission six years after Schultze and Dal. Bosse became a disgrace to the cause, for he gave himself up to drunkenness. At first his colleagues did not know what was the matter with him, thinking only that he was a very sleepy-headed man; indeed to make some use of him they gave him the charge of the money and accounts; but in 1737 their eyes were opened, for his drunkenness increased to such a fearful pitch, that it could not remain hidden from any one, and became a scandal both to christians and pagans. As there was a considerable deficiency in his accounts at the same time, the other Missionaries begged that he might be recalled, which was done; but Bosse refused to return home for the following reasons: — 1) He had not asked leave to go.—To this the Missionaries answered: that was of little importance, as the College had recalled him unconditionally; 2) That he had written about it in 1730 to Conferenzrath Schröder, who had advised him not to return. *Answer.* Because he thought better of him then. 3) He had now become ten years older, and had married a person who under the circumstances (she was a drunkard like himself) neither could nor would follow him to Europe. *Answer.* Neither age nor marriage could free a vicious priest from being deposed. 4) His sight had become very bad. *Answer.* If it had failed in the service of the Mission it would have been a very different thing, but if it had arisen, as Dal represented, from drunkenness and the incessant reading of story-books at night it made his recall so much the more necessary, as he was thereby unfit for service. 5) That the best members of the Portuguese congregation had now been much attached to him for 15 or 16 years. *Answer.* We know nothing of that. If any one who knew not his conduct wished to keep him, that wish could not be gratified; but if knowing his conduct, they still wish to retain him, we can scarcely express what we think of so depraved a taste.

Bosse's defence which he addressed to the College proves that he had not drunk away all sense, for it is very well composed. "The letter from the College," says he, "says that I am accused of leading a disorderly life; but as no particular point is mentioned except the deficiency in my cash accounts, I cannot enter into particulars in my answer, more especially as I willingly acknowledge myself to be the greatest sinner before

God:—with regard to my money difficulties I must remark that I do not think my colleagues did right in twice making me treasurer, which has led me into such a labyrinth of debt, that for 3 years more than half my income has been swallowed up by it. When Herr Schultze went to Madras in 1725, the Mission-money was given into my charge, though I was the worst accountant of all. When Worm and Richtsteig arrived in 1730, I begged to be freed from my charge, which was at last made over to Worm, and I made up what was then wanting, from my private property. The late Worm was a very good accountant, and yet at his death in 1735 there was a considerable deficiency in the chest, which was made up from what he and his wife had left in their wills. At Worm's death I was persuaded or rather forced by my colleagues to undertake the office of treasurer again, though I excused myself both on account of the little practice I had had in accounts and of my weak eyesight, and represented that any of my colleagues, but more particularly Herr Dal, would be able to manage it much better. I cannot account for the great deficiency in 1738 except by supposing that there was some mistake in the adding up at the bottom of it; perhaps too much has been put down in the receipts and to little to the expenditure." He moreover promises that his past conduct shall not be repeated, but that he will lead an exemplary life, and begs the College under any circumstances to leave him in his present position, until he shall be able to find some other situation in India. He was therefore allowed to remain, and seemed somewhat to improve, but this did not last long. "The change," writes Missionary Kohlhoff, "which I announced in Herr Bosse two years ago, was unfortunately only superficial and since then he has not lived as he ought. In a short time he gave himself up to the old vice without intermission for several days; public and private reminders and warnings have not been spared. Only two days ago, three of us represented to him that he was running headlong to ruin, told him that we had sent home a good report two years ago, and asked what we could now write? As usual he promised to improve by degrees, and intimated that he did not now commit such excesses as formerly. We answered that such a way of talking was of no avail, that he must not trifle with the sin, but that he must at once in the strength of Jesus Christ tear himself away from it, give himself up to earnest prayer and efforts, and take no rest until he had mastered his vice. He made many promises, but from our former experience we cannot trust to them." In the year 1747 they say "No prayers, no warnings, no threatenings are of any avail; we have been wrong in not acting with more severity, and it is to be expected that the Mission College after reading the reports that we have sent in will give us a sharp rebuke. He has to thank our dear old Mr. Dal for our over-abundant kindness, for we do not like to oppose him. May the Lord put an end to this evil." In the year 1749 Bosse was finally discharged, and as he had no fancy for remaining in Tranquebar as a discharged Missionary, he left his wife in the lurch (?) and sailed in a ship bound for Copenhagen, where he was received into the Orphanage, and dragged on a miserable existence for some years. I have seen a petition addressed by him to the College in which he begs for 24 *Schillings* monthly "as pocket-money for Tabacco, church-alms, clothes, shoe-and tooth-brushes, blacking, matches &c" or in other words—for brandy.

Thus the Mission in Tranquebar had suffered much from so unworthy a member, but the others who had come out with him, *Pressier* and *Walther*, were so able and zealous, that they made up for his deficiencies; indeed they are to be thanked for all that was done from 1725 to 1740, for though *Worm* and *Richtsteig*, who came out in 1730 promised well and set to work earnestly, they both died in May 1735. A longer season of labour was granted to *Obuch*, *Wiedebrock* and *Kohlhoff*, who arrived in 1737 and all died in Tranquebar, the two latter after many years of work. These, as well as *Zeglin*, who came out with *Fabricius* in 1740, belong to the list of faithful labourers, who, without possessing any distinguished intellectual gifts, carry on their work quietly and diligently. They continued what had been begun, but none of them were equal to a self-sustaining and individual activity. Pressier and Walther belong to a superior class; the journey of the first into Tanjore will be described on a future occasion; he died in 1738, about which time Walther obtained permission to return home. I have seen a letter to him from Francke the younger in Halle, in which he strongly recommends him to remain in India, as the cause was likely to suffer by his absence. "The most important reason," says he, "which you have adduced for your return, is that your health will be in danger if you remain longer in India: but health and sickness, life and death are in God's hand, and in such a case one ought rather to trust to God's providence than to any other circumstances whatsoever. Moreover one does not know what may happen in another place. I have ere this seen two such cases. One was the case of a pastor in my district (Francke was the Inspector and had the spiritual charge of the Pastors in the Saalkreis) who thought it very hard to have to attend to a chapel besides his parish-church, sought for a change, and was finally appointed to one church. But as he was leaving his new residence to go for the first time to visit a sick man, a dog ran out and bit him in the leg so severely, that he is lame to this day." We pass over Francke's other example. However ridiculous his moral to Walther may appear, yet events actually turned out with him as they had done with the man who wished for one church instead of two. He went home, arrived in Copenhagen in May 1740, and was appointed German preacher at Christianshavn; but there the dog rushed out and bit him, and that dog was death: he died at Dresden before he had been at home one year. When Francke heard of his death, he said "I heartily wish that God had given him a longer life, but before he returned from India, I told him that I feared he would not live long in Europe."

CHAPTER X.

NATIVE TEACHERS; THE APOSTATE FREDERICK CHRISTIAN; AARON THE FIRST NATIVE ORDAINED TO THE PRIESTHOOD.

Having thus taken a glance at the Missionaries who arrived from Europe in the interval between Ziegenbalg and Gründler's death and the year 1740, let us now turn our attention to the teachers who were forming amongst the natives themselves. In Ziegenbalg's time they had native catechists, but none of them were ordained as priests;—the early times of the Mission were full of difficulties, and Ziegenbalg did not think any of his converts so distinguished for their zeal and ability as to make him desire their ordination. I know of only one who was raised above the rest by his quickness and talents, and he, in time of temptation, fell away.

His heathen name was Kanabadi Wathiar. He was the son of the school-master from whom Ziegenbalg learned Tamil, but he far surpassed his father in knowledge, had kept a school from his youth and distinguished himself as a poet. He was very highly thought of in Tranquebar, where he had a large school for Mohammedan and Hindû children. In 1706 he composed some Tamil verses in honour of the Danish Royal Family, which were translated into German and sent to Denmark. In 1709, wishing for instruction, he entered the service of the Mission, but the Missionaries entertained very small hopes of his conversion. Meanwhile he translated the five principal parts of the Catechism into Tamil verse, and taught the school-children to sing it. They now began to see that some change was working in his soul; yet he did not say anything, but secretly learned the Catechism by heart, and continued to write hymns and songs for the use of the school. At last he avowed his wish of becoming a christian, begged for thorough instruction and that he might be soon baptized as his parents and friends with the most respectable heathens would be sure to oppose it with all their power. This soon proved true; for when he spoke openly of his intentions, his parents came, fell at his feet, wept and howled out their prayer that he would not thus disgrace them, for he was their only son to whom they looked for the continuation of their race. His father wrote one letter after another with his various motives for persuasion, but they were of no avail; the young man promised to assist his parents in all temporal affairs if they would not hinder him from becoming a Christian. They now tried another line of conduct, wished to take poison, and persuaded the most eminent Hindûs to oppose his wishes. These surrounded him whenever he went into the street, and used both promises and menaces, indeed once they shut him up for two days and would not release him until he took an oath not to become a christian. He worded his oath that he would follow what was good and not what was bad, and when he came out he declared that by the good he meant christianity, and by the bad heathenism. His father went with his friends to the Commandant, to whom a petition was also addressed by a great number of Hindûs. Meanwhile the Missionaries begged him to weigh well what he was doing, and represented to him what violent persecution he must expect; they also told him of the sins of which he was accused. He answered by letter that he could not by any possibility remain any longer in heathenism, that if they would not receive him into the church by baptism, he should wander forth as a pilgrim into some desert, and there serve the only true God as well as he could:—it was but too true that he had committed the sins of which he was accused, with countless others; and it was for this very reason that he wished to become a christian, that he might receive forgiveness for his past sins and strength to avoid them in future:—he held up the example of the Apostle Paul who would not give up his heathen converts when others opposed their entrance into the church, and reminded the Missionaries of the duties which their calling laid on them &c. This letter touched them to the heart, and they determined in the name of the Lord, to baptize him on the first opportunity. As the Hindûs declared that they should lay violent hands on him as he was led to baptism, the Missionaries avoided any outbreak by baptizing him in their own house, on the 16th of October 1709, in the presence of sponsors. He received the name of Frederick Christian, the King of Denmark being considered as his god-father. On the same day he received letters from the country promising him great things if he would give up his intention, but threatening him severely should be persevere. He answered them with much discretion, and petitioned the authorities in Tranquebar for protection. He then kept himself at home for some time, occupying himself in teaching the elder Hindû school-children. "People of rank," write the Missionaries, "both belonging to this place and others, often come to visit him at our house; he honours them with the entertainment of reading parts of the Gospels according to St. Matthew and St. Mark, on which he afterwards converses with them. Moreover he is very useful in the school." When he began to go about in public again, great outward persecutions and inward conflicts arose. He received no proper protection from the authorities, and fell into temptations which he did not mention to the Missionaries. The Roman Catholic Vicar Apostolic next attacked him, made great promises to draw him over to his church, and secretly conveyed him to a French settlement. At this, say the Missionaries, the enemies of the work were greatly delighted, but it caused great grief to us and great trouble to the soul of the man himself. The rejoicings of the enemies is shown by a letter from Bövingh, dated 22 September 1710. "Not long ago", says he, "6 of our people became Romanists, amongst whom one was Christian Frederick, his Majesty's god-son. Last year no doubt great things were written of this man but experience has shown that he was a godless man who joined the christian religion from worldly motives." The unfortunate man, however, did not long remain with his new friends, but fell back by degrees into heathenism. Dal and Pressier met him at Negapatam in the year 1727, and say, "Christian Frederick came to us on the 12th February, a lost sheep from our Tranquebar flock. He detailed his circumstances at great length, and that he had now fallen into such a labyrinth that he could not call himself either a christian or a heathen. He could not deny that, with his wife and children, he took part in the heathen ceremonies but he excused himself by saying, that in his heart he still felt that the christian religion was true, and that when after the Hindû custom he smeared himself with ashes of cowdung, he did not think of Siva, but meditated on his being nothing but dust and ashes." Pressier represented to him that if he held christianity to be the truth unto salvation, he ought not to settle in a heathen place, but in some town that was under European rule. He answered that he could not make a public profession of his belief, because his friends would persecute him and his wife would leave him, that God must give him sufficient grace and strength to bear it. Pressier spoke an earnest word of warning to him, and particularly pitied his two children who were growing up in heathenism. The elder had been christened in Madras when the father belonged to the Roman-Catholic communion, but the younger was still unbaptized. There was something which attracted Frederick Christian to Tranquebar, but there was still more which kept him back. In 1730 he came to visit the Missionaries, who exhorted him to humble himself before God and try to make up for his past faults; of his own accord he fell on his knees and begged God to forgive him; but it was only a momentary emotion. The last that we hear of him is, that Geister met him in the year 1740 as an idol-priest at a temple in the neighbourhood of Cuddalore.

So this man was lost both to the church of Christ and to the ministry amongst the Hindûs, and as we have said there were not many people of remarkable ability in the young congregation. The Missionaries never lost sight of the great object of forming a native class of ministers but they hoped to see them arise out of their schools, a hope, which was not destined to be fulfilled: it is true that they produced catechists and school-teachers, but in the early times not one priest. We may see the traces amongst the Missionaries of a certain anxiety to ordain natives, they were warmly encouraged to it by their friends. In the year 1725 the Archbishop of Canterbury writes to Schultze, "As you are so far from Europe, and there must always be a long delay and many difficulties in your obtaining colleagues from hence, it were much to be desired that you should select some from amongst those whom you have brought to an evangelical knowledge of the truth, and should give deeper and more complete instruction, in order to their teaching others in their turn and in their mother-tongue, not only in the schools but throughout the country, thus preparing the way amongst many who might come to you for further instruction and baptism. Such evangelists did much for the spread of the Gospel amongst the masses on its first publication. "Therefore they that were scattered abroad went everywhere preaching the word." They have easier access to their countrymen, and will find better opportunities for uniting them to their cause. When the number of disciples is thus increased, you will see how many young teachers are to be found amongst these proselytes, who will be suited for making known the faith which they have themselves believed." The Mission College also encouraged them to ordain native teachers as soon as they had expressed a wish on the subject; and this wish became very warm in 1727 when congregations began to form in the interior of the country, which by the next year were strong and flourishing. We shall have more to say about these congregations when we give the history of the catechist Rajanaiken; it suffices here to say that these country people received their first impressions from their christianized countrymen: they then came into Tranquebar, where they received regular instruction and were baptized. After this they used to come into the town for the three great feasts, and were sometimes visited at their own homes by catechists; but as Europeans were forbidden to travel into the interior, the Missionaries could not visit them themselves, and they were the greater part of the year without any teacher. No one will therefore be surprised to hear that the Missionaries thus wrote to the Mission-College in 1728:— "Our great desire now is to provide the congregations which have risen up in the interior with the proper means for the care of their souls. It is not easy to go ourselves into the country to help these people: thus they are obliged to come to us, especially when they wish for the holy sacraments; but there are great difficulties in the way of this and in some cases it is quite impossible. The best solution to all these difficulties would be to ordain a minister for these people from amongst themselves, if one could be found with suitable qualities. Therefore we wish to ask the College how far our power would extend in such a case?" The College answered "The good hope which you express of finding natives who may in time become the teachers and shepherds of their country people, has rejoiced us much; for we together with our best friends consider that with God's assistance this is the most certain means for extending and strengthening the congregations. With the most gracious permission of his Majesty we therefore give you power to ordain in the name of the Lord any person of Indian origin who shall be suitable for the work of the ministry, and to confide one or more districts to his care." The College further warned them to exercise great prudence, and to try any one whom they intended to ordain, with smaller services before instructing him with the care of souls. Five years elapsed before the permission was taken advantage of, but in the spring of 1733, the Missionaries gained sufficient courage to carry it out, and determined on ordaining that one from amongst their three town-catechists, whom they and the congregation should unite in choosing. This determination was made known to the catechists, who gave their consent in writing. The eldest, Schawrimuttu, answered, "As the things, which you our priests through the grace of Christ the chief Shepherd have determined on for the benefit of the congregation, is very necessary, it has caused me great joy. I hope that the person selected may receive the call of God the Father, the consent of the Lord Jesus Christ and the seal of the Holy Ghost." The second catechist, Aaron, wrote thus, "God be thanked, who has put this idea into the hearts of the priests by his Holy Spirit. It will be of great advantage and is really necessary for the country-people. May the Lord bring it to pass!" "The youngest catechist, Diogo, answered, "May our chief Shepherd Jesus Christ, himself select the one who shall please him for carrying out this holy work; may he begin, continue, and complete the work; may his holy name be praised!" The affair was brought before the congregation at Easter, as then many christians from the country would be present: the address to them ran thus:—

"Beloved in the Lord! After long consideration and having received counsel from our superiors in Europe, we have determined that a man from amongst you, and indeed from amongst our town catechists, should be chosen by the consent of ourselves and the whole congregation to be ordained a Priest, that he may with us undertake the care of souls in the country-congregations; for the congregations both here and in the country have grown to that extent that we can no longer bear the burden, or perform all things as it should be. It is the country-people especially who are in want of a true shepherd, who with the help of a catechist, shall make known the word of God to them, shall administer the holy sacraments, shall maintain christian discipline and order and show a parental care towards the rising generation. Hitherto God has sent priests to you from Europe, and we do not doubt that he will continue to do so, as long as the circumstances of the Mission shall require it; but you must not look upon it as if none of your own people were fit to be priests and shepherds. The principal thing which enables a servant of Christ to exercise the office of a preacher, is the anointing of the Holy Spirit, which God has promised to pour out on all flesh (Acts II. 17.) and Peter says "God is no respector of persons, but in every nation he that feareth him and worketh righteousness, is accepted with him." God has shown favour to all other nations, by awakening shepherds and teachers from amongst themselves; and why should it not be possible amongst you also? You may then confidently pray for this gift of God and you may do so the more earnestly as it will do much to strengthen christian religion in this country against the power of heathenism. Let us then in future lay this matter before God in our public services in church, and as it concerns you all, though more especially you who are from the interior, let your prayers for it arise with true devotion both in church and at home! May the Lord govern our undertaking, that for Christ's sake it may succeed to the glorifying of his great name, to the spread and support of his kingdom, and to the true benefit of you all. Amen."

From the beginning of the month of March, the three catechists were instructed in pastoral theology, to which instruction an hour of prayer was united. At Whitsuntide they preached their trial sermons: — Schawrimuttu had begged to be excused from the post of candidate, and the Missionaries had accepted of his reasons. Aaron preached on Whitmonday on Rom. VIII. 14—16: Diogo on Whittuesday on 1. Cor. III. 16, 17. The day after, the 27th of May, the heads of families were called into the church, and after hymns and prayer each one was requested to go into the vestry to give his vote; it so happened that there was an equal number of votes for each, and when the Missionaries had weighed the reasons which each man gave for his choice, they were also equally divided, three for Aaron and three for Diogo. There was certainly much here which spoke for the ordination of both, but to this the Missionaries could not make up their mind. They deferred the thing for some months, and at last in October they came to the unanimous resolution of choosing the catechist Aaron. He was the elder of the two, best acquainted with the country people, and most able to converse with them. His ordination was fixed for the feast of Christmas, and having been announced to the congregations in the country and to the Mission in Madras, it took place on the 28th December, 1733. Eleven clergymen were present; the six Missionaries of the place, Sartorius from Madras, the two Danish ministers of Tranquebar and two ship-chaplains. After the ceremony Aaron preached on Galatians IV. 4, 5, and afterwards partook of the Lord's Supper, together with the catechists who were to be under his charge. The catechist Diogo was ordained at Christmas, 1741.

Aaron was born of heathen parents in Cuddalore about 1698. His father Sockanada-Pillei was a merchant of a very respectable caste, had his son taught to read and write and kept him carefully to his idol-worship. Now it happened that the charity-school for native children, founded by the English in 1717, was exactly opposite to his father's house, so that it was very easy for him to make acquaintance with the catechist Schawrimuttu who then had charge of it. From him he obtained some biblical books, read them diligently, and "I perceived," he relates, "that God's word was working like a fire within me to melt my stony heart (Jerem. XXIII, 29), but this was only a small beginning. The earthly thought arose in me: Thou canst not leave thy father and mother, if thou goest away, who knows what evil may happen to thee?" In the providence of God, his parents got into some trouble with the company, were obliged to leave the town, fell into poverty and could not support him. Then what he had heard of christianity recurred to him, and he wished much to go to Tranquebar where he hoped to be taken care of both bodily and spiritually; he did not know the road, but met and accompanied a Pariah, who was on his way thither. On arriving there, he went to the catechist Schawrimuttu, who received him as one who was known to him and took him to Ziegenbalg, who instructed him and baptized him in the year 1718. Then came his parents and wished to take him away again, but he stood firm. The Missionaries first employed him as a school-master, then as a catechist, till in the year 1727 he began to make himself particularly useful amongst the country congregations. After his ordination he redoubled his activity, and after a time the Missionaries perceived a great awakening amongst the country people. Sartorius of Madras who was present at his ordination says of it: " he preached with great chearfulness from Gal. IV. 4, and particularly exhorted the Christians from the country (who were to be his especial charge) to be thankful for the benefits that would thus be bestowed on them; while he begged others to pray God to give him the gifts necessary for his office. By constant journies into the country he has gained great practice, and according to the testimony of all who know him, has hitherto proved himself very faithful. He has very dignified and agreeable manners, which gifts of Nature are rare amongst the Malabarians."

In order to give the reader an idea of Aaron's activity, I will give one of his accounts of his journies: — "After I had said my prayers and eaten a little food, I started on the 27th of March 1734, with the people who were to accompany me. When I came to P. I was received by a heathen to whom I read Acts XVII, 27—28. and then talked to him of the knowledge of God by his works, both in the support and creation of them, and showed him how they had left the only true God, whom they might thus have known, and worshipped many false gods, in whom they placed their confidence; in this indeed their heathenism consisted. He was so angry at this, that he showed us the door and began to abuse us, called us perverters of religion and seducers of the people, and so irritated the whole neighbourhood against us, that no one would allow us to enter into their houses, or even give us a place where we might eat. We were therefore obliged to sit on a bank near to take our mid-day meal. Thence we went on to M. where the christian Mutappen came to meet us with some of his friends. I said to them, "as God has led me to you, so let us have a short prayer together." Then we fell on our knees and prayed, but as I had to prepare my sermon for the next day, I could not then remain longer with them. On the 28th I preached a Lent-Sermon from the 26th Chapter of the Gospel according to St. Matthew, verses 1—35. Twenty nine of our christians were present, and 7 heathens. After the sermon was over, I examined the children in Catechism, and we then concluded with prayer. I asked our Muttappen especially, who has a very christian spirit, whether he had anything to complain of: to this he answered that his worldly affairs were going on tolerably well, but that it was bad for his soul to live in such a place; that was his only trouble: when I asked him what he meant, he answered, "You have christian parents and churches amongst you, and can hear the word of God at all times, but here we have nothing of the sort and are surrounded by heathens." An old woman said to me, "You see my necessities, and that I am now very old; I beg you therefore to tell the under-Catechist Schawri to take better care of my soul." I asked her, "When you die, to whom will you commend your soul?" She answered, "To him who was born of Mary! I took the opportunity of explaining this fully to her, and comforted her with promises from God's word. Then I announced that the coming feast of Easter would be celebrated in the country, for which purpose all christians were to assemble at S., where the service would be held; they were very much pleased at this. In N. I went into the house of a heathen, for the mid-day meal;—when I spoke to him on the folly of idolatry, he pointed to his stone idols and said, "You mean to say that it is nonsense to believe in gods of stone and metal; but it is an undoubted truth that this stone-god as he stands now before our eyes, grew out of the earth in former days." I tried to dissuade him from this superstition. In the evening I arrived at T. Our Adi, with five of his relations who were still heathens, came to me under a tree. I spoke to them of the knowledge of God, that he is Lord of our bodies and souls and of everything that we possess; and of the forgiveness of sins which they sought in vain from their false gods. On the 29th these people gave up their house to me that I might use it for a place of assembly. Forty-two persons came together there. I first spoke to the heathen listeners, and then preached to the christians on Matt. XXVI. 36—56. Adi's daughter and son-in-law promised to join our church."

"When I went to S. on the 30th, the christian Manickam came to me; I laid it to his heart to think properly of the blessings he had gained from Christianity, not to suppose that he owed them to his own wisdom or merits, but entirely to the grace of God. I reminded him to read a chapter in the New Testament for his edification daily, and each time to pray to God. He said that he did not know how to compose a prayer for such an occasion, and asked me to write one for him. I therefore gave him the following prayer, written on a palm-leaf: "Dear heavenly Father, my Lord and my Creator, as thou hast given thy Son for my sins, I bring my humble prayer before thee. I am of very weak understanding, and do not rely on my own ability. O merciful God! make me rightly to understand the Gospel which I am now about to read. Lighten the eyes of my understanding, that I may learn to know thee and to live to thy pleasure. Give me grace to stand as immoveable as a tree which is firmly rooted, and to find refuge and protection in thy Son. Hear me, O Lord, for thy Son's sake; Amen."

"After I had sent on the under-catechist Schawri, to assemble our people at the appointed place, I arrived at P. on the 31st. There I spoke to a heathen on the creation, and preservation and on the benefits which God has given to us in his Son Jesus. On the 1st of April I arrived at S. Here there is a Hindù who has built a house for travellers to rest in, has dug a tank in which he bathes daily, and has planted some beds of flowers from which he daily picks the blossoms and strows them before the idols, in the firm belief that his sins will thus be remitted. I tried to prove to him by the evidence of his own countrymen that these things could not be sufficient for the forgiveness of sins, for a Tamil song says, "By whatever path sins come, they must go away by the same." Now it is taught amongst you that sins are committed by the heart, the eyes, the mouth, and the hands:—if they are to be removed, they must be grieved for by the heart, wept for by the eyes, prayed for by the mouth, and as a sign of true conversion the hands must be used for good works. But if God will forgive us our sins, such forgiveness cannot take place without a Mediator and Saviour."

"On the 2nd I came to S: and held a discourse on Matt.

XXVI. 57—75 in the house of Devasagayam, a christian. There were thirty eight of our christians there, and 9 heathens. I particularly remarked to the latter that there was but one God, who had created us and the whole world, but they were like children who did not know their own father, but united themselves to strange false gods. I asked them whether the king of Tanjore, whose subjects they were, would allow them to keep back their tributes from him, and give it to some foreign lords; and further when death came, which of their idols would save them? after which I spoke of the resurrection from the dead. Then I spoke especially to each one of our christians. The relations of our Devasagayam are still all heathens. He begged me to speak a word of warning to them, which I did, and they promised to to join our church. His mother said to me, "If you cure my son's sickness I will come also." I represented to her that there were two kinds of sickness, that of the body and that of the soul. For our bodily sickness God had ordered certain means of cure which by his blessing would remove it, but we men ought to think far more about the sickness of our souls. It was like a cancer consuming all around it, and was the sinful corruption which clave to every one: she must not think that she had it not, but must examine herself and think over the sins which she had committed from her youth. After this the children repeated the catechism.

On the 3rd I arrived at S. Here I spoke with some of our christians who came to see me, and sent out Schawri and Njanajudam to call the people together to hear God's word. The heathen brother of our Sinappen was very sick;—he sent to me several times begging me to come and baptize him, or as he expressed it, to reconcile him to that God, whose feet he had kissed; but I waited for a time in order to awaken a deeper reverence and a more ardent desire for this holy ordinance in his soul; he was however so vehement in his prayers that I went to him in the night. I asked him, "What makes you so anxious to be baptized; have you no gods to help you in Mayaveram and Siarhi that you send for us?" *Answer.* "In order to be freed from my sins." *Question.* "What has given you these ideas?" *Answer.* "My brother Sinappen said to me with grief, brother, if you should die, how should I dare to burn you who are a heathen? you are dying in the name of the devil? Now in my days of health I never took any trouble to become a child of God, and my heart has become very heavy on that account: when my brother prays with me, I pray with my mouth and repeat after him, O Jesus." *Question.* "Shall I baptize you at once?" *Answer.* "Ah yes, let this blessing come to me at this time." *Question.* "If you die in this illness, do you think that you shall die in the name of Jesus your Saviour?" *Answer.* "Yes." *Question.* "But if you recover from this sickness, will you then, according to the covenant into which you are about to enter, remain unchanged in the christian religion until the time of your death, and like other christians watch carefully to the salvation of your soul?" *Answer.* "Yes." I then went through the five brief rules of the order of salvation, explained them, prayed over him and baptized him. On the 4th we had a meeting at the house of our assistant Njanajudam, at which 47 of our christians were present. A hymn on our Saviour's Passion was first sung and a prayer offered up and then an exposition given on Matt. XXVII. 1—26, after which followed some more verses of the hymn and prayer. In the afternoon I began my return journey, came to K. where I talked with the christians on the sufferings of Christ, and arrived at Poreiar in the evening. During this journey I have seen traces of much that is good and upright amongst many of the christians."

This is perhaps enough for a sample. On the working of Aaron's ordination the Missionaries write thus to the Court-preacher Ziegenhagen in London, who had for many years been a friend to the Mission. "Your Reverence will like to know how our native preacher is going on, and what effect his ordination has had on the heathen. You will see testimonials to his work in our reports showing how he preaches the word of God to our congregations in the country, administers the sacraments at various places, superintends the carrying out of proper discipline and order, manages and encourages the catechists, in which things he has made great progress, and will continue to make more as he gains experience in the things which belong to the kingdom of God and to the ministry. May God preserve his delicate health in these journies which on account of the heat, the wind, the dust and the wading through water, are very arduous in this country. With regard to the second point, we have had many instances both in the territories of the company and in the country, of the good effect which his ordination and the exercise of his ministry have produced on the natives, because they see that one of their own nation can be found, who devotes himself to teaching a congregation in the things connected with God and eternity, without seeking his own advantage. From the increased consideration in which he is held, the way to christianity has been made easier to many, for they have thus overcome the disgrace connected with it. His house in Poreiar is constantly visited, not only by members of the congregation, but also by Hindûs of different grades. He thus has the opportunity of making this intercourse conduce to the extension of the kingdom of God, some of the fruit ripening quickly, some after a time. May the Lord give to us and our work many more like him, yea better and better native Teachers! We trust in his mercy to accomplish this."

Aaron continued year after year in the exercise of his laborious ministry, occupied almost constantly with journies into the country. In order to relieve him of part of the fatigues, a horse was procured for him, but yet his health suffered much. He lived on the best terms with all his colleagues, but more especially with Diogo, and they divided the work between them. Missionary Wiedebrock, who speaks of this beautiful union, says that it arose from the humility of both. Aaron had once said to him of his colleague, "I am like a child compared to Diogo, with regard to knowledge and ability." And yet Diogo acknowledged that Aaron could manage the natives much better than he could.

In the last letter but one which Aaron wrote to the Mission College he says, "Though my bodily weakness is a great hinderance to my journies, I wish to work as much as possible for the benefit of souls. Sometimes when the Missionaries tell me to go to a strange place, I set off in fear thinking, "Who knows what misfortunes may happen to you?" But the Lord has always brought me back in safety; and I have most undoubting certainty that this safety is owing to his protection. Sirs, the worship and kingdom of the devil are falling into ruin: the dominion of the kingdom of Christ will be spread everywhere, the inhabitants of distant lands shall come to enter it in faith. The Lord alone can be our helper in the sufferings which lie before us. According to your advice I will patiently bear all crosses and trials that may come upon me for the sake of Christ, and will console myself in the thought that the rewards of a future world are far more considerable than the sufferings of the present time; in him alone will I seek for help and consolation. I am often cast down in my mind; but when we suffer thus the God of grace will send his Spirit to us, and come to help our weakness. (Heb. IV. 15.) Our country having now suffered from war and scarcity for several years, our people are in great distress. The French have brought some papist teachers to Carical, which is not far from Tranquebar, and there they have assembled a small congregation; they do not however build in the strength of Christ, but by worldly advantages, by mammon or money, by errors, by heathen ceremonies and the like wood and sand. What the mind of the Lord is on this point, we cannot tell."

In his last letter to the College, he and Diogo write: "The Hindùs wandered in many paths like sheep without a shepherd, took darkness for light, Satan for God, hell for heaven, and thus lost their souls, but God who is rich in mercy, not only sent them evangelical teachers for their enlightenment, but has also enlightened and selected us from amongst them ordaining us to teach our coutrymen instead of leaving them to the Brahmins, the Mendicants and the Exorcists, who like murderers of souls misled the people by external ceremonies and would finally have led them to the devil in the abyss. We do not consider this as a reward of our merits, but solely as a benefit which is given to us by the grace of God."

Aaron undertook his journies in 1745 in much suffering, but of this he took no particular notice; yet thoughts of death hovered over him. When he was told of the sudden death of one of his acquaintances, he said, "if that strong and healthy man is dead, how much ought I to think of it?" In all his latter journies he bade adieu to the Missionaries as if he should never see them again. He undertook his last journey in the month of June, to celebrate the feast of Whitsuntide in the district of Mayaveram. He assembled the christians at Tattenur, and according to the testimony of his assistant, preached very impressively though he was suffering great pain. He warned the assistants that they must not be like hirelings, and exhorted them to faithfulness. To the christians he said that it was the last time that he should celebrate the feast amongst them, and they must therefore be on their guard that it might become a blessing and not a curse to them. He returned home very ill, and said to a Missionary who came to visit him in Poreiar, "my country journies are ended." He however improved a little, and on the 23rd of June he came in to Tranquebar to be present at the marriage of his daughter to the son of Diogo; but the next day he lay on his dying bed in unspeakable agonies, yet with his full consciousness, and with his heart turned to the Lord who alone can help. He embraced his two sons-in-law, caused his youngest children to be brought and gave them a farewell kiss: then he said, "My Lord and my God; thou knowest that I have served thee without deception or hypocrisy, and thou art a witness that I have wandered through forests and fields;" his pain here became so severe that he could not say anything more, but cried out, "My Jesus, my Lord, draw near to me, draw near to me!" In the afternoon he received the Eucharist in the presence of the priest Diogo and many christians, and showed himself truly humble, penitent and believing. After 24 hours of severe suffering, he died, aged 47 years, and was buried in the old Jerusalem Church.

"We can in all sincerity testify of him," say the Missionaries, "that he worked with all faithfulness according to the knowledge and insight, grace and gifts, which God had given him, and that his services to the congregations both here and in the country have been very useful and much blessed. His loss (especially when we think of the country, and how few earnest workers are to be found there) almost affects our hearts more nearly than if one of ourselves had left this world; for he could go and work in places that we cannot enter. He was a man who conducted himself in such a way, that both christians and heathens not only felt respect for him, but also loved and trusted him. In difficult circumstances which might occur to the congregation he could give excellent advice both from his upright judgement and his experience. He possessed a peculiar ability for learning in a proper manner, even from very simple people, in what way God had first drawn their souls to himself. He could give a complete account of the congregation, and could tell what was wanting to each member of it, and how each one should be exhorted according to his circumstances. He warned and punished evil-doers earnestly and impressively; but the sick and suffering he treated with love. He bore his sufferings with extraordinary courage and firmness. Doubtless this faithful servant now enjoys the fruit of his works."

CHAPTER XI.

NATIVE TEACHERS.—THE CATECHIST RAJANAIKEN.—THE MISSION SETS FOOT IN THE STATES OF THE KING OF TANJORE.—STATE OF THE MISSION IN THE YEAR 1740.

We have already related that Ziegenbalg had turned his attention to the states of the king of Tanjore and that he did not succeed in entering them for the preaching of the Gospel. When Schultze was at the head of the Mission, its fame reached as far as the Court of Tanjore, and a Prince of the name of Telungurasa, who was nearly related to the King, sent a Brahmin to Tranquebar in the year 1721, in order to inquire into its regulations. Schultze profited by this circumstance to begin a correspondance with the Prince, in whom he gained a friend and protector for the Mission. Schultze even received an invitation to visit him, but he could not leave Tranquebar where he had so much to occupy him. When Schultze went to Madras, the other Missionaries wrote to the Prince and renewed the communication with him; but it was neither the Prince nor any of the mighty of the earth who were to open the way for the Gospel into the kingdom of Tanjore;— a poor outcast Pariah was to be the instrument of this great work.

His name was Rajanaiken; he was an under-officer in the service of the king, and generally lived in the city of Tanjore, though sometimes sent into the country on different duties. We will give particular attention to this remarkable man, who was in the service of the Mission for more than forty years. As he was brought up in the Roman-Cotholic church, he may be taken as a representative of those natives, who left that communion for the Lutheran and attached themselves to the Mission. In a letter dated 1732 he relates the events of his life in such a lively manner, that I will here give it at length:—

"My grandfather remained a heathen until he was 30 years of age, and then joined the Romish church. When my Father was born he was baptized, and I also received the holy rite soon after my birth. We loved the holy Xavier very much, and built a chapel to his honour, in which service was performed morning and evening. When I had reached my 22nd year, and together with my younger brother Sinappen, had learned to read, I took a great fancy for reading the books of the Romish church; my brother followed my example. All the palmleaf books which were given to me to read, contained the papal histories of Saints, the miracles of the Virgin Mary, and a few of those of Christ. When I read of what Christ had suffered for us, God caused such an emotion in my heart that I began to meditate on what sin really is, and began to fear his judgement. Then I became very anxious to know what had happened before Christ, up to the time of Moses. I tried both flattery and presents on the catechists to induce them to lend some books descriptive of this, but they declared that they neither possessed nor knew of any such books. When I pressed them to beg them of the priests, they answered that it was of no use to apply to them, for as the books of Moses do not exist in Tamil, why ask for them? But the desire of obtaining them gained the mastery over me. It happened at this time that a Catholic mendicant monk, of the name of Sittananden, came to Madowipatnam in the year 1725. He had a book in which the four Gospels and the Acts of the Apostles were bound up together. (Ziegenbalg's Translation of the New Testament, 1st Part. Tranquebar. 1714.) He could not read it himself and had no taste for what he had heard out of it: on the suggestion of some one else who could read, he had torn out the title page, on which were printed the name of our king and of the town of Tranquebar. As soon as I saw the book, I showed him great respect and said, "Eh, what is that? He said that he had got it in Mailapur.* I begged him to leave the book with me for a few days;

*This was clearly untrue. He had received the book from Schultze in 1724. I will give the account of the two visits of this beggar monk from the Halle reports, as some light is thereby thrown on the Roman Catholic Missionaries in India. Schultze writes in 1724 "A catholic mendicant monk visited me, to whom I gave a short explanation of yesterday's Tamil sermon, but it seemed to be a complete mystery to him. After he had been some time in Tranquebar he came to say goodbye to us before starting again on his journey. This man had been a heathen priest, and not only joined the Papists himself, but persuaded all his hearers, whole villages and hamlets, to become christians, for he represented to them that hitherto he had been deceiving them, but now that he had found the true religion, they ought to follow him and become what he was. He carried a great piece of linen with him, on which was a short series of pictures of Scripture history. There was represented a tall naked man in whose back, hands, feet, sides and everywhere little children were to be seen: when I asked who it was meant for, he answered that it was Adam and that the children seen through his skin represented how many nations had sprung from him. I wished to talk to him on the Christianity of the heart, but he considered himself as a great Saint, and that nothing was wanting to him but to convert more heathen. If this had but been the case! I gave him the four Evangelists and the Acts of the Apostles in Tamil, with the One hundred Rules of life, (according to Wilken's Communion-book, Tranquebar, 1721.) He asked me why I remained quiet in Tranquebar, and did not travel into the country, by which means I might gain many more converts. I answered him that I was now alone, and that even if I wished, I could not be away for a day. If time and opportunity came God would point out the way, and also those whom I ought to help."

In October 1726, Missionary Walther writes, "The Catholic begger monk came to see me. Amongst other things he showed us a picture of Christ complaining to Joseph of having been struck by the Jews as a child, and another of the burial of the Apostle James in Spain: I told him that these tales were not to be found in the Bible; then he showed us Adam and Eve standing under the forbidden tree, and opposite to them Christ on the cross; this he explained by saying that as Eve used her feet to approach the tree, the feet of Christ were nailed to the cross, and that it was because she stretched out her hand to pluck the forbidden fruit that Christ's hands were pierced:—moreover that as Eve had been made from a rib out of Adam's side, so Christ must be pierced in the side. I said to him that when he showed these pictures to the people he should particularly point out to them that thus sin and death came into the world through one man, and that there was no salvation but through Christ. He said that it was much more difficult to convert the people and as I supported him for several days and gave him a turban, he granted my request. He started off again on his begging journey, left me the book and said, "You can keep it for your own reading, but take care that the Priest does not see it." When I had thus obtained the book, my longing was satisfied by it. I used to read it all day and then from evening till midnight by a light. When I had read it through, the Lord had given me great light in understanding it, I wished to begin it again, but then the troublesome thought arose, "When Sittananden returns and wants his book, what will you do?" I therefore determined to copy it all out on Palm-leaves and make a book of them, and so began to write. I copied the gospels of St. Matthew and Mark and part of Luke, but being but little accustomed to writing, my hand was so tired that I could do no more. Moreover as Sittananden did not return to Tanjore, I left off writing. I did not know that it was the Gospel which had been printed at the Tranquebar Press, but supposed it to be one of the books of the Romish Priests. The texts which struck me most while I was reading poured like oil upon my faith and caused it to burn brightly. In the year 1727 I was commanded to go to the villages which lie near Tranquebar; in Tirukadeiur I met with a man named Schawrimuttu, a papist, who possessed a small printed book in the form of a letter addressed to all Malabarians

on the coast than in the interior; that since he had last been in Tranquebar 2000 people living about Madura and towards the dominions of the Mogul had become christians, and that in the country the people did not lead such a godless life as on the coast. He asked whether I was married, adding that he and his priests were not so. I explained to him that it was very well if this gift were given by God to a man, but that is was a human decree to enforce celibacy and explained to him what St. Paul says to Timothy on the subject. They hold marriage as a sacrament. I asked him whether he still had the book which Schultze gave him. He said that he had and that Ziegenbalg, whom he praised highly, had once given him 26 sermons. I gave him the Epistles, the first part of the Old Testament, and two little books, because he said that he wanted something to discuss with the heathen. He finally admired the efforts that were being made here for the conversion of the natives, so much greater than in other places.

(written by Ziegenbalg, Tranquebar 1717), and though he could not read, he pretended to read out of it anything that camè into his head, for which his ignorant (Romish) hearers gave him alms. I bought the book from him for one fano, and asked him how he came by it? I got it from a German priest, answered he. A German priest, said I, what does that mean? Those who do not pray to our holy mother are German priests, said he,·there are two kinds of priests. When I heard that, I thought whether it were possible for christianity to be divided into two sects, and I began to doubt as to which of them might possess the gift of salvation. Then I said, I must enquire into this thoroughly; make me acquainted with these German priests; if you bring me another book I will repay you. He brought me another book, treating of heathenism (also written by Ziegenbalg, Tranquebar 1713.) As soon as I had bought it from him, I wrote a letter to the priests, and sent him off with it. He brought me another book called Theology (Theology by Freylinghausen, Tranquebar 1716), but he had not given the letter to the priests. I paid him for the book but as I saw that he was a deceiver I sent him back again with a letter, and said, this time you must bring me back a very large book from the priests. This letter he also put aside, and came back with all sorts of lies, telling me that the priests required 4 Fano before they would send the book: I saw that this was false, yet I gave him the money together with a letter, but I sent a man after him to watch him and see where he went. When this messenger returned and brought me news, I sent a letter by him to the book-binder Johann. He sent me an answer and the large Catechism (Abstract of Spener's Explanation of the Catechism, Tranquebar 1719.) All the letters which I had written before, had been kept back by my messenger. When I had read Johann's letter, I wrote another letter to the priests and sent it by my new messenger. The priests immediately sent me an answer with the books of Moses which I had so long desired, and moreover the second part of the Old Testament. (Tranquebar, 1720 and 1726.) My wish was therefore most comfortably fulfilled. I then went myself to Tranquebar with my brothers, visited the priests, and received the Epistles and Gospels bound up together (the whole New Testament.) Moreover I had the opportunity of talking with them on the difference between the Romish and the Evangelical creeds. After I had had about six month's intercourse with them, partly by writing, partly by word of mouth, and had studied the Bible after I returned to Tanjore, the evangelical texts which shine like stars in heaven had awakened and strengthened me. I was thereby persuaded to leave the Romish church. When I returned to Tranquebar in 1728, I joined the Evangelical congregation, and became a servant of the church. This is what has happened to me, a poor sinner, but God has shown himself merciful even to such an one and has made me a partaker in the salvation of his most holy Son; to him and to our Lord Jesus Christ be honour and praise for ever and ever."

As soon as Rayanaiken had thus received enlightenment in the christian faith, he was anxious to communicate it to others, and even before he had formally joined the Evangelical Church he came to Tranquebar in the summer with three of his soldiers, whom he had taught himsef as well as he could, and who having given up the worship of idols wished to be baptized. The Missionaries told him that these men must be better instructed first, and learn the most important parts of the small Catechism: he therefore determined to leave them in Tranquebar for some days, and see whether he could not answer for their absence to his superiors; if they were not satisfied he would send a messenger for them, but he begged that the Missionaries would do their utmost to finish their instruction in a week, and then to let him know when they were to be baptized. All possible diligence was given to teaching these catechumens, who made use of the time to the best advantage, asked questions when they did not understand, and in ten days had learned the commandments, the articles of belief, the Lord's Prayer and the explanation of Baptism in the short Catechism, one of them also what is said there on the Lord's Supper, and this when they could not read for themselves but were obliged to learn it as it was repeated to them. They sent a messenger to Rayanaiken, who speedily came. The Missionaries pointed out the 10th Chapter of the Acts of the Apostles to him, where mention is made of the Centurion Cornelius, and his God-fearing soldiers, and as the word centurion was rendered "Sêrweikâren" in the Tamil translation, which was his own rank in the army, he was very much pleased and exhorted his soldiers earnestly. These latter professed their faith openly before the congregation, were baptized, and returned the next day to their duties.

In the same year, 1727, the catechist Aaron was sent forth to inquire into the state of things in Tanjore, and to make the way easier to him, he had a letter and some small presents for Prince Telungurasa, who received him very kindly, and invited the Missionaries to come to see him at Pulliruckumwölur (Vyteesurenkoil), a town which lies about one day's journey north-west from Tranquebar, and to which he was going in the course of the next year to a heathen festival. Before the end of the year, the Missionaries baptized fifteen heathens from Tanjore who were brought to them by Sattianaden, a son of the

Romish catechist Surappen. This Sattianaden was placed as catechist over this young and small flock.

In March 1728, Missionary Pressier started to meet Telungurasa according to his invitation. He was very kindly received by him, and had an opportunity of speaking of the principal points of christian faith before him and a number of Malabar learned men. Telungurasa cared for his entertainment; and invited him to visit him in Tanjore during the ensuing summer when the marriage of his son was to be celebrated. Pressier accepted the invitation with pleasure, as it would be the first occasion on which the gates of the heathen capital had opened to a Missionary of ours. Telungurasa sent a carriage for him which brought him safely to Tanjore just at the time when the newly-married Prince was making his entry. Pressier's coachman advised him to cover himself that the guard at the gate might not perceive that he was an European, but he having made known who and what he was, during his whole journey, determined to do so here, and advanced into the town without difficulty, where the Prince received him into his house and showed him all the friendship he could desire. Pressier had an opportunity of speaking to him in the presence of a great many others, and declared to him the intentions of the Tranquebar Mission, and afterwards when he spoke to the prince alone he told him freely that though he was seeking for salvation, his idol-worship was not the true path to it; that he must advise him to leave the service of idols and of sin, and to turn to the true God and the only Mediator Jesus Christ, for whose sake God had promised that all who should believe in him and be baptized, should be saved; but that all men who had not this faith should be given up to eternal condemnation. His calling would not allow him to be silent on this point, lest he should feel guilty when they should meet before the judgement-seat of God. Telungurasa did not say much to this, indeed he was always a man who spoke but little, but he continued to show great friendship to Pressier, permitted him to go into the town and to speak to any one in his house. It was a great delight to the evangelical christians in the suburb of Tanjore to see Pressier, for the catholics had reproached them, saying, that their priest sat in a corner and never came near them. As he always made known the word of God whenever a suitable opportunity offered as he was passing through the town, he was very near being forced out of it in a hurry, for the Mohammedans who formed the town-garrison, and who were perhaps urged on by the Roman Catholics took his free speaking in very ill part; and one day as he was passing by the principal guard and saluted the Mohammedan soldiers, one of them called out to him, "You live on the fat of the Mohammedan religion, and are come to throw sand in the eyes of the heathen," by which they meant that whatever the christians might advance against heathenism was borrowed from Mohammed and that they were strutting about in borrowed feathers. Immediately after this he was stopped by the Mohammedan Cutwal or Town-bailiff who spoke to him very sharply, and sent to the Commandant to know what was to be done with him. Towards evening an order came to take him out of the town, and the Cutwal and his soldiers wished to carry out this order immediately; but meanwhile the affair had come to the ears of Telungurasa who immediately sent some soldiers to release Pressier: he was close to the gates when they stopped him, and after some altercation with the people of the Cutwal, they led him back to the Prince, who arranged the affair with the Commandant and warned Pressier not to speak on religion when he went out in future; though he gave him full leave to speak to those who should come to visit him in his house, and visiters were not wanting. When he wished to return home, Telungurasa had some difficulty in getting the necessary pass from the Commandant, but it was finally obtained and he left Tanjore in the same carriage which had brought him there. On his way he began to speak with the heathens one day on the text, "And this is life eternal, that they might know thee the only true God and Jesus Christ whom thou hast sent," but Telungurasa's people interrupted him hastily, being fearful of the consequences. Pressier remarks on this, "The help and protection which one enjoys from man, may be a great assistance, but on the other side, it is also an obstacle. May God therefore cause the labourers in his work to be ever less and less in need of outward help, and particularly cause faithful and enlightened men to arise from amongst the people, who, armed with the gospel of Christ and freed from those difficulties which beset the path of Europeans, may turn their country-men to the Lord." This wish was partly fulfilled that very year when Rayanaiken began his service in the Mission. He could no longer support himself amongst the Roman Catholics, who, unable to oppose him in argument or to silence him by fair promises, took refuge in threats and maledictions. Rayanaiken therefore went with some of his friends to Tranquebar and having given up his military position, was employed by the Mission as a catechist in the Tanjore territory; his brother Sinnappen being assigned to him as an assistant. After he had partaken of the Lord's Supper for the first time, he left the Missionaries who exhorted him to steadfastness, and promised to pray for him as there was no knowing what his opponents might do. "I shall represent to them," said he, "that it is very unwise to throw stones at one who has a very important and powerful man as his protector, for it is very likely that the powerful man himself may come out to meet them. Thus I have taken refuge in Jesus."

Thus he went forth to his work in Tanjore, and if he had before been a thorn in the eyes of the Roman Catholics, he now became doubly so. "To what church do you belong?" he was one day asked scoffingly before his last journey to Tranquebar. "Ah, how many churches are there?" asked he. "Two," said the mockers, "the romish and the heretic." "I belong to neither of these," said Rayanaiken, "but to the one holy church which is mentioned in the catechism." Even then he understood how to answer thus intelligently, but he asked and received from the Missionaries further instruction in Church-History before returning amongst his angry opponents, whose conduct may be imagined from a letter which he wrote soon after his return. "After I had said goodbye to you," he writes, "I returned to Tanjore; but even before I left Tranquebar the catechist at Tanjore had written to the Priest at Elakuridschi (Father Beschi, an European) to tell him that Rayanaiken, his brother, Schawrimuttu and Sandiar (a sub-officer and a soldier who accompanied them) had all four joined the heretical priest at Tranquebar. Thereupon the priest called his catechists together, and sent them into Tanjore with orders to call together the elders and principal people of eighteen villages and to bring them to his house. If any one hesitated about coming, they were to give him some food. The catechists assembled the people and led them to Elakuridschi. The priest said to them, "Rayanaiken has joined the heretics, do you think that right?" They asked him what they ought to do. The priest answered, "If Rayanaiken were to come to me, I would make him know my mind but he does not come: you can do what you like." Then one said, "I will kill him;" but the priest answered, "If you were to kill him it would give us a bad name, so we must go to work in another way, and we will gain our end as certainly as if you were to kill him." Then they returned to Tanjore, and the catechist assembled the people of 18 villages. They went to my native place, Sinneianpaleiam, troubled my parents very much and wished to pull my house down: but the inhabitants of all castes interfered to prevent this outrage. This happened on the very day that I started from Tranquebar. As they could not succeed in pulling my house down, they declared that I had lost my caste, and forbid my relations to hold any intercourse with me. Now that I have arrived in Tanjore many despise me and behave towards me as enemies. They threaten the heathen telling them not to speak to me, which distresses my parents very much. I wished to let you know this and to beg you to send me some good advice."

The Missionaries wrote to Father Beschi on the subject, and exhorted Rayanaiken to show patience, to keep quiet for a time, and meet his opponents with gentleness and humility, but though he followed this advice, and would not dispute with the Roman Catholics, his persecutions continued with great bitterness for many years. It would take too much space to particularize all that he had to suffer; we can only find room for some of the more prominent features. His parents and some of his relations joined the Evangelical Church in 1728 and partook of the Lord's Supper in Tranquebar. This step cost his father his life, for in 1731 a number of armed papists attacked him and his relations under pretext of a quarrel about some property, and while the old man was trying to defend his youngest son from the murderers, he was himself overpowered and sank under their blows:—two hours afterwards he expired, crying out, "My Father!" His sons exposed the corpse at the gates of the town, hoping thus to attract the attention of the authorities, but as they had no money to give, they could not get justice. Rayanaiken himself was in constant danger of his life, for his enemies did not satisfy themselves with branding his name, but in the year 1732 sent assassins to his house by night, who however failed in their aim. The year after, he and his companions were attacked by papists on the road to Tranquebar; a sword was drawn against him, when his wife threw herself between him and it, and he escaped from his enemies with rough treatment only. It happened thus almost every year: and he tried to take all these troubles as useful exercises for patience. "As I have to bear so much contempt, abuse and threatening," he writes in 1735, "I will tell you how I console myself. The Lord means well towards me both for time and for eternity: the sufferings which he sends me will work for me a far more exceeding weight of glory, for which I look with anxious trust. I have not been able to hide these thoughts from my people. God has graciously granted me this relief, and without his will nothing can happen to me." His patience and long-suffering were blessed, for he won many souls, and amongst them some of his most violent enemies. He possessed a thorough acquaintance with the Bible, and an excellent delivery. He even ventured on a connected discourse, for I find it remarked that in 1736 when one of the Missionaries was ill, he took his place in Jerusalem Church, and preached on Matt. XVI. 18, showing that the church is built on the rock of Christ and that the gates of hell shall not prevail against it. He was not however ordained, because his caste was so contemptible, that people of consequence would not pay any attention to his words. As this remarkable man lived long after the year 1740, we shall return to his activity and development in the latter part of his life.

If we cast a glance at the condition of the Mission in the year 1740, we find that it had reached its highest point about that time, from which it did not sink down suddenly, for it remained in full activity for some years after, and spread so to speak, though it did not develop itself further. In 1740 it had spread northwards to the English settlements on the coast, Cuddalore and Madras, and in the interior it had spread into the kingdom of Tanjore. Ten European Missionaries were in full activity, with about 30 natives under them. One native, Aaron, was already ordained, and another, Diogo, was soon to be. The number of those who had been converted since the foundation of the Mission was above 5600. The entire Bible had been printed in the Tamil language, and translations of it into other Indian tongues were in the course of preparation. Before we begin to consider the time from 1740 to 1840 in which we shall see how the Mission stood for a time, then became sickly and almost died, we will devote the next Chapter to seeing how it was managed in Europe.

CHAPTER XII.

THE MISSION IS SUPERINTENDED AT HALLE.—NO DESIRE FOR DANISH MISSIONARIES.—SILENCE IN THE PRINTED REPORTS.

It has been already remarked that the Tranquebar Mission was a result of the cooperation of the Danes, the English and the Germans, and this cooperation lasted throughout the time that we have been considering. The original gift of King Frederick IV of 2000 Rix-dollars yearly, had been increased 1000 R. D. by King Christian VI. The English did not merely show sympathy and give their manifold assistance to the Mission in Tranquebar, but they undertook the support of any mission-stations which should be established in their settlements along the coast. Much assistance was sent yearly from Germany, and it was there that everything was arranged, for though a cursory observer might suppose that the Mission was directed by the Mission-College in Copenhagen, and that Francke, father and son, were only sympathetic advisers, a more careful inquiry convinces us that the real spring of the complicated machine was at Halle. The counsel of the counseller had become so indispensable in many respects, that he might fairly be considered as a law-giver.

I will point out one important arrangement in which Halle gained the mastery over Denmark;—that the Missionaries were chosen almost exclusively from that city or the adherents of the Halle school, and this notwithstanding the wish that was expressed in many quarters that they should be Danes, or at least

German subjects of the King of Denmark. This question was often agitated, but it was rarely of any use. It is true that the Court-preacher Masius recommended two Danes as Missionaries, Johann Wilhelm Petersen, who was afterwards Pastor near Rendsburg, and Peter Claussen of Töndern, who was afterwards Preacher at Rodenäs in the provostship of Töndern, but that was before the establishment of the Mission and we cannot but remark that about 1711, when Professors Trellund and Lodberg were made Inspectors of the Mission and recommended two Danish candidates, they were not chosen, though they had already applied themselves to learning Tamil. We have no precise account of the reason for this, but it is certain, that it was the general opinion in Denmark that no Dane could enter the mission owing to the influence of Halle, and on the other hand the people of Halle did not hesitate to ascribe this discontent to the national vanity of the Danes. Dal was a Dane by birth, and was sent to India in 1719, but then he had studied at Halle and was thoroughly imbued with the opinions taught there: in fact he himself was against Danes being sent out to Tranquebar. "I should speak against myself," says he, "were I to advance anything against Danes being fit for the East India Mission, for I am not only a Danish subject of his Majesty by birth, but I scarcely knew any other than my Danish language till I was thirteen years old." He then goes on to show, that many men in Denmark are really converted to God, that they have good opportunities for applying themselves to theology and that learning a foreign language is not difficult to them, but yet he adds, "On the other hand the Missionaries have been nearly all Germans from the very beginning, and no one can deny that this has been the means of procuring us much assistance both from Germany and England. All our affairs are managed in German, the conferences are carried on in that language, it is used in the Collegiis biblicis and in the prayer-meetings; every one reads German books, writes in German to the other Missionaries, to England, to Denmark, and to our superiors, and receives German letters from them in return. If the Missionary is a Dane he is the more likely to be attracted into wordly society, and therefore we may declare this paradox: that in English places a Missionary should not be an Englishman, in Dutch places not a Dutchman, and in Danish places not a Dane. If a single Dane is to be taken, he ought to understand the German language and to be acquainted with Halle and with England. This is the decision of several Danes here on the spot who have the welfare of the Mission at heart. This only applies to Danish-born subjects; but if we look for Danish subjects in general, the Duchy of Schleswig or Southern-Jutland where I was born, the Duchy of Holstein and the country of Oldenburg might be taken into consideration. Danish subjects might therefore be sought for in Halle, as it happened in 1717, when the Mission-College wrote expressly on this point to Profr. Francke, saying that it had heard that there were two Danes, Hammerich and Dal, then studying there."

The Mission-College was very earnest on this point, and in the year 1740, when Missionary Walther returned home, it engaged him to teach Tamil to two Danish candidates, Ole Maderup and Elias Naur Fabricius, and this teaching was to lead to the foundation of a Seminary for the Tranquebar Mission; Francke took this very ill, and according to him the news of it occasioned much apprehension to the Missionaries in Tranquebar, even to Dal, from whom he had least expected it. When one of these Danes, Maderup, was ordained in the year 1741 and sent to India, Francke expressed his disapprobation in a letter to the Mission-Secretary Finkenhagen, and he thus expresses himself in a later letter, "I am very much pleased to hear that the Mission-College agrees with me that it would have been far better if Maderup had not been sent out." Finkenhagen writes on the margin of this, "This was not written to Francke concerning the College but concerning me privately, in order to content the good man, who had been much troubled by this affair." Francke goes on to express that it would be much better to leave the choice of the Missionaries to him, instancing how well the last five Missionaries turned out, and how unitedly they lived together and with Mr. Dal, and representing what a good opportunity he had at Halle for knowing a man before he recommended him. With regard to Bosse and Schultze (whom he calls "not altogether well-advised Missionaries") he does not consider them as resident in Halle, for both had been away for some time, and both were accepted because they offered themselves and there was nothing to be adduced against them, and Schultze more especially on account of his command of languages. When he was accepted, the rule had been followed of allowing the Missionaries to offer themselves, to which Francke the elder encouraged them in his *Collegiis päraeneticis;* but in 1724 by the advice of Francke the younger, they followed the different plan of looking round for suitable people, because they thought that the most sincere minds would be unwilling to forestal the work of God by coming forward themselves, while the unsuitable were ready enough to offer themselves. Thus Francke had chosen Pressier and Walther, by whom the Mission had been so much invigorated, while Bosse, the drunkard, had come forward of his own accord. Francke says that he cannot see any divine guidance in the sending forth of Maderup, and that he does not think that any one chosen at Halle would have been in such a hurry to marry before going out; they could not say that there was no opportunity for marriage in a country where Herr Dal said that there were twenty Danish young ladies who could not get husbands. He adds that he had good reason for supposing that some one had proposed the idea of a Seminary to the King out of ill-will towards him (Francke) and that Maderup was wishing to return home, which would be the best thing he could do as he was unsuited to his place.

These opinions of Francke's received the most complete refutation; for Maderup remained in Tranquebar till his death in 1776, and was on excellent terms with the other Missionaries. One year after Francke had thus confidently expressed himself, he received a severe humiliation : — he had recommended two men, Klein and Göring, who had just been ordained at Copenhagen, when a letter came into Francke's hands which Göring had written that year to a girl who lodged in the house at Zeiz at which he had been teacher, and which contained the most tender expressions, ending with the postscript, "Adieu, my dear heart:" — he had confided this letter to the care of one of his former scholars at the Pedagogium, who kept it back and opened it and thus the news reached Francke. When Göring returned, he was called to account, but as he involved himself in contradictions the result was that his appointment was cancelled. Francke writes soon after this, "I must say that this event, taking place in spite of all my discreet care and usual forethought, has hurt me very much and has been a great humiliation to me." But this humiliation had no lasting influence on his turn of mind, for ten years afterwards when Maderup fell ill and wished to return, and the College was thinking of choosing another Dane in his place, Francke, when his opinion was asked, sent a long answer advising that body to spare itself the trouble, as he could choose best: forgetting what had happened, he says, "I am sure that *all* who have been recommended by me in the last 27 years, have devoted themselves *entirely* to the Mission, and that none of them have left Europe with the idea of ever forsaking it." The end was that though Maderup remained, Francke chose another Missionary from amongst the German-Danish subjects, Peter Dame of Flensburg, who was not yet 24 years of age, and whose father was very much opposed to his going; but at last, after much trouble, he gave his consent.

There was another cause which contributed to the management of the Mission being conducted at Halle, and this was that all its reports were published there; the Mission-College in Copenhagen published nothing, but was satisfied to receive all the accounts from Halle, which were read also with great avidity, not only in Germany, but in all Evangelical countries. These "Detailed Reports from the East Indies" as they were called will always be a principal source of information for those who wish to inquire into the history of the Tranquebar Mission, and I can with truth testify to their reliability, if a report is to be called reliable because all that it contains is true: but if on the other hand a reliable report is considered to be one in which nothing essential is omitted, I cannot recommend these, because all that might hurt the christian public or bring the work into discredit, is evaded. I can easily believe that Francke was very slow to receive the less agreeable news, such as the quarrels amongst the Missionaries, some scandal in the life of one or other of them, and their misunderstandings with the temporal authorities, because he might hope that these things would smoothe down with time, and he would not wish to hurt any one by an unfavourable public mention of his name; I can easily imagine further that the inclination of representing those who are engaged in a work which depends on public charity in the most favourable light, has had the influence on the Halle reports of filling them with that which is agreeable and encouraging, rather than with that wich is disagreeable and saddening. But with every desire to judge fairly, I must declare my conviction that any one who should write an account of the Tranquebar Mission from the Halle reports *alone*, would not give a true picture of it as it was, because many important particulars are carefully left out. With all my respect for the Franckes, father and son, I must declare that any one who compares their public reports with their private letters, cannot resist the unpleasant impression of a sort of clandestine caution ; — I have noticed this more particularly in the younger Francke, with whose private letters I have the more complete acquaintance, but there is no reason for thinking that he did not imitate his father in this; indeed when one considers that there is nothing to be found about Bövingh's quarrel in the Halle reports, it seems that it was the custom already in the time of Francke the elder to suppress what ought to have been mentioned.

In order to put the reader somewhat in a position to judge in this matter, I will give a letter from Francke to Höjer, the Secretary of the Mission-College, which is remarkable also in another particular:—"I cannot blame you for wishing for many improvements in the management of the Mission. Much would be far better if the spirit and remarkable zeal of Ziegenbalg showed themselves amongst the Missionaries; but you will yourself acknowledge that these gifts are not the same in all, as God distributes them according to his good pleasure, and one must take people as one finds them ; — we cannot get them as we would wish to have them, for God from the beginning has carried on our work amidst many trials, thus using feeble instruments, as he often does, to show that the honour is all due to him. When my late father asked me about 15 years ago to take charge of the affairs of the Mission, it appeared as if the sad quarrels between Herr Schultze and Herr Dal had brought it to its last gasp, if one was to judge from their sentiments and from the complicated state of external affairs. I can truly say that I was like Peter (Acts X, 10) when my father gave me the letters from which the 19th Report was to be abstracted. When I said so to him, he answered me that I must not lose heart under such circumstances, but must accustom myself to such trials, as God could awaken his work even from a death sleep. I did not venture to answer, but could not enter into it, especially when for several years we sought for Missionaries at the request of the College, but could not find any. But now God led my thoughts to the late Herr Pressier, whose remarkable sincerity, faith and ability I had long remarked at the Pedagogium. He and another, who now has a living in Brandenburg, determined to accept the call, but as the latter drew back, we looked to Herr Walther by whom I knew that the Mission would be far better served than it would have been by the other, though he was also a good man. Herr Bosse was then added to the number whom we certainly recognized as far the weakest in the gifts both of nature and grace, but as he wished to go and we were in want of help, we would not repulse him. On the arrival of these three in Tranquebar, we heard much more on the state of the Mission, by which, as well as by his subsequent conduct, Dal appeared in a far more favourable light. The Mission then took a turn for the better, and though Schultze's quarrels with the new Missionaries again hindered the improvement and finally obliged him to leave Tranquebar, the result proved that it had not been injured thereby, but on the contrary a blessing was clearly seen when the remaining three were thus enabled to act freely and began the work in the country. Though Schultze could not agree with his colleagues in Madras, but brought on the same confusion there that he had done in Tranquebar, God made use of the two others and so ordered it, that they commenced the Cuddalore Mission at the desire of the English Society. I expect a great blessing of it, for I know them to be two good men. Poor Schultze on the contrary has shown his character so unfavourably, that both I and the Court-preacher Ziegenhagen lose our confidence in him more and more. I still firmly hope in faith in God that he will take care of the Mission in Madras as he has done of that in Tranquebar, though I do not see how it is to be done."

So far Francke. Now I must request the reader to turn his attention to this 19th Report, which was printed at a time when, according to his own account, the Mission appeared to be at its last gasp:—any one who reads, sees nothing of this, there is no sign of its being in the last extremity, or of any unusual obstacles being in the way; indeed Francke tries in the Preface to contradict any unfavourable rumours, and does not say one word on the confused state of affairs, though he promises on the title-page to describe the state of the Mission consistently with truth. I would further ask any one to go through the many Reports which were published during the period of Schultze's long services, and ask whether he could point to a single place in which mention is made of any disagreement between him and his colleagues. It may be said that the fault of this should not be laid on Francke alone, but also on the Missionaries, whose original letters and journals are published in the Halle Reports, but all that was printed passed through

Francke's scissors, who expressly says in a letter to Finkenhagen, "It has been my custom to omit *odiosa* from all journals when they were published." But this kind of report of course gives but an one-sided view.

To give one more proof of Francke's suppressions, I will add that, when the fallen Missionary Bosse at his return from India wished to come to Germany, Francke writes that it cannot be allowed, as his offence, which *until this date is unknown in Germany*, must be noticed on his arrival; it would thus become known, and scandal would arise to the work, as many would take occasion to scoff, and many springs of benevolence might be choked. Here we have Francke's own acknowledgement of what must strike every reader of the Halle Reports, and see that Bosse's vicious conduct, which caused so much trouble for so many years, was not touched upon with one word in the Halle publications, and we also see that the reason of this silence was the dread of diminishing the contributions which flowed into the Mission.

It would be very easy to increase examples of this, but what has been already adduced sufficiently proves that the Halle Reports must be used with caution, and that they are by no means sufficient for any one who wishes to give a true (full) history of the Mission.

Having shown Francke's failings we must remark that he showed a warm zeal, an untiring diligence and a remarkable unselfishness which greatly redound to his honour, indeed he gave up his time and strength to the cause till his very latest breath. It is true that there were many friends to assist him, but there were also many enemies, and the powerful support given by the Halle theologians to the founding and continuance of the Mission, led all those who were not favourable to the one to oppose themselves to the other. Besides that, we have seen how the Roman Catholics attacked the budding evangelical Church in India and they did not fail to do the same in Europe.

CHAPTER XIII.

C. F. SCHWARTZ IN TRANQUEBAR, TRICHINOPOLY AND TANJORE.

We have seen how the Tranquebar Mission was first conducted by Ziegenbalg and Gründler and then by Schultze and his colleagues; amongst the latter there was not one who so raised himself above the rest that the history of the work could be united to his name. The first name of consequence that we meet with, between 1740 and 1840, is Christian Frederick Schwartz*, who worked in the East Indies for nearly half a century, not so as to become the centre of the whole, but so that all eyes were turned towards him. He did not lead the Mission one step further in its development, but many steps in its extent, and therefore we think it right to devote this Chapter to his history, even though it will lead our attention from Tranquebar into the interior of the country.

Schwartz was born at Sonnenburg in Neumark on the 26th of October 1726. His father's name was George; his mother who was one of the Gruner family, died during his early childhood, but on her dying bed she told both her husband and her Confessor, that she had dedicated her son to the service of the Lord, and begged them to promise that at all events they should not hinder the boy if he wished to study theology. He was first

*Life and Acts of the Evangelical Missionary Schwartz, in Schmidt's concise Biographies of remarkable Evangelical Missionaries, Leipzig. 1886. Dr. Pearson's detailed Life of Schwartz which has been translated from English into German I have not seen; but it was made use of by Schmidt.

sent to the school in his native town and then to that at Küstrin, and the good impression which he had received in his childhood, though darkened at times, was never entirely extinguished. A. H. Francke's book entitled, "Footsteps of the living and all-ruling God," made a powerful impression on him, and gave him the desire of visiting Halle, where he arrived in 1746, and met his countryman Benjamin Schultze, who had just returned from India and who advised him to give up his intention of joining the Latin school and to enter the University, as he already possessed the knowledge necessary for such a step. He now attended theological lectures, became teacher at the Orphan-house, and received instruction from Schultze in Tamil, in order to be useful in the correction of the Tamil Bible which they were then preparing to print in Halle. Francke the younger then made his acquaintance, and offered to send him as a Missionary to Tranquebar, an offer which he accepted and to which he kept firm, though a few days after he was offered a good living in the neighbourhood of Halle. Great hopes were entertained of him from the hour that he was called to the work. Francke writes to Finkenhagen, the Secretary of the Mission-College:— "With regard to new labourers, I have not only taken much pains to find suitable men, but have the pleasure of informing you that the Lord has so far given us his blessing that we have already found one, of whom I nourish the hope that he will be approved by the Honourable College, not only on account of his ability and great talents, but also for his other good qualities, and that he will work as a blessing to the Mission. This is C. F. Schwartz of Sonnenburg in the Mark, one of the two students who have begun to learn Tamil in order to make themselves useful in the printing of the Bible, and this, though a small beginning, is yet some preparation. When I first made him the offer, there were some difficulties in the way, but by God's assistance they have all been removed, so that he feels the more certain of the will of God, and has undertaken the work in full confidence in his name and with the complete approbation of his father." In another letter he says that Schwartz had gained such freedom in Tamil, that he could expound the Gospel according to St. John fluently, and also that he made himself a great favourite by his cheerfulness and remarkable purity (*candor*), and being at the same time very diligent in study, it was to be hoped that, with God's blessing, he would become very useful to the work.

In August 1749, Schwartz was ordained at Copenhagen together with the Missionaries Poltzenhagen and Hüttemann, and started for Tranquebar *via* England, arriving in July 1750, and preaching his first Tamil sermon before the end of the year. By his gentle and modest manners as well as by his zeal and ability he won the love and respect of his colleagues, but during the first ten years of his stay in India, there was nothing to distinguish him particularly from the rest. He was, like the others, diligent in the church and in the schools, taught the catechumens and undertook several journies into the interior. "Oh that the Lord would bless my work!" he writes in 1757 to a friend in Europe. "It is certain, and I learn it more thoroughly every day that neither he that planteth nor he that watereth are of any consequence, but God, who giveth the increase. He who does not lean on himself or his own strength, but undertakes the Mission-work in all humility, going forth with prayers and tears to seek the lost, and waiting on the Lord for the early and the latter rain, shall receive a blessing from God, and be preserved from many needless cares. And even if the blessing is not shown immediately, God enlivens the heart and in the

16

mean while we can say "Nevertheless at thy word I will let down the net — *and when they had done this they enclosed a great multitude of fishes.*" This sentence often comes into my mind, more especially as it was the text of my first sermon, and God has wrought humility and a childlike confidence in his word by it. Oh may he ever impress it more and more on my heart by his Spirit."

I must however relate one trait of Schwartz at this time, which does honour to his heart. That he was a great friend to children, though he was never married, is well known, and though far removed from his father's house, he yet remembered his filial duty, of which we have a beautiful little example in the following letter to Justizrath Finkenhagen:—

"I have this year received the sad news of my native town having suffered from a severe fire, by which my father's house has been reduced to ashes, and I have been thinking of some means of performing my duty as a son in sending him some little assistance. I have a watch which was given to me in England, and as I make little or no use of it, I have taken the liberty of sending it to you by Herr Bram, Chaplain of H. M. Ship Bornholm, with the humble request that you will sell it to some watchmaker, and send the proceeds, together with the enclosed letter, to my parents, who live at Sonnenburg in Neumark.

Most respectfully

Tranquebar, 6th. Octr. 1753. C. F. Schwartz."

Finkenhagen remarks on this letter "the watch mentioned herein was sold for 14 Rix-dollars 3 Schllg. at the auction held at the Orphan-house, January 27, 1755."

In the year 1760, Schwartz went by invitation to Ceylon, to strengthen the Lutherans who were employed there in the

Dutch service and to administer the Lord's Supper to them. The journey was quite successful, but when he arrived at Negapatam in September, he heard the extremely surprising news that a wife had arrived for him from Copenhagen. I will relate the whole history of this extraordinary event, as it throws some light on part of the daily life of the Missionaries. It has made an unpleasant impression on my own feelings, but that would not justify me in concealing it. Schwartz's sincerity and energy are remarkably shown from amidst the infirmity and anxiety which surrounded him.

Missionary Kohlhoff was a widower and very delicate. It was with great difficulty that he could take care of his children, though Zeglin's wife was of great use to him. As none of the ladies in Tranquebar seemed suitable for him, he thought that he should like to procure a pious wife from Europe, and Madame Zeglin directed his attention to some of her relations in Colding and Sönderburg. It was then desired, that two of these relations should come out: one was to become Kohlhoff's wife, and the other was to live with the Zeglins who promised to provide for her if she feared God and conducted herself well. And the Ship-Chaplain Böhme, who left Tranquebar in 1754, was requested to arrange this; but he seems at first to have given himself no trouble in the matter. The relations of Madame Zeglin declined the offer, and Kohlhoff was willing to forget the whole affair, though Zeglin was constantly reminding him to make another effort. In the year 1758 Böhme put himself in communication with the Mission-College, and represented that he had received a commission from the Missionaries (indefinitely) to procure wives for them, and that they reminded him of it every year: in consequence of his remarks, two girls, Pernille Thors and

Anne Sophie Pap started for Tranquebar, under the care of the Mission-Assistant Bliesner and his wife. Böhme had in his own mind assigned Pernille Thors to Kohlhoff and Anne Pap to Schwartz, though there is not a trace to be found in any of his letters of a desire to be married. Böhme had certainly overstepped his commission and led the College to do what it never ought to have done without a more complete written expression of what the Missionaries wished. As soon as Kohlhoff heard from Copenhagen that Böhme was selecting a wife for him, he wrote to forbid it, but his letter probably arrived after the girls had started. Bliesner wrote even from Helsingör complaining of the improper conduct of Anne Pap, and again from the Cape a still stronger account enclosing a lampoon on her, apparently written by one of the sailors. When the ship arrived in Tranquebar, the first thing that Bliesner did was to write to the Missionaries and tell them that one of the girls was quite unworthy of entering the house of an honest man. The Missionaries were in great consternation. The bride intended for Kohlhoff, to whom Bliesner gave a good character, was received by the Zeglins into their house; but no one would have anything to say to Anne Pap, except the Dane Maderup, to whom she declared with bitter tears that all that Bliesner had said was false and calumnious, that his wife had taken a dislike to her from the beginning of the voyage and had scolded her in the most frightful way. Anne Pap had not been in any way behind hand with abusive words, so that Maderup considered them as much about equal in that respect, but Bliesner's grave accusations against her could not be proved, though it was clear that she had been thoughtless to the highest degree. What would be the end of it all? The bridegroom, Schwartz, was in Ceylon and had not the slightest idea of what was awaiting him on his return. As soon as he heard the news he wrote the following energetic declaration:—

"I, Christian Frederick Schwartz, testify in the presence of God, to whom all things are known and who will bring all to judgment, that I never, either by word or by writing, either lately or in times past, have given to Herr Justizrath Finkenhagen or Herr Böhme a commission to choose any woman as a companion for me and to send her here from Copenhagen. Thus I declare before God that what has taken place in this affair, is without my knowledge and without my having given my permission by a single word, so that it is not binding upon me either before God or man. I wish that this declaration should be considered as the strongest oath which can reasonably be required of me, for I could not answer otherwise if I were asked on the bed of death itself. I add moreover, 1) that in the beginning I knew nothing of the commission which the dear Brothers Kohlhoff and Zeglin gave to Herr Böhme and Justizrath Finkenhagen, but only heard of it a long time after; 2) that if I had said a word on this subject to Herr Böhme, my name must have appeared; and yet during the seven years correspondence on the subject, my name has not once been mentioned. 3) Justizrath Finkenhagen has not one single line in my handwriting to prove that I have given power to any one to advance any thing from my pay to such a person; neither can Herr Böhme produce such a document. 4) Had I harboured any such intention I should have acted in a most deceitful way not to make it known to one amongst my dear Brothers. 5) If this young girl Anne Sophie had conducted herself properly on board ship so that not a word could be said against her, I yet could not determine to marry her. I am open to conviction as to what happened on board ship, or what is said to have happened, but even if she could prove in a trial that she had conducted herself well, I yet declare that I will not marry her. 6) As I am perfectly innocent in this affair, and have not had anything to do with her being sent out, either by word of mouth or by writing, I will not pay one farthing towards the expenses which may have been incurred thereby. The shame and scoffing which I, even though guiltless, must bear, I forgive from my heart.

May the God of peace tread down Satan, the disturber of peace, under our feet. Written at Negapatam, 9th September, 1760."

Things thus looked very dismal, but when the confusion was at its height, better days appeared, and the history ended with marriage, for not only did Kohlhoff decide on marrying Pernille Thors, but Anne Pap was also provided for. She had been untiring in intruding upon Governor Forch, who seems to have been a right minded man, till at last the happy thought struck him of inquiring privately amongst the Company's servants whether any of them were inclined to marry Miss Pap, as in such a case he should provide for the wedding, the bridal presents &c. Behold, an old Lieutenant, Haldager, appeared as wooer. Naturally enough he was not refused, and the marriage was solemnized with great pomp at the Castle. Maderup was particularly glad that the Governor had thus saved the girl's reputation, and that the mouth of Bliesner's wife should be stopped. The Missionaries thanked God that the affair took this turn; but none of them would pay for the expense of her voyage out. She died the year after in child-birth.

We now return to Schwartz's missionary-work. The time had now arrived when he, who for ten years had lived quietly in Tranquebar, was to become the instrument for strengthening and spreading the branches of the Mission in the interior of the country. It has already been related how native catechists were placed over the different congregations which were formed in Tanjore, how they were visited by native priests, and how one Missionary had been so fortunate as to conquer the difficulties which opposed themselves to a journey into the interior. The next who undertook it, after Pressier's journey in 1728, was Wiedebrock, who accompanied the suite of Captain Sivers as interpreter in 1753, when he had an audience with the King of Tanjore as a Danish Royal Commissioner and Chief of two men-of-war. Wiedebrock made use of this opportunity for communicating with the Christians in Tanjore, preached before the heathens, and recommended the Mission and its congregations to the King. The recommendation was graciously received, the King saying, "They are my people". From the year 1755 we may suppose that the way into Tanjore was open to the Missionaries, for in the same year Johann Wilhelm Berg, a native of Hamburg, who was a Captain in the service of the King of Tanjore, obtained permission for one of the Missionaries to come to the capital to administer the Lord's Supper to himself and others of the Evangelical Church who were residing there; a permission which was often repeated in following years. Thus in the year 1762 the Missionaries Klein and Schwartz went to Tanjore on Captain Berg's invitation and afterwards to Trichinopoly. This town belonged to a Mohammedan Nabob, to whom the King of Tanjore was in some measure tributary, but there was an English garrison there, and many of the officers were so rejoiced at the arrival of the Missionaries and so willing to help them, that Schwartz determined on remaining there. This visit was the origin of a complete change in his position, for Trichinopoly and Tanjore became the centres of his activity during his long and useful life.

A letter from Schwartz to the Mission-College, dated the 10th of July 1766, gives an account of his first year in the interior. "I have now been absent a considerable time from Tranquebar," he writes, "and have lived here in Trichinopoly, and now and then in Tanjore. It would have been right to inform the College of all that I was doing, and I have often thought of it, but the uncertainty of my position and the hope of soon having some thing certain to say, has delayed me so long that I must now with shame ask forgiveness for my negligence, and promise in future to be more careful in my duty."

"My dear brethren have made known by their letters that I have remained in the country, with their consent thereto. At the beginning of my residence here (in Trichinopoly) I preached before a small Native and Portuguese congregation; on week days I tried to instruct Hindoos, Mohammedans and Roman Catholics in the Gospel and thought that I should very soon return to Tranquebar. Not long after, the English Commandant requested me to conduct public worship for the English on Sundays. I asked counsel of the brethren, and they advised me to do it in gratitude for the protection which I enjoyed here, but to take care that the Portuguese and Tamil congregations were not neglected. A few months after, a sorrowful event led to the erection of an English school. The powder-manufactory here blew up, robbing many soldiers of their lives, and many children of their fathers. The Commandant, Major Preston, set a collection on foot for the orphans, which amounted to 300 Pagodas; this he gave into my hands, asking me to select a schoolmaster from amongst the old soldiers. I found one who had ability but not sufficient perseverance, and I therefore determined to send the money and the children to Fabricius in Madras. The English army now marched upon Madura, to take the place from the rebels. The siege lasted long, the number of sick and wounded increased, and Major Preston often begged me to come to him for a time for the sake of the sick. All the brethren gave their consent; and I therefore went to the camp, and remained there for two months.* When Madura was given up to the English, the Nabob made a present to the army, of which (without any request on my part) 600 Pagodas were given to me, which I dedicated to the Tamil congregation and school. A pious soldier had been wounded in the hand before Madura, which made him unfit for service. When I had left the army, and returned here to Trichinopoly, this man whom I did not know before, was brought to me and recommended as a school-master. I engaged him. Not long after, the Nabob gave 300 Pagodas for the orphans, so that I now had 600 Pagodas for them, with which I supported the school-master and four children. The other children only received instruction, books and paper. After the taking of Madura, the army returned, and remained for some weeks in Trichinopoly. Some of the officers

*This was in the summer of 1764. On his arrival in the camp Schwartz found 500 sick and wounded in two hospitals. The smell was most repulsive, but the entrance which he found for the Word, made him forget everything else. He sat beside the straw beds of the soldiers, showed to them the way of repentance and faith, reminded them of their father's house which most of them had left, and to which they now wished to return with shame and grief. Many were humbled, listened willingly and promised improvement. Schwartz visited the hospitals in the morning, and the sick officers in their tents in the afternoon. Madura was stormed on the 26th of June. Major Preston led the attack and mounted the wall, but he was wounded and carried back into the camp covered with dust and blood. "My friend," said he to Schwartz, "I am now punished for my sins." He died of his wounds a few weeks afterwards. "When I came into the hospital after the assault," says Schwartz, "I saw such a scene as I had never witnessed before in my life. Oh, war is a terrible punishment from God! I went from one to the other, talked with them; and prayed with them but at times I felt dumb, for the misery was too great. Some prayed, some cursed their enemies, some moaned, the instigators of the war were not forgotten. Schwartz remained in the camp till he fell ill himself and was unable to visit the hospital.

remarked, that the place where Divine Worship was performed for the English was most unsuitable: this awoke the desire of building a church here and a subscription was opened, which soon amounted to 2000 Pagodas: the church was also to be used for the Tamil and Portuguese congregations. The Governor in Madras helped both by advice and deed. The Nabob when his permission was asked, declared that he had nothing to say against the building of the church, but only wished that it should be outside the fort, in which case he would give a good stone-bungalow for it; but the Commandant feeling that such a plan would make it almost useless to the garrison, determined on building it within the fort. The foundation was laid on the 13th of March last year, and on the 13th of March this year, the upper vaulting which forms the roof, was completed. The present Commandant, Colonel Wood, superintended the building, whilst I had charge of the materials and the accounts. It was finished in May, and consecrated at Whitsuntide. The school-house, in which I live, is to be enlarged and improved by the consent of the Nabob. The service is conducted in this way:—on Sunday morning from 8 to 10 the Tamil christians assemble; at 10 o'clock the English, and at 4 the Portuguese. In the evening there is another prayer-meeting. I have as yet taken no pay for the slight service that I perform for the English, and do not intend to do so, as it leaves me the more free.* On week-days I work in the congregation, and try to awaken the heathen by constant conversations; both amongst them and the Roman Catholics traces of conviction are beginning to appear, which I trust that God will strengthen by his Holy Spirit into a real conversion. This year I have prepar-

*He afterwards received a salary from the English as Garrison-Chaplain, all of which he gave up to the good of the congregation.

ed two little bands of heathen for baptism, and have instructed two Portuguese women who voluntarily left the Romish church to join ours. In this way I have occupied myself here as a Royal Danish Missionary, and rejoicing as I do in having received a regular appointment from the King of Denmark, I should feel much grieved if any change were to take place; and to do anything which would lead to such a change would be against my conscience."

"Further, as there is now a spacious Church here in Trichinopoly, and a Missionary has full freedom in publishing the gospel; as there is both a Tamil and a Portuguese congregation and school, and as the English, at least in all that belongs to the Fort, have full power here and will keep it unless a more powerful enemy should drive them away, my poor opinion is, that Trichinopoly is a very convenient place from which to make known the Gospel to the country-people; added to which, a Missionary stationed here might visit the congregation in Tanjore at least once a year. I wait now for orders as to whether I should remain here or return to Tranquebar; but if the College should decide that a Danish Missionary ought to remain here, I should think it an advantage if an exchange could take place from time to time."

The Dane Maderup was the only one amongst the Tranquebar Missionaries who was anxious for Schwartz to be recalled, and who murmured at his remaining away so long. The others declared that his cheerfulness, sincerity, intelligence and experience were extremely useful to them, and that therefore they had often wished to recall him, more particularly since their numbers had been diminished by the deaths of Dame and Wiedebrock, but that they could not decide on calling him away from the great harvest which appeared to await him in Trichinopoly. Even Francke gave it as his opinion that Schwartz had better remain where he was, as he was a great favourite with the English, the Nabob, the Christians and even with the Heathens, and that therefore he was likely to work more effectually than any one who could be put in his place. Schwartz then wrote to the College as follows: — "Your Excellency and the honourable gentlemen wish me to say whether I will return to Tranquebar, or remain in Trichinopoly on the appointment of the Society in London. In my last letter I expressed that if I looked to my own feelings, and particularly to the delightful intercourse with my brethren in Tranquebar, I should certainly wish to return there, or at least to be able to make an exchange sometimes. But as all the brethren there say that they do not feel sufficiently at home in the English language to be able to change with me, and fear that the work might be thereby obstructed, I will follow whithersoever God shall call me, and trust that he will in his mercy remain with me and near me in this desert.* But I would rather be passive than active in this change. I have written to the Society that I am not entirely disinclined to take up a regular appointment if God should will it, but that it would be quite against my conscience to cooperate thereunto, as I consider your Excellency and the honourable Council as my appointed superiors, and could not undertake anything against or without your consent. If I am to be given up to the Society, it is my humble request that I should not be considered as separated from the Tranquebar brethren, but as being still in union with them." Attention was paid to this request, and the Missionaries wrote, "The wise resolution adopted by the College with regard to our honoured brother Herr

*Schwartz often grieves at being alone in Trichinopoly, and says that experience has taught him why our Lord sent out his Apostles by two and two.

Schwartz, may set him at rest. He can thus retire to us at any time, if it should please God to alter the state of affairs in the country." The letter-books of the Mission-College show the greatest good feeling in all connected with Schwartz. In a letter to the Missionaries dated 1768, the College says, "With regard to Herr Schwartz, we are so convinced of his zeal, his unselfishness and his other merits, that we have determined not to cut off anything from his pay, but to grant him his full allowance together with the 100 £ sterling given to him by the English Government in Madras, until he shall think fit to enter the English Mission-service." In Schwartz's own letter to the College from which we have quoted above, he says, " I have hitherto received my pay from Tranquebar; but as the Society has this year sent an annual salary for a Missionary in Trichinopoly, whoever he might be, my brethren in Tranquebar have, since the beginning of August, received that which was otherwise intended for me. All that the Company has spontaneously given to me has been devoted to building the Church and the Mission-house." Thus we have the pleasing sight of a threefold reward pouring in from different sides on a worthy and active Missionary, and that he, wanting but little for himself, gave up his abundance for the good of the Mission.

Yes, Schwartz was contented with very little. On this we will take the testimony of a trustworthy and excellent man, the Englishman William Chambers, who was then living in Bengal, but who knew Schwartz well and thus describes his life and activity in writing to a friend:—"Before I went to Trichinopoly I had often heard Schwartz spoken of as a man who united great piety and zeal with a thorough acquaintance with the native languages. But as accounts of this kind were generally given to me by those who looked at the features of a religious character through the dark glass of their ruling prejudices, my ideas of him were very imperfect, and having no better guide for my judgment, I mixed up what I heard in his praise with an idea of gloomy melancholy and extravagant severity. But the first sight of this man made me give up my preconceived ideas. Certainly his dress was worn and of a very old-fashioned make, but in his whole appearance there was something exactly the reverse of what one could call dismal or repelling. Picture to yourself a well-grown man somewhat above middle height, holding himself naturally yet erect, of rather dark yet healthy complexion, with black curly hair and a powerful manly glance expressing unaffected modesty, uprightness and benevolence, and then you have an idea of the impression which the first sight of Schwartz makes on a stranger. A plate-full of rice, boiled after the fashion of the country, with few vegetables (curry) formed the daily meal to which he sat down with a cheerful countenance: and a piece of native cloth, dyed black, formed the material of his dress for a year. Thus raised above all earthly cares, his whole attention is turned towards spreading the Gospel. He was untiring in making it known both to the natives in town and in the outlying villages, and before long a congregation of converted Hindûs was assembled round him. Amongst these were three or four who soon became assistants to him in his work. These he fed daily at his table, and did all that he could for their support out of his own income."

Now we shall see how this plain and simple but sincere and earnest man had the good fortune of preaching the Gospel to the very heathen King of Tanjore himself. He relates it in a letter to Francke of the 3rd of June 1769. "After the English," says he, "had concluded a peace with Hyder Ali, I went to Tanjore. I left this on the 17th of April, and returned on the 6th of May. I preached three times almost every day that I was there, and had many conferences with the heathens. The King sent word that he wished to speak to me. On the 30th of April after I had preached to the Tamil congregation on prayer, I was summoned to the fort. From 11 o'clock in the morning till 5 o'clock in the afternoon I was at the castle talking to all sorts of people, till I was quite tired. A Brahmin asked me how we could overcome our fleshly lusts? I pointed out the Saviour of the world to him, to his sufferings and death, and to the power of the Holy Ghost which he had thereby won for us. To others I preached on the deep-seated corruption of man, on the gracious deliverer from sin, death, and hell, and on the life of godliness. When I arrived at the castle there were many hundred writers, accountants, and servants, who were very friendly to me and wished that I might preach in such a way that unjust and godless manners might be annihilated. Till 5 o'clock I remained in a place where the King sometimes shows himself in public. Then I was led through many dark passages to the King, who sat in a four-cornered space on a bed, which was made fast at the top, so that he could rock himself. His servants were ranged at his feet on both sides. Opposite to him, at a distance of 10 or 12 feet, a chair was placed for me. The Persian interpreter said that the King had heard me very well spoken of, and that he had sent for me on that account. I thanked the King for his good will, and wished that God might richly bless him with all blessings. The Persian interpreter would not say that I had blessed the King, but one who stood near him, said, "he blesses you." The King kindly answered, "He is a priest." I was then asked whether I was married, to which I answered, No. The King asked why some Europeans refused to worship images, while others, as the French and Portuguese, worshipped them. I begged permission to speak in Tamil so that those who were near me might understand, and said, "The worship of images is expressly forbidden in the word of God; and it is because the word of God is not given into the hands of the people that they fall into idolatry, and go wrong." To the question how man could attain to a knowledge of God, I answered, "God has in his great mercy revealed himself to men in two ways; first, by the great works which he has created, heaven, earth, sun and moon, by which he shows his power, goodness and wisdom, and thus these great works are given for our teaching; yes, God manifests himself daily by his daily care of us. All that we eat and drink requires us to acknowledge God and to worship him gratefully. The second means which God has mercifully given us is his word, which he caused to be written for us by certain holy men whom he had prepared and called to the work. From this we can learn with certainty what is necessary for our salvation, and what we could not have understood by meditating on the creation. If the King will permit, I will give a short acccount of its principal doctrines."

"The King answered that he permitted it, and wished me to mention some of the principal doctrines, on which I said, "The main doctrine concerns the only true God and his glory. The word or law teaches us that God is a Spirit, who possesses infinite wisdom, but no form or mortal body like ours. Therefore it is contrary to his glory when men represent him by any image: by this they mock him instead of doing him honour as they think. The word says further that God is omniscient, holy and just, kind, benevolent and omnipresent. (These qualities were explained at full, and one of the King's most distinguished attendants always repeated the explanation). The true God then being a Spirit, omniscient, holy, just, omnipotent and omnipresent, judge for yourselves whether it is possible to make an image like him. Is a figure of stone or a block of wood, which has neither sense nor holiness, nor power to do anything, a suitable representation of an all-powerful, holy and omniscient God? Is not the true God dishonoured thereby, and the knowledge of him obstructed? We Europeans used in former days to make images of gold, silver, stone, and wood, we used to bow down before these idols, and rambled about in error; (this expression seemed to appear too lively to the King, for he smiled, but said, Go on!) but God took pity on us, sent us teachers of the truth, and brought us to the knowledge of Himself. Here I introduced the first teachers of Christianity in Europe as interlocutors, made them bring forward their arguments against heathenism with very strong expressions, warning the Europeans most earnestly to forsake their idols, and turn to the living God; for this I thought would be the least obnoxious way of laying the truth before them.—We then turned to the great doctrine of the corruption which is to be found in the heart of every natural man. I said: a soul which fears God above everything, which loves and trusts him, whose thoughts, desires, and inclinations are all turned towards God to honour and to praise him, such a soul is healthy. But let us look into ourselves, and examine ourselves, and we shall find that our inclinations and desires are all set upon earthly, carnal things. We may feel sure from this, that our souls are not in a right state, that they are not pleasing to God, but altogether corrupt. God's word teaches us this also, it agrees with our own sad experience.—We then came to the third great doctrine, of our being freed from grief and misery by our Saviour. I said that if he would permit me I would first lay before him a beautiful simile which is contained in the word of God. The King said, "yes, let us hear it." It was the parable of the prodigal son * which I first related and then applied. I showed how we had fallen away from God, and had thus ruined ourselves in understanding and will, in body and soul, that husks were the best reward one could expect in the service of sin and the devil, and that the consideration of the good gifts which our gracious Father will give us, and of the misery which we reap in the service of sin, ought to induce us to arise and return to him; finally I showed how God in his unspeakable love is always ready to receive us. Here I was interrupted, for pastry was brought in, of which I was required to partake. I ate a little, and said that we Christians, when we enjoy bodily comforts or meat and drink, thank God for his goodness towards us, and beg him to give us grace to use to his service those powers which we receive by the enjoyment of his gifts. At the King's request, I then said a prayer. Then he wished to hear a hymn, as he had been informed that it was our custom to sing. As I had expected such a request, I had the hymn "*Mein Gott, das Herze bring ich dir*," translated by our brother Fabricius, with me, of which I then sang the three first verses. The remainder I read to him, adding some explanations. The last verse was the 15th "உபத்திரங்கள் வரச் சேகீர் ஆதரித்திரும்" &c. The King expressed himself much pleased, and said that he had never heard such things from an European before, adding that I must not take it ill that he had kept me waiting all day. I answered that I wished him all good things and all blessings from my heart, and then took my leave. Then Captain Berg and I were conducted to another part of the palace, where supper was prepared for us."

* The 15th Chapter of St. Luke was Schwartz's favourite portion of the Bible which he used constantly both in teaching and preaching.

Shortly after this Captain Berg had an audience with the King, and informed him that Schwartz had left (he had returned in haste to Trichinopoly on account of the approach of Whitsuntide,) to which the King answered, "I expected, that he would always remain here." When the Captain remarked, "he would not venture to do that without your permission," the King said, "It is my decided will that he should remain near me, that I may have the benefit of his advice." The Captain immediately wrote an account of this to Schwartz, who felt very uncertain as to whether it were not therefore his duty to go to Tanjore; he asked the advice of the other Missionaries, who thought that he ought at least to go to the King for a short time. Schwartz went therefore, but though he visited and preached before the Minister, so many difficulties were put in the way of his seeing the King, that he had but one audience, yet when Schwartz left Tanjore, the King sent word to him, saying: "Remember that you are my Padre."

It was by the gracious Providence of God that Schwartz did not settle in Tanjore, for the relation between the King, the Nabob and the English became less and less friendly, till finally war broke out. The capital was twice besieged, first in the year 1771, when the King begged for peace after a breach had been made in the walls; this he ratified by giving up one of his most important forts, and paying a considerable sum of money, by which the country was frightfully drained. In the year 1772 Schwartz went to Tanjore, and united Captain Berg's daughter to another European Captain at the castle, in the King's presence. It was easy to see that the King wished to keep Schwartz, for he talked with him five times; but it was still more clear that he wished him to be his advocate with the English, for he said, "Padre, I trust you, because you do not care for money." "I told him," says Schwartz, "that there would be no sin in trying to cement a friendship between him and the English, but it was a dangerous thing to have anything to do with his people in such affairs because they were so full of lies." The servants of the King feared any interference from Schwartz, expecting that it would bring to light their unjust practices, so the affair fell to the ground, and Schwartz departed after having faithfully witnessed to the truth in that corrupt court. "Looking at this people from a distance," says he, "one thinks that their conversion cannot be very far off, and one is strengthened in this idea when one sees them so often willing to hear the Word of God; but when you learn to know them better, you see that the enemy holds them prisoner in so many nets and traps, that you are thoroughly frightened. But the Lord's arm is not shortened. I seek for his grace to publish the Gospel to high and low, and hope for the blessing of him who has said, " I am with you alway." One day, when he was earnestly exhorting the King to give his heart to God, he answered, "Padre, that is not so easy as you think;" Schwartz showed him that by the grace of God it might become both possible and easy, but he was unable to convince the weak King, who was unnerved by luxurious living and quite dependant on heathen associations.

In the year 1773 Tanjore was stormed and taken by the Nabob and the English and the King himself fell into their hands. "Thus," writes Schwartz, "fell Tolossi Rasa in the 10th year of his reign, and by his own fault, for he had allowed the Brahmins and Mohammedans to persuade him to such a dissolute course of life, that he had forfeited the love of his subjects, and thus lost his great earthly power. The imprisoned King sent for me. As soon as he saw me he was very much affected, as indeed was I. At last he said to me "Do you not know me,

Padre?" I answered that I knew him well and was much grieved at what had happened to him, and that I could only wish that God would give him grace to bear his misfortunes with patience." The Nabob kept him in prison for about two years and a half, and would willingly have got rid of him in order to bring the whole country under his own dominion; but that was contrary to the policy of the English, who at last determined to free the King and replace him; the Nabob, after a long delay, gave a reluctant consent. Schwartz followed the English regiment, which was to relieve the Nabob's guard in Tanjore, and announce freedom to the imprisoned king. He had allowed his beard to grow and neglected his appearance altogether. "O Padre," said he as soon as he saw Schwartz, "how often I have thought of you when I laid down to rest at night. I have repented on my couch that I did not follow you and take the advice which you gave me." "Very well," "said Schwartz, "suffer yourself to be led to the Lord by the humiliation which his hand has laid upon you, and by the unexpected help which he now offers you;—pray to him and free yourself from the worship of idols." His answer, says Schwartz, was like a dagger through my heart: he said, that he was a man of the world and that he acknowledged that there was but one true and highest God, but yet that mythology had originated with very great men. "Not great, but very foolish men," answered Schwartz. He translated the King's letter of thanks from Tamil into English, but he stopped almost at the beginning when he found that the happy change in the King's circumstances was to be attributed to the idol Rama. "What," said Schwartz, "has Rama done this? he who is unable to do anything for himself." "Write that the true God has done it," answered the King. Another time he declared that the Brahmins had been the cause of all his misfortunes, or as he expressed it, that they had drowned him. Another time when Schwartz related to him the history of Joseph, he remarked that it had some similarity to that of Jesus. "I cannot say what is passing in his heart," Schwartz remarks, "but there are no external signs that his sufferings have done him any good." Immediately after his restoration some heathen festivals were celebrated with great pomp.

And such as Tolossi Rasa then was, he continued to be. He had seen the power of Christianity, and felt the greatest respect for Schwartz, who took up his constant residence in Tanjore from about the year 1778 (the care of the congregation in Trichinopoly was confided to Missionary Pohle, who had arrived the year before, and who conducted the Mission at Trichinopoly for 40 years), but he not only did not join the Church of Christ, but he kept up his old life of idolatry and vice. He was very kind towards Christians, indeed he even told general Munro that he was sure that Christianity was a thousand times better than idolatry, but—he yet lived and died a heathen. When his end approached he determined on adopting a child of nine years of age to be his successor. He then sent for Schwartz, showed him the child and said, "this is not *my* son but *yours*; you must be his guardian and protector, I lay his hand in yours." Schwartz represented to him that this arrangement was unwise, and advised him to confide the guardianship of the child to his brother Amer Sing. This advice was followed and all the parties at the Court were satisfied. Tolossi Rasa died in January 1787, and his brother succeeded him. Amer Sing, though an idolater like his predecessor, was favourable to the Mission, and soon after his accession presented to its school a village in the neighbourhood of the Tranquebar district, which brought in 1000 Rupees yearly. This gift was to be for ever, and a formal deed to that effect was made out, and signed by the King and his ministers. As Amer Sing behaved in a very suspicious way to his pupil after this, and Schwartz even thought that his life was in danger, he did not forget the request of the deceased King, but persuaded the English to send the Prince in security to Madras, where he received a good education under the superintendence of Missionary Gericke (1793—97.) This was the Prince Serfogee who ascended the throne in 1798 in the room of the deposed Amer Sing, and who could never forget Schwartz, whom he called his father and his benefactor.

It is in truth a very remarkable fact that a man in such a humble position as Schwartz, who had neither time nor wish to mix in politics, was yet so well thought of by the rulers of the country, both English and Native, on account of his uprightness, unselfishness and ability, that he was often able to render them considerable service. I cannot stop here to describe his embassies to Hyder Ali and Tippoo Saib, nor to relate how by the power of love he was often enabled to help those who were much above him in station, but must refer to the accounts printed in England and at Halle, and particularly to one of his letters which he felt it necessary to write in answer to a general attack on the usefulness of the Missionaries, which had been publicly made by Mr. Campbell, formerly Private Secretary to the Governor of India, who however had expressed a very high opinion of Schwartz's private character. Schwartz therefore wrote a letter* to prove that the facts adduced by Campbell were distorted, and pointed out the fruits which the labours of the Missionaries had already borne to the blessing of the country. As he was thus obliged to bring forward some of the events

*Abstract of the annual Reports and Correspondence of the Society for Promoting Christian Knowledge. London 1814. 8, P. 739.

of his own life, he said in conclusion, "I feel that some may accuse me of self-glorying and am quite willing to agree that there is an appearance of it, but the fault lies at the door of him who has forced me into this vanity. I stand on the brink of eternity, and declare at this moment, that I do *not* repent having spent 43 years here in the service of my divine Master."

It has been already related, that from the year 1778 Schwartz's principal residence was in Tanjore, where he worked in conjunction with Kohlhoff, a son of the Tranquebar Missionary, who had been with Schwartz from his childhood and been educated by him for the Mission-work; he was ordained at Tranquebar in 1787, and trod closely in the footsteps of his teacher. With them Tanjore took the place of Tranquebar, and became the head quarters of the East India Mission, whence it spread to distant places. Schwartz, in 1778, was the first Missionary who visited Palamcotta, and he never lost sight of it and its neighbourhood. He appointed a visitor to the congregation there in Sattianaden, who was a Catechist at that time, but was afterwards ordained a preacher, and laboured diligently in that neighbourhood, where also Missionary Jänicke laboured, who arrived in India in 1788 and died in 1800. I shall have much to say of the great awakening in that neighbourhood in 1802, when I speak of Missionary Gericke.

With regard to the Mission-congregations formed by Schwartz, almost every arrangement was the same as it had been in Tranquebar. As we have before said, his Mission was, properly speaking, an extension and not a development of the parent one, and yet his personal character is so amiable that we like to linger awhile over his labours. He was always simple in his intercourse with Heathens, Mohammedans and Christians, though he well understood how to bring in striking remarks and to make suitable answers. I will adduce a few examples. One day he met some Mohammedans who asked him to what caste he belonged.— "I am a sinner," answered Schwartz, "like yourselves;—your question should rather be how we may free ourselves from sin." Once on a journey from Trichinopoly to Tanjore, he met several Brahmins; one of them asked him why he was going to Tanjore? "To admonish the Christians," answered he. "Do they not know their christianity then?" asked the Brahmin. Schwartz answered, "Why do you water a tree when you have planted it?" to which the Brahmin replied, "That is enough, I understand you now".—He was preaching one day before some Hindûs on the parable of the prodigal son, and exhorted them to return to their Father. One of them said, "We also worship God; the images are our interpreters who make known our requests, and enable us to speak with the Lord." "You speak truly," said Schwartz, "they are like the thievish interpreters of this country and deceive you."—In the year 1773 a Hindû aged 18 came to Trichinopoly. Schwartz's catechists began to talk with him; he was very passionate and said, "If a priest talks to me about heathenism, and advises me to leave it, I can bear it with patience, but if you mention such things to me, I will strike you over the nose and mouth." Schwartz called him and said, "I hear that you are very passionate and violent. But I do not despise you on that account. I can assure you that I have better hopes of you than of those who are ready to consent to everything that is said. Now here are many heathens, both of high and low castes who are about to receive instruction; I dare say your pride will not allow you to sit down amongst them, but go to a distance of 20 steps and listen attentively. When you have heard everything in this way, you will be better able to pass judgment on what is taught; and you can then receive or reject it according to your own convictions. And you catechists, let a day or two pass over till his violence shall be a little abated." He listened to this advice half-pleased and half-angry, first went away, then came nearer, and finally placed himself at Schwartz's feet, who sat in the midst. He soon began to read a little, and was a most attentive listener. When three months had expired, Schwartz asked him what his intentions were, whether he would put on Christ by holy baptism, or return to his former ways? "I wish now to be baptized," said he. He was therefore publicly baptized and chose the name of Samuel. "He is," adds Schwartz, "a very serious young man, and keeps steadily to daily prayers. May the Lord confirm, support and strengthen him more and more."—One morning he met a Brahmin in the palace of the King of Tanjore who asked him, "Do you think it wrong to touch a Pariah?" "It is certainly very wrong," answered Schwartz. The Brahmin who had not expected this answer, said further, "And what do you understand by a Pariah?" "A thief, a liar, a calumniator, a drunkard, a fornicator, a proud man," answered Schwartz. "Alas," interrupted the Brahmin, "then we are all Pariahs."

As Schwartz's life had been the means of edification and blessing to many, so were his last days, his illness and his death. I cannot find space for all the interesting particulars that have come down to us, but I will give Gericke's letter describing the close of his life. "I returned to Tanjore," says he, "on the 17th February 1798 from a journey to Trichinopoly, and found that Schwartz's foot had become very bad and was full of black spots which were constantly increasing. The Surgeon had begun to use fomentations of Peruvian bark. As we might expect the death of our dear brother at any hour, the other brethren begged me to remain with them, to help them to bear the burden.

It was a great benefit to me also, for our dying friend presented a most encouraging example of faith, patience and hope. Whenever he spoke of spiritual and heavenly things, when he prayed, exhorted, consoled, or talked of the rest and peace of the soul, he was always in the most happy frame of mind. He often quoted texts of Scripture and verses of hymns, and always in the language of those that were round him. On the Friday evening he said that he did not consider himself to be so very near his end, but that it would probably be accompanied by great sufferings; later he said several times, "I think I shall now soon depart and go to my heavenly Father." When he was asked if he hoped that God's kingdom would be much spread in this country after his death, he answered, "Yes; but it will be accomplished through sufferings and trouble." Again when he was asked whether he had any wishes with regard to the converts, he answered, "Help them all to go to heaven." Another time he said, "Many have made a good beginning in Christianity, and if any one is surprised that the work has not been brought to perfection, let him examine himself." When some one showed pleasure at his patience and content, he answered, "Human misery is universal and indeed I suffer very little." He often repeated, "Our faithful God helps us and punishes us with moderation. How should we be able to bear it if he punished us according to our sins. But on the other side of the grave there will be no more grief, for which may the Lord Jesus be thanked." He was very grateful to his Native Assistants who served him gratefully, and often said to us, "for the sake of these poor people, who certainly do all that they can, one must not complain too much, lest their duties should grow burdensome to them."

"On the morning of the 10th his tongue was quite dry

and blackish and his breathing very much oppressed; at his request we prayed, and thought that it would be the last time that he would join with us; but towards evening he rallied and the fever abated. The next day the Doctor (Samuel) said, "The Lord has done wonders; the signs which predicted speedy dissolution are all gone." The English Surgeon also said when he looked at the foot, that he was quite astonished at the unexpected improvement, that he now no longer feared that the sick man would die from external causes, but that his recovery was not possible. On the 12th I wished to depart in the afternoon. Schwartz bade me adieu and said, "So you are going away today. Salute all the brethren from me, and tell them all to look to the one thing needful. I am now going to my Lord Jesus: if he accepts me, forgives me my sins and does not enter into judgment with me, but treats me according to his mercy, all will go well with me and I shall praise him. He might reject us on account of our works, for sin hangs to all of them." He thanked God that he had the companionship of dear brethren in his last hours, and that it had been ordered that I should be with him in his great weakness to praise Jesus as the Saviour, the Resurrection and the Life. Now, he added, pray once more. I knelt down with Kohlhoff, who had come in meanwhile, and formed my prayer on the hymn, "*Allein zu dir, Herr Jesu Christ.*"

"When he had had some fresh fomentations applied to his foot, and we had moved into another room, we saw for the first time how weak he was, and his last hour seemed nearer than ever. I therefore determined to remain. In the afternoon he talked long with Jänicke. In the evening I went to him with the Surgeon; he knew him very well, and said, "let us all take care lest any of us remain behind!" He expressed great gratitude to the Surgeon, to his brother Missionaries and to his Native Assistants. These latter did all that they could with the greatest willingness, love for their father and teacher made everything easy to them, they eagerly received every instructive word which he addressed to them and always wished to be with him. The Surgeon was much moved, and said as he went away, that he hoped that I would not leave the invalid now that he was so weak. He suffered more this evening than before, for the constant moving of the foot (which was necessary on account of the repeated fomentations) and even sitting and lying in bed were painful to him; but his patience and contentedness remained the same, it was only by an occasional sigh that we knew how much he suffered. I said, "May God give us such peace and happy resignation in the approach of our last hours, as we now rejoice to see granted to you." "Yes," he said, "may he give it to you in a measure which passeth utterance." Our hearts were much moved by the love and earnestness with which he expressed this wish. In the night of the 13th he had a little sleep, but in the morning of the following day he was oppressed with torpor and his pulse was very weak. When he was awake, he spoke certainly, but we could scarcely understand what he said, yet he seemed to understand all that was said to him. We thought that he would thus probably sink into the sleep of death, but towards mid-day he became more cheerful. We sang the hymn "*Jesu, meines Lebens Leben*" and he began to sing with us, spoke very humbly of himself and affectionately of our Saviour, and wished to be allowed then to depart and to be with Christ. "If it had pleased him," said he, "to support me a little longer it would have been very pleasant to me; I might then have said a word to the sick and poor, but may his will be done! May he only in his grace receive me. Into thy hands I command my spirit, thou hast redeemed me, thou faithful God." The Native Assistants then sang the last verse of the hymn "*O Haupt voll Blut und Wunden.*" He often joined, rested a little, wished to sit up, opened his mouth from which for 72 years so much doctrine and consolation and so much hearty prayer had poured forth and died in the arms of his faithful and grateful Native Assistants at 4 o'clock in the afternoon. The weeping and sobbing of the people in the two Christian villages was most touching; they were close to his garden and we could hear it all through the night. The grief was universal at the loss of their teacher, comforter, instructor, benefactor, counsellor, pastor. It was not only we, the congregations, the schools and the Missions who had lost a father, but the whole country. Wherever he was known, tears were falling. The following afternoon his body was lowered into the grave which had been prepared in the garden near the church. Serfogee, his pupil and Prince of Tanjore, came to look at him once again before the coffin was closed, wetted him with tears and followed him to his grave. The Native Assistants wished to carry the coffin, but as that duty had been assigned to Europeans the day before, no change was made. They wished to sing a hymn on the way, but the grief of the people made it impossible. A hymn was sung in the church both before and after the burying, and when the English had gone, the Natives sang a hymn and expected a discourse from me, but I could scarcely speak more than a few words and needed all my strength for reading the prayers. The servant of the departed stood near me and said in a low voice "Now is our beloved gone!" This went to my heart; for this was not the saying of one, but of many, old and young, high and low, friends and strangers, Christians and Heathens, all spoke alike. When I had dressed again,

I went to the Prince who still remained near and tried to console him. The principal servant of the widowed Queen begged me to go to her to console her, but she lived too far away. The next morning we all went to the Surgeon and thanked him for the kindness that he had shown to the departed in his last illness. I looked through the papers that were left, in order to fulfill the will and found that the Tanjore Mission with the poor and the institutions belonging to it, had been left his heirs. In the afternoon I talked and prayed with the Assistants. Towards evening the native congregation assembled in the church and wished to hear a discourse. I took the words of the dying Jacob, "I die, but God is with you." I mentioned much what the departed Schwartz had said about the congregation and about his hopes that the kingdom of Christ would come; I sought to awaken them to show the same spirit as he had done, whose grave was now before us. The next day I prayed with the brethren and departed."

So far Gericke. Two monuments were erected to Schwartz; one in Madras at the expence of the English Society which he served, with a Latin inscription:—it was placed in the Fort Church, and consecrated by Dr. Kerr in 1807 with a sermon on 1 Sam. II. 30. "Them that honour me I will honour." The other monument was erected by the King of Tanjore in the church in his capital. He wrote a letter on this occasion to the English Society, which ran thus:—

"Gentlemen!

I have asked your Missionaries to write to you, their leaders and friends, to ask you in my name to procure a marble monument which may be erected in their church in my principal city and residence, to keep up the remembrance of the departed revered Father Schwartz, and to testify the extreme respect with which I regard the character of that great and good man, and the gratitude which I owe to my father, my friend, the protector and guardian of my youth. I therefore take the liberty of addressing you and begging you to procure such a monument at my expence and to send it to me, that it may be fastened to the pillar which is nearest to the pulpit where he used to preach. The pillar is about two yards broad. O Gentlemen! that you were but able to send Missionaries here who should resemble the departed Schwartz.

Serfogee Rajah."

Tanjore, 28th May 1801.

The monument was the work of the celebrated Flaxman. It is a bas-relief, on which the King of Tanjore is represented paying his last visit to Schwartz: some of his ministers and three boys from the school which Schwartz had superintended for so many years, follow him. The inscription is in English.

I must confess that not one of those, whose acquaintance I have made in studying the history of the Tranquebar Mission, is so dear to my heart as Schwartz. I have followed him through the long space of 50 years, have read many of his letters and many accounts of him, and from beginning to end he is always the same, upright, humble and untiring in his Master's service. It has often struck me as remarkable that *all* agree in speaking of him with respect, love and admiration. His employers, his colleagues, his scholars, his congregation, Germans and Danes, Englishmen and Hindûs, Christians and Heathens, high and low, are unanimous in honouring him. Amongst the many opinions that have been passed on him during his many years of usefulness, not one voice has said, "Schwartz is not fitted for his position." The servants of Christ cannot generally rejoice in such universal approbation; indeed it is not promised to them, for our Lord has said to his people, "if the world has hated me, it will hate you also." Neither Ziegenbalg nor Gründler won such general love as Schwartz and the question naturally suggests itself: did he belong to those weak characters who will not speak the truth, and who therefore repel less than those who call everything by its right name? To the best of my belief I must answer, No. He did not belong to those timid characters who anxiously turn their cloaks towards the wind, and always ask what people will say and what they may gain or lose by their approbation. His history, even the short account of it which has been given here, abundantly proves, that he never feared to give his testimony to the truth, even where it might prove offensive; but he did not give his testimony only in words, but in his whole conduct, which was so remarkable for purity and love that it could not fail to win respect. We often think that we are suffering for the sake of truth, when, if we examine closely, we shall find that we are suffering for our sins, which contradict the very Gospel we are preaching. If we walked more in the light, our amiable conduct in the Lord would win souls without preaching, and this was the case with Schwartz. It is not said only of our Lord and Saviour that he grew as in stature so in favour with God and man, but it is also said of Samuel (1 Sam. II. 26) that he was pleasing to both, and therefore I think that though Christians should not of course be anxious for the approbation of man, they should not make themselves uneasy if the world praises them, only they must not build their content on these praises, but remember that the world really loves her own servants only, so that its applause and approbation may change as easily as the wind. But Schwartz belonged to the few amongst earnest Christians and witnesses to the truth, who escape the calumny and blame of the world, and truly I think because he knew how to bear praise, and could preserve the blossom of humility unfaded.

In another respect it is much more difficult for me to defend Schwartz. He died a rich man. There is an old proverb which says, "The niggard has money," or more mildly, "The careful man has money," and I should be very unwilling that Schwartz should lie in his grave with the reputation of one who was too careful to use the money which he had, but rather laid it out to interest; for he was supported by the benevolence of European friends to the Mission, and certainly had opportunity enough for spending all the money that he might receive for the public good in India. I cannot deny that after so often taking pleasure in Schwartz's contentedness and unselfishness, and in seeing how all parties hastened to assist him, I was very much surprised when I learned that he had left a considerable property behind him, which he had not brought with him to India or gained by inheritance, but had accumulated by degrees; and I was not at all satisfied with his having left his property to the Mission and to the poor, because why should he have had it at all? I cannot answer this quite satisfactorily, but will not keep back what may be adduced. We must remember that the close of Schwartz's life embraces a period when the zeal for Missions was growing cold in consequence of increasing infidelity, and that the subscribers were diminishing every year: this would suggest the idea that the Missions in India might be entirely given up by their European friends, and Schwartz might probably wish therefore to collect a fund from what he could spare from time to time. He gave up the care of his money affairs to his friends in Madras, and once lost all that he possessed (as we shall describe when we come to speak of Missionary Fabricius),

CHAPTER XIV.

C. W. GERICKE.—THE SUBSEQUENT HISTORY OF THE MISSION IN CUDDALORE, (KIERNANDER IN CALCUTTA) AND MADRAS.—PALAMCOTTA.

Next to Schwartz I know no name in the latter part of the last century which adorns the Mission-history so much as that of Christian Wilhelm Gericke, and as Cuddalore as well as Madras was the scene of his labours, we may unite the history of these two Missions to his name. Gericke was born at Colberg in Pomerania in the year 1742; in 1760 he went to the University of Halle, where he became a teacher at the Orphan-house and inspector of the girl's school. In the year 1765 he became a Missionary in the service of the English society, was examined and ordained at Wernigerode and went immediately after to his home at Colberg to say adieu to his family and friends. Agreeable as it was to him to be once more with them he was much grieved that the greater part of his friends were quite opposed to his journey and reproached his father severely for having given his consent to it. His father answered nothing, for, said he, these people mean well, and only judge thus because they know no better. But after Gericke had preached three times and explained the objects of his journey, all reproaches ceased, and his farewells were eased by universal sympathy. His friends all said as he was going that they should pray God to bring him back again, but his father did not join in this.

Gericke begged them to make themselves quite easy on his account, and simply to pray to God to conduct him to his destination, to keep him there in health, and to give him a heart full of love to Jesus and of wisdom so that he might not work in vain, to which his father answered, "Yes, that is right, we will do that." He then went through Hamburg to England, where he remained till the early part of the next year, and then began his voyage to India, a voyage such as few have made. The ship experienced fearful weather from July till November 1766, and just as she had cast anchor in Madras she was obliged by a fresh gale to slip her cable, and only escaped shipwreck with the greatest difficulty. She now sought the open sea, but the further she went the fiercer was the raging of the storm, which lasted for 32 hours with a roaring like the loudest thunder. The sails were torn to pieces at the very beginning; then the mainmast went over the side and next the foremast, while water was streaming in everywhere. One of the pumps broke to pieces, the other five were choked, while the water was rising so high that a man might have been drowned in the hold. Soldiers and sailors then gave way. All came on to the upper deck, expecting the ship to go to pieces and thus to escape a more horrible death below; but when their troubles were thus at their height, help was near. The clouds were suddenly rent, like the tearing of a garment, and there was a calm. The light of the mid-day sun, says Gericke, had an effect on us all equal to that of the word "Pardon" on a culprit condemned to die and already standing on the place of execution. Cheerfulness reigned throughout the ship, the pumps were put in order and water pumped out, but the storm began anew and the ship drifted a helpless wreck at the mercy of the winds and currents. They could not get back to the Coromandel coast, but thought themselves very fortunate in reaching the Dutch fort of Galle in the south-west of Ceylon. Gericke landed there, remained some time in Ceylon, passed through Negapatam and Tranquebar and arrived at Cuddalore in June 1767.

There is not much to tell of the history of the Cuddalore Mission since its first foundation, which we have already related. It had often appeared as if it were going to flourish, but external obstacles were added to internal, for the French and English were fighting for supremacy in India, and Cuddalore shared in the uncertainties of war. When the town was threatened with an attack from the French in 1746, Missionary Geister* left it, went first to Batavia and thence started for Europe, but died on his passage home. Missionary Kiernander remained in Cuddalore, which successfully resisted three French attacks in the two following years, and received Hüttemann as an assistant in 1750.

I will here relate an incident of Kiernander's ministry in Cuddalore, which is characteristic in several ways and proves what many have cast a doubt on, that for those who have anything to lose, conversion to Christianity is attended with temporal losses. In 1745 a young man of a respectable caste, 20 years of age, came to Kiernander who instructed and baptized him. His heathen name was Tripulli, but he was christened Isaac. He then wished to go to Tranquebar, partly to escape from the

*This Missionary had also left Cuddalore in September 1743 in obedience to the directions of the English Society, and had gone to Madras to assist Fabricius who was alone there. I here meet the first trace of the disagreements between German and English in the East India Missions which have broken out in our own times. In 1746 the Tranquebar Missionaries in writing to Finkenhagen, add this postscript: "Fabricius writes to us from Madras, four days ago Geister introduced the English catechism. The next day I began to take my meals alone, as I had been obliged to keep away from the conference for several weeks." Francke in his letters expresses himself much grieved at this disagreement between English and German which seems to have been broken off by the bombardment of Madras, and Geister's journies to Cuddalore, Batavia and Europe, for one hears nothing of it for many years.

anger of his heathen brother, partly to be able to receive further Christian instruction in peace, for which Kiernander gave him a letter of recommendation to the Missionaries there. But now a tumult arose. His heathen brother, Rangen by name, made a complaint against Kiernander with the Governor declaring that he had enticed his brother and sent him away. Not satisfied therewith he got together 300 of his relations and friends who assembled round the Mission house, crying out that Rangen's brother must be restored and his baptism taken away, else they would do something that neither the Governor nor the Missionaries would like. Kiernander was not at all alarmed, but went out to them and assured them that he was very much pleased to see so many of them together as it gave him the opportunity of preaching the Christan religion to them, and he only hoped that they would receive his instruction. On this some cried out that they had not come there to be instructed, but to carry out their intentions which they had already announced to him: on this Kiernander represented how unreasonable they were as they must know that Isaac was not his brother's slave, but that according to their own customs he might leave his brother and require his own portion of their patrimony whenever he pleased: that his journey to Tranquebar had been undertaken entirely of his own free will and that he certainly would not wish to have his baptism taken from him as he held it in the highest honour. Some were convinced by these representations and went away, but others said that unless they had what they wanted, they would lie down by the Mission house till they died. Kiernander told them that he should be very glad if they would remain and listen to his instructions. Soon after they all went away, but laid the complaint before the Governor the next day, who, finding that Isaac had acted entirely on his own free-will would not interfere. The storm then abated, Isaac became an able catechist, and was an active member of the congregation for many years, while the bitterness of his heathen relations so far abated that he was allowed to divide in equal shares with his brother the inheritance which their father had left them, consisting of a house and a piece of land. Isaac however did not wish it to be divided but left the use of the property to his brother, even contributing his share towards the repairs of the house. But when his brother died in 1768, the heathen relations refused to give Isaac his share, saying that he could not hold property as he was a Christian and had lost his caste. The Missionaries tried in vain to get any redress for him from the English authorities; even a Member of Council, who was very much in their favour, thought that there was nothing to be done. "In this case the laws of the Natives must be followed; and if they had a law that any who had lost his caste could not inherit, so the English had a similar one that any one joining the Romish Church could not inherit. One must be impartial, and the Natives who become Christians, must be prepared to give up everything." Isaac therefore did not receive any portion of his inheritance, but he was just as well satisfied as if he had done so.

In May 1758 Cuddalore was at last taken by the French. Missionaries Hüttemann and Kiernander received permission to leave the town with their own property and that belonging to the Mission, and a great part of the congregation followed them to Tranquebar, where Hüttemann remained for two years until he was able to return. Kiernander on the contrary carried out a long-talked-of plan of founding a Mission in Calcutta, whither he went in 1759, but though it seemed to begin well, there were many obstacles and it was never firmly established. I must stop here for a few minutes to describe Kiernander's personal and public character, and think it best first to give the account which was published at Halle after his death.

Kiernander was born in East-Gothland in 1710; he first studied at Upsal and went to Halle in 1735, to complete his theological studies. Here he was made Inspector of the German and afterwards of the Latin school at the Orphan-house, and in 1739 he accepted the calling of a Missionary to Cuddalore, where he was soon rewarded by flourishing Hindù and Portuguese congregations. When he was driven out from Cuddalore on its being taken by the French, he went to Calcutta, and soon succeeded in attracting a congregation, which increased year by year. All went on as well as could be wished; he was a blessing to his congregation, and from his uprightness, unselfishness and humility won universal love and respect. In the year 1774 Missionary Diemer was sent to assist him, and in 1778 Gerlach joined him from Tranquebar; but by his (second) marriage he became a man of so much property that he was considered one of the richest capitalists in Bengal. The Mission had until then struggled against great poverty, and he proved his earnest desire to make good use of his temporal gifts by building at his own expense a Church, a large school-house, and a residence for two Missionaries; indeed it was calculated that he had devoted 100,000 Rupees to the Mission. But by degrees his wealth brought him in contact with many rich and fashionable people who did him much harm. His mind seemed to be more and more set on earthly things, while his grandeur and extravagance exhausted his property. To put a stop to this, he built a great many houses though he was obliged to borrow money for the purpose, hoping thus to retrieve his fortunes, as house-rent was very high in Bengal. But this undertaking, by which many of the English had enriched themselves, failed in his case; he was completely ruined and was obliged, at the age of 78, to leave Calcutta, and take refuge in the Dutch settlement of Chinsura. Here he spent the remainder of his days in poverty and useful activity, and recognised it as a great mercy from God that he had been humbled and saved from the snares which had held him captive, and here he died in the year 1799 in consequence of breaking a leg.

So far the Halle Report as given after his death; but if we turn to the opposite side and follow both English and German accounts during a series of years we find a most encouraging account of the progress of the Mission, an excellent report of Kiernander's activity and benevolence, and of his success in converting a Roman-catholic priest, Pater Bento, who finally became his assistant; the English Report of 1786 speaks of the increase of the congregation amongst Bengalees, Malays &c., and that of 1787 of his conversations with Bengalees and Mohammedans. After reading all this how surprised are we then in 1788 to find it mentioned (p. 278) that from age and weakness he has been obliged to give up the service of the Mission and has sold the church and church-yard with the school to the Revd. Mr. Brown and Messrs. Chambers and Grant, who have taken the charge of the congregation upon themselves until the Society shall send another Missionary. The above-mentioned Brown writes immediately after, that according to all that he can learn of the other Missionaries of the Society, they are faithful men, full of zeal and good works; but his remarks on the Mission in Calcutta are not flattering. The English and German accounts agree as to the cause of the breaking up of everything in Calcutta. A Mr. Owen,* who had formerly been a Chaplain, says

*He is said to have returned to England after a 10 years' residence in India with 2½ lakhs of Rupees.

on a later occasion, "Some, who formerly took an active part in these things, were seized with an unfortunate desire to grow rich, and fell into temptations and snares. I knew two Missionaries with noble talents and of excellent character in other respects, who allowed themselves to be led into such earthly troubles by the avaricious Natives, that they only ended with their lives. In the East, as everywhere else, there are lawful gains for every one in their different positions; but in truth, those Missionaries ought to have known that when a Priest has food and clothing he should not require any further gains."

Owen's words no doubt allude to Kiernander as one of the Missionaries, but I do not know who the other can be; perhaps Diemer, or Pater Bento, or if Owen was acquainted with Madras, it may have been the old Missionary Fabricius (!?), of whom we shall have more to say hereafter. A strange ill-fortune pursued the Calcutta Mission, which would seem to prove, that there must have been something unsound in the bud. Diemer left Calcutta in 1785, visited Tranquebar and returned to England. The Tranquebar Missionaries say of this, "Herr Diemer came here on the 12th of January with Captain Clemens, and went away on the 31st to England with his little son, in order to lay the state of the Bengal Mission before the Society in England, and to make some new arrangements. Such a representation ought to be very useful from one who has had so many years experience of the real wants of the Mission and who has devoted himself so entirely to it, but yet we doubt whether the right aim will be attained, as Diemer, from ignorance of the language, could not take part in the care of the Portuguese congregation, and not one (?) of the Missionaries there has studied the native language."

Such was Diemer: and the sad fate of Pater Bento and

Gerlach is best shown by a little note (dated 26. Dec. 1788) from the latter to the Secretary of the Mission-College, "I cannot unfortunately give you any more agreeable accounts from here. The Mission is in the most pitiable state, and appears to have been quite abandoned by the English Society for the last six years. No money has been received during that time. Pater Bento died in great poverty and in miserable circumstances. Kiernander has been obliged to leave Calcutta on account of his debts, and has taken refuge at Chinsura. I have been obliged to support myself by making almanacs." One year later Gerlach died; he had come out originally to assist Missionary John in his schools at Tranquebar, but as he did not give satisfaction he went to Bengal. John says of him that he might have been a great school-man in Europe, but that he had not the smallest talent for teaching Indo-european children. The English Society now determined to send an Englishman to Calcutta, and sent out a clergyman of the name of Clarke, but he had scarcely reached his destination before he gave up the service of the Society. They then had recourse to the Germans again, and sent Ringeltaube to Calcutta in 1796; but he was soon tired of it and returned to England in 1799. This is the more surprising as he was a clever man, and was afterwards very active in the service of the London Missionary Society. At the close of the century the Calcutta Mission was empty and deserted.

We will now return to Cuddalore, where Hüttemann was alone from 1760 to 1767, when Gericke who afterwards became his son-in-law, joined him. Gericke worked diligently for ten years, but just as the Mission was beginning to prosper, war broke out again; indeed a double war both with Hyder Ali and with the French. A very trying time followed both for the Missionaries in Cuddalore and for their congregations. There were wars and rumours of war, famine, sickness, and all those calamities which are sure to follow wherever war rages. Hüttemann died in the midst of these troubles in 1781, and one year after the town fell into the hands of the French. Gericke was attacked with a very dangerous illness, and his native assistants were in such a state of fear that he received very little assistance from them. We will let him speak for himself in one of his letters. "An English prisoner of war is about to be sent to France and therefore I have an opportunity of informing you in a hurry, that Cuddalore has been in the hands of the French since the 3rd of April. Since then it has pleased God to reduce us even lower than we were before. Only two of the native school-children remain; the rest are all dead. An epidemic fever has carried off one third of our congregation, while I was myself lying on what was supposed to be my dying bed from the same disease. Tirusiluwei left me last year in our troubles. Isaac, who loses his presence of mind in danger and cannot keep up under difficulties, is gone to Tranquebar. Rayappen is in weak health, and suffers much from the wretched food with which he has had to support himself for the last year and a half. Manuel visits the few remaining Christians with great diligence, and talks much with the heathen, but gets no encouragement. The English schoolmaster is always sickly, but perseveres. Our Church was changed into a powder-magazine directly the town was taken, and the poor assistants who live near the Church have not been able to have any fire in their houses since then, nor even dared to light a lamp and yet they cannot get any other house. We hold the Tamil service in the school, and the Portuguese in my house, where we also continue to have the English; for besides my own family there are many English prisoners of war here who attend Divine Worship. The garden, which we thought would have produced well, is laid quite waste, and now the trees that remain will probably be all cut down, as a battery is to be built on this side. The houses in which the late Herr Hüttemann lived have been taken possession of by the French:—in other respects the officers have behaved very well towards me. General Duchemin received me in a very friendly way, when I went out to him in the camp, before the place was given up. Hyder's troops wished for Cuddalore as much as the French did, and our not falling into the hands of that tyrant has been attributed to my intercession with the General. The French have always listened kindly to my requests for others, particularly for the English prisoners and have assisted me whenever it was possible. Admiral Suffrein has written a very kind answer to a letter I addressed to him, and the Governor in Cuddalore always seems pleased to be able to fulfil my wishes. Yet we are in a very unpleasant position. The scarcity is increasing, and the whole country has become a desert. At least three quarters of the inhabitants have fallen by the sword, hunger or disease. I have heard nothing from my brethren and friends in Madras, and very little from Tranquebạr, and the misery is so great everywhere that on the whole it seems best that I should continue my work here. God has hitherto protected us wonderfully, and he will continue to do so. It is a time of suffering."

Gericke did not however keep his resolution of remaining in Cuddalore through all difficulties, but lived a wandering life until 1788, when he settled in Madras; he was sometimes at Madras, sometimes at Cuddalore, but principally at Negapatam, whence he could superintend the Cuddalore Mission, which was first conducted by Natives, and afterwards by Horst who was there at first as a Reader, was ordained in 1806, but died in 1810. His successor was Holzberg, a clever but immoral man, who died in 1824. After him came David Rosen who is still living in Denmark as Pastor in Lille Lyndby in the Bishopric of Seeland; and at the present time (1842) the Cuddalore Mission is for the first time under the charge of an Englishman; his name is Jones. Having thus taken a brief view of its history and with the remark that it never displayed great activity, we will return to Gericke, and relate the history of the Madras Mission (of which he undertook the charge in 1788) from the time when its founder, Benjamin Schultze, left it to return to Europe.

This time, from 1742 to 1788, is occupied by one man, *Johann Philipp Fabricius*, who, though originally intended for the Danish Mission in Tranquebar, received permission after he had been a few years in India, to enter the service of the English Society; he went to Madras, thus enabling Schultze to return to Europe, and during the long series of years that he remained there was principally assisted by Missionary *Breithaupt*, from 1749 to 1782.

Fabricius was a skilful and learned manager for the Madras Mission as long as he retained his youthful vigour. His thorough acquaintance with the native languages was acknowledged, and his lexicographical labours deserve praise, but his particular gift lay in translating hymns into Tamil. His translations were used in all the congregations and are still famed as being really excellent. But the Madras Mission shared the same fate as that in Cuddalore in suffering much from the war between the French and English. In the year 1746 Madras was taken by the French. The Mission-house was pulled down, and Fabricius with the catechists and school - children took refuge at Paleacatta (Pulicat) which belonged to the Dutch, and where they met with a very kind reception. In 1749 they were able to return to Madras, where everything was in a state of desolation, and they hastily erected a hut for the school in the church-yard which was the only possession remaining to them. The congregation assembled under some large trees for Divine Service, and the servants of the Mission were received into private houses. Thus they managed as well as they could and waited for better times.

In the year 1752 the English Government gave up to Fabricius a new and handsome Roman Catholic Church with all its adjoining buildings; it had been built by an Armenian Romanist a few years before in Vepery, close to Madras, but, on account of treachery committed, it had been taken from the Romanists. Their still more magnificent Church in the Fort was pulled down. Whoever knows anything of the Roman Catholic persecutions of the Madras Mission, will recognize a judgment in what thus happened to the persecutors, but one does not like to see our Mission in the possession of the property of others, neither is it surprising that the possession of the gift was much embittered in later times. In the year 1758 when war again broke out, the Church and Mission-house were so entirely plundered that even the clothes were taken from an infant of Breithaupt's, and he had to turn his pockets inside out several times to prove that there was nothing in them. Both Missionaries again took refuge in Pulicat, while the French besieged Madras, which happily they did not succeed in taking: on the contrary they lost the advantages they had already gained and were obliged to give up Pondichery to the English, who took a printing-press on this occasion which they presented to the Mission. Scarcity and famine succeeded the war, and the town had scarcely begun to recover when it was troubled by Hyder Ali, by the Mahrattas, and again by the French, so that the difficulties of the Mission were unceasing. It was blessed with conversions both amongst

Natives and Roman Catholics, but it wanted rest. Breithaupt died in 1782 in the midst of their greatest trials, and Fabricius had become weak from old age and fatigues. This weakness in an otherwise upright and unselfish man had shown itself sadly before Breithaupt's death in great disorder in his accounts.

In the year 1778 Schwartz and Gericke had both gone to Tranquebar to assist the Missionaries there in the ordination of the Native priest Rayappen; but immediately after the ordination Schwartz was obliged to go to Madras for a very sad reason, for Fabricius had been induced by a native Canacapoly to lend large sums of money which had been intrusted to his care to the son-in-law of the Nabob and other natives of high rank without sufficient security. No Missionary, not even his colleague Breithaupt, had been informed of his proceedings. Schwartz found that he was quite unable to repay anything on his own account, and that the money which had been confided to him must be considered as completely lost. The Tranquebar Mission lost 2000 Pagodas, the Trichinopoly Mission all that it possessed, which Schwartz had entrusted to Fabricius. An angry letter to Fabricius from the Missionaries followed, but he had only empty promises to offer. This loss caused much offence along the whole coast.

Under these circumstances it was most fortunate that Gericke was at hand that he could first assist the Madras Mission, and in 1788 take the management of it, for wherever he was, no confusion was allowed. In the year 1795 Missionary John says of him, "He is not merely a real blessing to the Mission in Madras, but is the teacher, father, and counsellor of many children and grown people in Vellore, Negapatam, Cuddalore and other places. I am astonished and delighted when I behold the labour, sufferings, patience, gentleness and earnest piety of this man." Schwartz said of him, "He works so hard and in so many places that one cannot but wonder that he is able to go through it." John admires his patience which was put to many proofs, not only by outward obstacles which impeded his career of usefulness for many years, but by internal dissensions in the congregation which caused him great uneasiness. It is touching to see his much-enduring patience rewarded at last:— he had longed from his earliest youth to win souls of heathens to Christ, and for a long course of years he worked in many places with untiring zeal, though the impediments that were raised against him prevented his gathering in much fruit; the storms which had beaten against his ship on his voyage out seemed to be emblems of those which were to rage against himself when he commenced labouring in his Master's service, but in the latter part of his life (1802) when it seemed as if he had laboured in vain and spent his strength to no purpose, he was blessed with winning hundreds of souls to the Church of Christ.

The southern point of India from Palamcotta and Manapaar down to Cape Comorin had been formerly visited by native catechists and priests from Tranquebar; but we have heard that Schwartz was the first European Missionary who visited this district, that Jänicke worked amongst the congregations who were there assembled, and that the native priest Sattianaden was one of the most useful instruments in spreading the Gospel. The native priests and catechists had often written to Tranquebar describing the ever-increasing readiness with which the Gospel was received, and the great effects which might be expected if a Missionary would go there and settle for a time amongst the country-people; but these accounts were considered as over-drawn, the journey was expensive and the Missionaries fully occupied with their congregations. Gericke however devoted the evening of his life to preaching the Gospel to the poor in the southernmost point of India. It is well known that the Lutheran Missionaries were accustomed to be very careful and circumspect in administering the rite of baptism, themselves instructing those who desired it. Gericke had acted thus hitherto, but in the extraordinary and far-spread awakening in the South it was not possible to continue the same plan of operations. We see him going from place to place to visit those who had formerly been instructed by the native priests and catechists, who had determined on being baptized and who had built churches or had changed their Pagodas into Churches. He examined them, exhorted and then baptized them, placed elders over them, and journeyed on. Some pages from his Diary for 1802 will give the reader the best idea of what he was doing.

"1st October. We started after morning-prayers, and arrived at Naduwakuritschi, where some Christians came to meet us, amongst whom were some of those who were baptized yesterday at Mudelur. We exhorted them as well as the heathen inhabitants, who came out, and prayed with them. After this we went to Bethlehem, a new village, where there is a Church built by the Catechumens who have settled here, in which baptism was to be solemnized. They assembled directly, and I preached on the man with the palsy, pointing out to them that if they truly accepted Christ, he would give them forgiveness of sins and power to lead a holy life: I told them that they should now by faith in Jesus Christ receive grace and become children of God. Their heathen names were then written down according to their families, and the new Christian names placed beside them. Towards evening they assembled again; I then preached on the history of Cornelius, and baptized 203 Persons, who belonged to 48 families. We did it in this way. The native priest read the Formulary; after I had asked them whether they gave up heathenism from their hearts, believed in the Christian truths and would live according to the same, one family after another were called up by their heathen names. When the whole family was collected they knelt down and I baptized them in the order in which the catechist repeated their Christian names. It sometimes occurred that the head of the family addressed a few awakening words to some member of it about to be baptized, which was very affecting. The service altogether lasted from 6 o'clock in the evening until midnight. The native priests and catechists said "We have received new life; such a thing as this has never happened in this country before."

"October. 2nd. The congregation assembled again this morning for prayers, and the four elders whom they had themselves chosen, were presented to them. We visited several Hindùs of rank, who though they could not exactly determine on becoming Christians, showed much pleasure in what they had seen and heard. After this we went on to Nageladi. All was here very much as in the last place: there was no Church here, but when the inhabitants determined on embracing Christianity, they had themselves prepared their idol-temple for the service of God. Here too they have been taught by the native priests and catechists. I brought the example of Lydia before them, and then baptized all the inhabitants of the place, amounting to 220 persons in 53 families. It was 11 o'clock at night, before the elders were determined on. We then went on to Kundali, where we rested till morning."

"October. 3rd. The whole village was waiting to hear God's word, and to be admitted by baptism into communion with the Christian Church. The idol temple had been for some time converted into a house of prayer. I brought the example of the jailor before them in my address, and afterwards baptized 62 families, consisting of 248 persons. The whole service lasted from 8 o'clock in the morning until 2 o'clock in the afternoon. We then went on to Karikowil, where in the same way all were awaiting us, and had already written down their names together with the christian names they wished to be called by. The Catechist had proposed the latter to them, and they were, as much as possible, similar in sound to their former names. .After an address I baptized 46 families, consisting of 204 persons. The service lasted from 7 o'clock till midnight. The village consists of one long street, at the southern end of which stands the temple, now converted into a house of prayer. It looked very noble when the people with their children streamed towards the temple of God from all the houses in the village; the Catechists and Christians from other places who had followed us here, said when they saw it, "They never used to come in this way, when it was an idol-temple. God has brought them to the true Vedas and to baptism."

"October. 4th. The congregation assembled again in the morning, and I prayed to God for their elders, catechists, and assistants, whom I left in this and the neighbouring villages, together with a young man educated in Vepery. We then went on to another village, Uwari. These 4 villages are on the sea-coast between Manapaar and Cape Comorin, and the piece of land on which they are built is called Karei-Suttu. The inhabitants of Uwari had began only the day before to purify their idol-temple and to convert it into a house of prayer. They had erected a covered room before the temple and expected an assemblage of 500 persons. But as they had not arrived by the afternoon, I represented to them how short my time was, and advised them to be baptized by the native priest, or else to go to Mudelur and there receive baptism; on this some of them came forward and begged me to do here what I had done in the other villages. In the afternoon we heard that a wicked heathen who had already caused great troubles, and had tried by severe persecution to force the Mudelur Christians back to their idol-worship, had taken great pains to keep these poor people away. Those who were not influenced either by his threats or his promises begged me to remain till morning. I addressed them in the evening on the parable of the four different kinds of ground, and had cause to rejoice in the attention of the people."

"October 5th we occupied with instruction, and the names of the inhabitants together with their new Christian names were written down. One man came to speak to me guarded by two native soldiers. He had been accustomed to listen to the teaching of one of the Catechists, but on account of being present at the plundering of a village three years before he had been thrown into prison. He wished to be baptized as he had gained much knowledge of our religion by reading our books whilst in prison. I preached on the tares amongst the wheat, and then 23 families, consisting of 102 persons, were baptized. I did not go to rest till 2 o'clock in the morning."

Thus Gericke, in spite of bodily weakness, travelled about sowing the seed of the Gospel. After he had left the district many more heathens came forward to be received into the church of Christ, but almost immediately on his return to Madras he received letters from these very places, some complaining of the conduct of the native priests, the catechists and the christians, and others from the christians sighing under the severe persecutions to which they were subjected. "In the midst of my bodily weakness," Gericke writes on the 24th December, "I receive most grievous letters almost every day from one or other of the suffering Christians in the South, and I cannot help them with letters, nor by returning to them. The heathens have treated them with all the rigour due to those who have lost their caste from misconduct. They have forcibly smeared their foreheads with ashes, they have broken in armed into their houses of prayer on Sundays, have seized men, women and children, beaten and imprisoned them, plundered their houses &c. We must wait in patience and humility to see how and through whom God will help them. I hope that he will not permit the enemy to disturb the work which is begun; this unexpected and severe persecution will purify our people and their firmness will cause others to reflect. I trust, that God will give them courage rather to suffer everything than to assist themselves by unlawful means."

The Tranquebar Missionaries write as follows on this persecution:—"Soon after the joy which Gericke spread amongst us on his return by his account of the thousands who had embraced the Gospel in the south, events took place which might have been expected, for they had accompanied the first foundation and spread of the Christian Church and were therefore nothing uncommon or surprising, yet they struck and grieved us. The enemy sowed his tares amongst the wheat, the heathens began to rage and to fear that a still greater number of heathen temples would be converted into Christian houses of prayer. Universal complaints were brought forward against the new Christians, that they neither worked nor brought in their taxes regularly as before. Many were forcibly dragged away from Divine Service, were beaten, plundered and thrown into prison, and a new Christian Church was set on fire and burned to the ground. A Hindû of consequence who had not been able to repress his inimical feelings even while Gericke was present, showed the greatest zeal in persecution directly he was absent; and amongst the new converts, there was an overseer, who having embraced Christianity with Jewish ideas of the kingdom of God, and having promised great worldly advantages to all who followed him, no sooner found himself disappointed, than, like a second Julian, he joined the opposing party and distinguished himself in it. A few examples of bad Christians spread their ill-fame over *all*, and heathen Dubashes represented to the English Resident that the spread of Christianity was very bad for the revenue and for all civil arrangements, so that the native priests received orders not to accept or baptize any one who should announce himself to be converted. The most sorrowful letters and reports came in, accompanied by earnest requests that we would assist the oppressed Christians and send them a Missionary to strengthen and console them. Meanwhile a pious-minded Englishman had undertaken to see justice done in their case, and a new and noble-minded Collector who was appointed followed his example, instituted rigorous inquiries, suppressed the riots and punished the guilty without respect of persons. Some of those who had burned the Church, were condemned to several years imprisonment by the English Judge. The greater part of the inquiry took place while Herr Kohlhoff was there, for he undertook a journey to visit these congregations in 1803, and was kindly received by the good Collector and other English Gentlemen. He inquired into and brought forward the real state of affairs, found much attention and assistance, reconciled opponents, recommended the Christians to be very careful in their conduct, exhorted them by faithfulness, courage and patience to imitate their Saviour who through the cross had entered into his glory and encouraged them with the hope that those, who cheerfully bear his cross, will also be admitted to share in his glory!"

Gericke died at a distance from the work which had been begun in the southern regions, but before giving an account of his death, I must remark that it was in the very district in which Gericke preached a year before his death that Rhenius afterwards laboured in the service of the English Church Missionary Society. Any one who has been interested in the progress of Missions in our century will of course have heard of the name of Rhenius,* and of the thousands won by him to the Church of Christ in Southern India; but very few know that it was the Tranquebar Missionary John who caused Rhenius to be sent out to India, and that Palamcotta and its neighbourhood had been well ploughed up by the old Lutheran Missionaries, even though neglected after their death.

Immediately on his return home from his remarkable journey to the South, Gericke was attacked with fever, from which he recovered indeed, but his increasing and ceaseless labours did not allow him that repose which his weak health and age (he was then 61) called for. His malady preyed on him inwardly, and hoping that a change of air might be beneficial, he went to Rayacotta at the repeated invitation of some English friends. On his return he came to Vellore, where there was a small congregation of his, and while staying there in the house of Colonel Cammel, took advantage of the opportunity of having the advice of an English Surgeon. He saw that he could scarcely hope to go on, and yet wished to be at home, and by the ad-

*Karl Gottlieb Ewald Rhenius was born at Graudenz in 1790, went to India in 1814, to Palamcotta in 1820 and died in 1838. See the "Life of Missionary Rhenius" in Schmidt's "Biographies of celebrated Evangelical Missionaries;" Leipzig, 1842.

vice of the Doctor took a bath, but it only seemed to increase his weakness. He baptized Colonel Cammel's child, though so weak that he could only sit up in bed to administer the sacrament. When the baptism was given he said, "Now I must start at once, for I long to see my catechists, my children (these were the children of a school founded by Lady Campbell for European orphans, called "the Female Asylum" which Gericke superintended) and all the members of the congregation." When he found that the Colonel, the Doctor and all the other gentlemen opposed his going, he was much distressed. Towards evening he ordered his palanquin to be prepared, and said to the Catechists, "Go to the authorities and bring me the necessary passport for my journey," but when it was brought to him he said, "I shall not require it, keep it, I am going!" A boy, who was standing near, asked, "O Sir, where are you going?" "Be contented, my son," answered he, "I am going." He then drank a little rice-water and said, "Now let no one disturb me," and laid down. About 12 o'clock he cried out, "My God, my Jesus, my Jesus," and lay quiet as if asleep. No one liked to wake him as he had asked not to be disturbed, but when the Catechist at last spoke to him he found that he was dead.

When the corpse was brought into Vepery on the 6th of October 1803, the bell was tolled and great numbers of people of all classes assembled; it was calculated that there were between 4 and 5000 people at his funeral. "Rest softly," say his colleagues in Tranquebar, "thou amiable, faithful, ever memorable brother! after thy long and severe sufferings, after shining here as a christian and a teacher amongst thy brethren and the servants of the Gospel, enjoy the reward of thy faith and patience in the home of the blessed. Christ was thy life, and death was gain to thee, now art thou with Him whom thou hast served and followed so truly, and with whom thou didst often long to be. Thy example in humility, disinterestedness and untiring labour in the cause to which thou didst devote thyself, should be ever present to us and encourage us to a like zeal."

He was everywhere loved and respected, so that his company was much sought after by people of distinction. This was very useful to him when he had any request to make, and he was very seldom refused, as every one felt sure that he would not ask what was unsuitable or unreasonable. He would not refuse to assist any one, even if it cost him time, trouble and expense, nor even if it led him into danger. He gave remarkable example of this in 1782 at Cuddalore, when he hid in his house seven of those English officers who were given up by Admiral Suffrein to Hyder Ali, and fed them till they could fly to a place of greater safety, thus saving them from the imprisonment and misery which the others suffered for the two years during which they were at the mercy of that tyrant. In his housekeeping he was frugal, spending little on himself, but much on his fellow-creatures who were in need. The more disinterested he was, the more presents flowed in upon him, which he distributed generously on all sides. If he could do some good or turn away some evil, he did not hesitate to give away hundreds of dollars.* He lived most simply himself, and when on a journey was always satisfied with a curry of dried fish with rice, which he called his pilgrim's curry. Though many poor people, widows and orphans shared his property during his life, he left his family

*The Tranquebar Missionaries received a proof of this in 1801 when a most unworthy and vicious Missionary, Früchtenicht, had been sent by them to Madras to go home from thence: he spent all his money and would certainly have returned to Tranquebar, had not Gericke come forward, paid his debts and taken a passage for him in a ship bound to the Cape for 200 starpagodas, declaring moreover that he did not wish to be repaid, for he had given it freely, wishing to remove such a scandal from the Mission. The Mission-College ordered him to be repaid and sent him also a complimentary letter, but Gericke was dead before it arrived.

properly provided for, and had also remembered the Mission-establishment in Vepery.† He spent and ended his valuable life in activity for mankind. He died without a long and painful illness, like a pilgrim on a journey.

†Gericke says in his will, "My greatest troubles have occurred during the last seven years. My daughter Dorothea Sophia Hunter died aged 20, and my son Captain George Frederick aged 30."

CHAPTER XV.

THE MISSION IN TRANQUEBAR AFTER THE YEAR 1740.—MISSION EXPERIMENT AT THE NICOBAR ISLANDS.—MORAVIANS IN TRANQUEBAR.—JESUITS IN TRANQUEBAR.—BETHLEHEM-CHURCH.—NATIVE TEACHERS.

It has been already shown how the Mission spread along the coast from Tranquebar to Madras, from Madras to Cuddalore, from Cuddalore to Calcutta, and in the interior from Tranquebar to Trichinopoly and Tanjore, and from Tanjore to Palamcotta. We will now return to Tranquebar, and see what has been going on there since 1740. We will first notice an attempt to spread still further, over the sea and salt-water to the Nicobar Islands, to which the Danes laid claim, and which they had often tried to colonize, but unsuccessfully as sickness and death amongst the colonists had always stifled the undertaking in its birth. It is not my intention to describe these expeditions, but I must mention that at least in one of them some one thought that the conversion of the Nicobarese should be attempted, for in February 1756 the Government requested the Missionaries to send one of their number in the Company's ship that was about to start for those islands, to try whether the heathen inhabitants could be persuaded to embrace the truth, and also to take the spiritual care over those white and black Christians who were already there, or who might go hereafter. This request was at first refused, but when it was repeated in the same year shortly before the departure of the ship, it was thought better to take it into more serious consideration, and they selected by vote Missionary Poltzenhagen who was also willing to go. He was born at Wollin in Pomerania in 1726, had studied at Halle, and given instruction in the school of the Orphanhouse there. In 1750 he went to India with Schwartz and Hüttemann and attached himself particularly to the Portuguese congregation. He was a quiet pious man, whose turn of mind may be seen in the following letter written the year before he started for the Nicobars. "So far as my insignificant person is concerned, through the mercy of God my Saviour I have been kept tolerably fresh at my post. He also works in my soul by his Spirit, preparing me both for my employment and for a blessed eternity. My constant prayer therefore is, "Lord Jesus! drive out everything, take everything away which might separate me from thee and which might hinder me from belonging to thee." Both inwardly and outwardly I have great cause for praying thus with a daily-renewed zeal. If the faithful Saviour will help me through unto salvation, this will suffice me." As we have said he was quite ready to undertake the voyage, and when some difficulties occurred and he was again asked whether he remained firm to his intention, he answered, "No difficulties shall be made on my part, but in God's name I will go in the ship to the Nicobars, as an explorer, and may God give, a good one, of the country." On the 1st of September 1756 he started in the ship "Copenhagen" and arrived at his destination after a voyage of eight days. He employed his time admirably in trying to become well acquainted with the natives, in visiting the many sick and dying (as we see by his journals) but fell ill himself and died on the 28th of November, at the early age of 30. In two of the following expeditions Danish priests were at the head of affairs, Engelhardt in 1790, and Rosen in 1831, but as their primary object was not the conversion of the natives, and as they did not belong to the Mission though they sailed from Tranquebar, I cannot stop to relate their fate. The attempt of the Moravians at colonizing the Nicobars will be spoken of directly.

While the Tranquebar Mission was thus trying to spread, it was exposed to some immigrations which caused the Missionaries much more disturbance and trouble than was desirable. The first of these arrivals was that of the Moravians, as I glean from some of Francke's letters of the year 1759; writing to Finkenhagen, he says, "Another piece of news which I have received has struck me very much, and troubled me not a little, namely that the Moravians are trying to establish themselves in Tranquebar. Whoever knows the intrigues with which that sect is always connected, will feel sure that not only the advantages which they will have promised to the King or the Company will consist in empty words, as experience in Silesia and other places would prove, but it is also to be feared that they will spare no pains to distract the congregations gathered, which has ever been the consequence of their making their way into a place and trying to spread their cause under cover of the Saviour's name; for they seek out the least steady and most pliable of the congregation, and take great pains to draw them over to their party, by which they are torn away from simple Christianity. I could bring forward innumerable examples of the damp they have thus thrown on all that is good." Thus Francke continues, and from his other letters it is easy to see how violent he was against the Moravians, especially on account of their duplicity. He relates examples of Count Zinzendorf's untrustworthiness, and declares that the Moravians had boasted, especially in Switzerland, that the management of the Danish Mission had been confided to them.

But if Francke took the idea of their going so ill, how startled were the Missionaries at the place itself, when, in the year 1760, 14 Moravians arrived in the same ship which brought out Governor Forch, made preparations for settling there, bought a garden near the town for 1100 dollars, began to learn Tamil and Portuguese, received encouragement from Herr Husum, the Pastor at Zion-Church, who was considered by the Missionaries to be a thorough Moravian, and were not discouraged by the new Governor. The Missionaries were very unfriendly towards these strangers and would have nothing whatsoever to do with them. As they feared that a Mission would thus be established within the Mission, they wrote to the Governor and asked for an explanation as to whether the Moravians had received permission to act thus from the King or the Company. They received the unconsolatory answer, that so far as he knew these colonists had been invited by the Royal Danish Court to settle in the Nicobar Islands; that they had received privileges* and permission to settle in Tranquebar or its territory and to enjoy those advantages which had been promised to them in the Nicobars; that it was the King's will that they should have liberty of worship according to their custom, and that it would be pleasing to the King if they could assist in the conversion of the blind heathens; that they would have free permission for preaching the Gospel to the natives, for forming into Moravian

*The Missionaries received further information on this point from the Government Secretary Falck. The Moravians had received permission to settle in the Nicobars, and to be free there from all taxes for 20 years; they might enjoy the same freedom for 12 years in Tranquebar or indeed in any of the Danish possessions in India. All Christians or Heathens who would join them were to enjoy the same freedom, Government promised to assist them, to assign land to them, to give them introductions when they went to other places &c.

congregations those, whom they should bring into the communion of the universal christian Church by baptism. The Governor concluded by saying, that, as it was his duty to see that the Evangelical brethren avoided all causes of disagreement with the justly-famed Lutheran Missionaries, he hoped that these would in their turn also act in the same spirit.

It is difficult to understand how the Moravians had obtained these privileges; yet I think I can resolve the difficulty. Knowing that the Mission-College would be opposed to them, they applied to the King through another channel, viz the Direction of the Asiatic Company and Count Moltke. They would naturally represent at first what an advantage it would be to the Company to have them as colonists, and as soon as the Company showed its wish to secure them, they required privileges which were drawn up as if one of themselves had written them; but I have seen it asserted that it was done with the help of the book-keeper of the Company, Bornovsky, and these privileges were then confirmed by the King, who, never suspecting that there were any obstacles in the way, did not communicate with the Mission-College. When the College now heard of the arrival of these unexpected guests,it sent in most earnest representations of the consequences of such a step, and a Royal Rescript of the 16th of November 1762 ordered, that the Moravians must go to the Nicobars within a twelve month, or else return to Europe. This order was harsh and unjust, for it contradicted their privileges, which they had not forfeited by overstepping them in any particular. But it was not carried out, for they remained for six years in Tranquebar without troubling themselves about the Nicobars, and during the whole of that time were very attentive to their own interests: yet they were partly restricted as the Direction of the Asiatic Company informed the Mission-College in 1764, that Government had repeated an order to the Moravians not to meddle in the slightest degree with the conversion of the heathen, much less encourage any one to leave the Lutheran congregation to join theirs.

Amongst the Moravians were two well-educated men, Buttler and Völkel, who applied themselves to the study of the native languages, and began to translate Zinzendorf's sermons into Tamil and Portuguese. The Missionaries relate that they tried to become acquainted with the members of their congregation, and to imbue them with a bad opinion of the instruction they had heretofore received and with a good one of what they could give, that they never attended Divine Service when it was performed in German, but only the Tamil and Portuguese services in order to perfect themselves in those languages. At last they report that, in addition to the fourteen Moravians who came out in 1760, 9 men and 4 women had arrived from Europe on the 22nd Aug. 1761, and that it was rumoured that a large party of them was coming out in every ship that should leave Denmark, "from which," say the Missionaries, "may God preserve us!" They made themselves such general favourites in Tranquebar that Wiedebrock relates that the arrival of the Royal Rescript had made a very unfavourable impression on the public, who looked upon them as useful colonists. Even their opponents bear testimony to their irreproachable lives. Maderup expresses himself still more strongly on the general favour in which they were held. "I cannot describe," says he, "how the Moravians have insinuated themselves in so short a time into the good will of Danes, French and even Hindûs by their voluntary humility and angel-like conduct as they consider it; in a place where there are so few who can try the spirits, it is no wonder if the shell is preferred to the kernel. If they were as pure in their doctrine and teaching as their life is outwardly to the eyes of the world, there would not be a sect or race to equal them in the whole of Asia. The Natives therefore call them the "Saints" or the "Nyanigöl" which means "the wise men," that being the name which they gave here to some of their own holy men." The two elder Catechists, Rayanaiken and Schawriappen, often went to visit them, even after the Missionaries had told them that they did not approve of it;—they showed a great liking for them and one even took up their peculiar modes of speech, so that it was much feared that he would join them altogether, which however did not take place. The Moravians next gained the favour of Captain Berg in Tanjore, the great patron of the Mission, for Wiedebrock says of him that he had asked and obtained permission from the King of Tanjore to allow twelve of them to settle in his dominions. Wiedebrock spoke to the Captain, warning him of the errors of the Moravians which he explained to him, but without effect, for the Captain was quite taken in by them. It is difficult to say why, under such favourable circumstances, they remained in Tranquebar instead of going to Tanjore. Perhaps they wished first to be on a better footing with the Missionaries, for which purpose they made several attempts. In the Archives of the Mission-College I have seen an account of a conversation between an Assistant of Francke's, Inspector Fabricius of Halle, and the Syndic Koeber, who had been sent there by the Directors of the Moravian brethren to persuade the Halle party not to work against them. I have also seen the representation of the Moravian Stahlmann to the Government in Tranquebar and the counter-representation of the Missionaries. Finally there is a document in the writing of Frederick, Baron von Watteville, who addresses the Mission-College in the name of the Directory of the United Brethren to complain of the quarrelsome disposition of the Lutheran teachers towards the Brethren and to beg the College to write to the Missionaries and to try to remove their suspicions; the whole is instructive in many respects, but being too lengthy to be inserted here, I must be satisfied with saying that it did not produce any favourable results. In 1766 the Missionaries relate that two of the Moravians had gone to Colombo in Ceylon and one of them had died there, wherefore one of their Missionaries, Buttler, had left Tranquebar to join him; and that the Moravians were more and more known and loved on the coast. "Some," say they, "are very much surprised at their going on so mysteriously, but many become very anxious in consequence to know what their secrets are." In 1767 it is said of them that they keep within bounds, that the Missionaries have no communication with them, neither do they talk of them to others, so that they can scarcely complain, but that real unity is not to be hoped for, because the Missionaries felt perfectly convinced of the unfair dealings of this party. At last on the 7th of August 1768, six of the Moravians, including one of their Missionaries, Mr. Völkel, embarked on board a sloop belonging to the Company, and sailed for the Nicobar Islands, with the understanding that more were to follow, if they gave favourable reports. The news soon arrived that two of the six were dead. The remaining four extolled the fruitfulness of the country, and thought that they should do very well when they had got over the fever. They did indeed remain there, and the colony lasted for nearly twenty years, but in 1787 it was given up. They remained much longer in Tranquebar. In 1772 the Halle Reports say, that the newspapers relate that the Moravians have taken advantage of the state of affairs to obtain new privileges and ask whether anything that has been done will be prejudicial to the Mission? The Missionaries say in 1773, that more Moravians have arrived, and that the Danish priests had made known an edict in their favour from the pulpit. In 1774 it is told, that they are not making public attempts to spread their doctrines, but that one of their elders, Woltersdorf, who had come out the year before, had, in an Indian dress, baptized one of their heathen servants, that this had often occurred with persons in their service, but had never been known before. Freylinghausen, who had taken Francke's place at Halle, especially requested the College to keep a watchful eye on the Moravians, as he had reason to believe that their minds were bent on mischief, and that they were doing all in their power to obtain a share in the Danish Mission-work. "As the Moravian party," says he some years later, "have suddenly taken a more refined appearance, and seem to find more entrance every where amongst well-meaning people, it requires great care that none of their adherents should be selected as Missionary, for it is quite clear that their intention is to get the Mission entirely into their hands." After this time we hear very little of the Moravians. They are only spoken of in a cursory way, and in 1803 it is said, "The two who still remain here, Weber and Ramsch, have given up their establishment, sold their garden and fields, and intend to return to Europe by the first opportunity."

About a year after the immigration of the Moravians, we hear for the first time of Jesuits in Tranquebar. When Pondichery was taken by the English in 1761, eight or ten Jesuits with other Frenchmen fled to Tranquebar, where the Franciscans have long had a Church. At first they only erected an altar in their own house and performed their worship privately, but afterwards they had a piece of ground in Poreiar allotted to them as a churchyard by Governor Forch, where they built a little hut and collected stone, in order to build at some future opportunity; they even rented a house in Poreiar and requested the Government to allow them to perform Divine Worship publicly. On the representation of the Missionaries this was denied them, at least they were told that they could only obtain such a permission from the King of Denmark. They then rented a large house in Tranquebar and began a school. The Missionaries made a representation against this also, and begged the College to do everything to prevent the Jesuits who had fled with many native Catholics from Pondichery, from building their nest in Tranquebar: and then they go on to speak of the change which the English victories had produced. "Three years ago the Jesuits boasted publicly in their church at Pondichery that they made such progress in persuading our Christians to embrace their errors, that the *heretical* Missions in Madras, Cuddalore and Tranquebar would soon fall to the ground. They began skilfully enough; for as the French were then conquering whole kingdoms, they could bring in Christians every where, and give them all sorts of emoluments and employments, by which means they could of course easily attract the worldly-minded. Their strength lay in General Lally having arrived from Europe with 3000 men, who sought to bring everything into their power by violent means. When our brethren in Cuddalore fled for refuge to us, and those in Madras to Pulicat, our prospect was dark and dreary certainly; but how suddenly it has all altered! Where is the great and terrible army? has it not melted away? Where is Pondichery, the great Babel? Have not the English, or rather has not God, the Holy and the Just, thrown it down to the ground and made it desolate? Where are now the numerous and proud false teachers?

Have they not been obliged to take refuge in Tranquebar? And our Mission-establishments are still standing. Let us not therefore be highminded, but rather let us fear, for we know that if we do not turn his goodness and the blessings of his grace to better advantage, still greater trials may fall upon *us*. We acknowledge with thorough humiliation before God that among our Native assistants, in our congregations, and in our schools, there is so much indolence, such earthly and carnal customs, and such a disgraceful want of faith, as cannot be pleasing to a holy God. Yes, we ourselves are not pure before him! He has good reason to cast us off, and to make us desolate, and who can say what he has determined in his holy counsel?"

The Missionaries complain again of the Jesuits in the following year, and call the attention of the College to the fact that, in spite of the Danish prohibition, they have now been in Tranquebar for two years. A Jesuit school-master, who had gone out for a walk with his children, had entered into a dispute in the public street with the children, and teachers of the Mission-school, and had said amongst other things, "You do not know the truth; none of you can be saved, only we know the way to salvation. All who do not pray to the Mother of God, but say that she was a sinner, will certainly go to Hell." He also spoke contemptuously of Luther. This conversation went on till they were close to the gates of the town, so that two of the Missionaries, who were just passing by, heard it. Meanwhile the Romanists increased the pomp of their religious services, to which the number of refugees from Pondichery, contributed; some of the native Romanists in Tranquebar were very rich, and had plays acted in Poreiar at their own expense; probably on scripture subjects as is often the case in Roman Catholic countries. This storm however passed away sooner than had been expected: as early as 1765 the Missionaries announced that since Pondichery and Carical had again fallen into the possession of the French, both they and the Jesuits had left Tranquebar.

We will now turn our attention to the state of the congregation in Tranquebar since 1740, and remark that it had increased so much that it became necessary to build a new Church. It was in the year 1717 that Ziegenbalg had consecrated the one which was called New-Jerusalem. This had soon become too small, and the Missionaries had to consider how to make room for the people, who on festival days when many came in from the country, and even on Sundays, were obliged to sit outside the door. They thought at first of adding to the Church, but there were difficulties in the way of this and it would not be a sufficient change. With the consent of the Government they therefore determined on building a new Church in the Mission-garden at Poreiar amongst the villages of the Company, so that the Christians there might have the Church close to them, and the foundation was laid in October 1743. The building went on but slowly, on account of a want of materials, but it was finished in 1746. It was in the form of a cross, and received the name of Bethlehem, because, as it is said in the consecration-sermon, "it lay not far from Jerusalem-Church in the town, just as the ancient Bethlehem was not far from Jerusalem. Bethlehem was a little village and yet the Son of God did not despise being born there. Also the little insignificant Bethlehem Church will be thought worthy of the gracious presence of Jesus, and as the Redeemer was born in the flesh in Bethlehem, we may hope that he will be spiritually born in the souls of many believers if the Gospel is properly published and accepted here. Bethlehem means a house of bread, and deserves its name as Jesus who is the bread of life (John VI, 35) was born there, and our Bethlehem Church may be a spiritual house of bread, wherein Jesus will communicate himself to hungry souls by the preaching of the Gospel and the receiving of the Lord's Supper." These words of David's were placed over the principal entrance, "O come let us worship and bow down, let us kneel before the Lord our Maker" (Psalm XCV, 6). Over the pulpit was written with reference to the preacher, "We preach Christ Jesus the Lord" (2. Cor. IV, 5), and opposite to the pulpit with reference to the hearers, "Hear the word of the Lord" (Isaiah LXVI, 5). Over the font, "The washing of regeneration" (Tit. III, 5), and over the altar, "The table of the Lord" (1 Cor. X, 21). The consecration took place on Wednesday after Whitsuntide, the 1st of June 1746. Besides the town-congregation 400 Christians from the country were present, also the Danish priest of Zion Church, Herr Schiönnebölle, the Commandant, the Council and other people of distinction. The text for the Tamil sermon was, "Mine house shall be called a house of prayer for all people" (Is. LVI, 7), and the service was concluded by a Tamil hymn sung by the school- children, which had been composed for the occasion by the native priest Diogo. The Church received many presents for its further adornment, and the Missionaries determined to preach alternately there on Sundays and Festivals.

But it is not enough for us to know that the actual members of the Church were increasing, we wish to know something also of their spiritual life and growth. It would be of little use to extract examples from the Mission Reports of those converted heathens who were now leading a godly life, bearing opposition with patience, or bidding adieu to the world in the hour of death with a noble and Christian resignation; for such examples, though they are very numerous, only tell us of the state of individuals, and give no idea of the general state of feeling in the congregation. Therefore we seek for more general signs of Christian feeling and development, and come at once to the question, whether with the advance of time the natives had shown themselves better able to teach, and whether the more talented amongst them were fit for collecting and managing a congregation; or whether at least the Missionaries had worked on steadily towards this aim, and with what success? It has been remarked before that the Archbishop of Canterbury amongst others zealously exhorted them to turn their attention to the education of native teachers; neither were such exhortations wanting afterwards. An anonymous letter was sent in to the Mission-College with the superscription of "Immanuel" intended for the consideration both of Francke and the Missionaries. "According to my humble opinion," says the anonymous writer, "the main design of the Mission from the beginning has been, not so much to enlighten a confused crowd of Asiatic heathens by means of European Missionaries, as to obtain and to instruct a sufficient number of inquiring Indians who might be educated in an Evangelical Seminary at Tranquebar for the Ministry among their countrymen; and until this design is more effectually carried out than hitherto, even much sowing will produce but very little fruit. Thanks be to God we have had an Aaron,* and we have a Diogo still, and it is through their means that most of what can properly be called a conversion of the heathen has taken place; but according to my ideas, we ought to have twenty such, and our God to whom the cause belongs will grant them to us though he does not give them immediately. I am willing to believe, that our good Missionaries of whom there are now 7

* See Chapter 10.

or 8 besides the Catechist Hutter, faithfully endeavour to follow out the plan which is laid down to them by the Instructions of the King, but if by the blessing of God the plan is to be carried out in right earnest, then that what now seems to be their principal aim should be but secondary, (namely to give a general instruction to the children, and now and then to journey about) and that what they now treat as secondary should be their great and principal object, namely, by God's grace to select and prepare a much greater number of teachers from amongst the natives; and for this purpose their greatest strength must be given to establishing a seminary in which 10, 20 or 30 young Indians should be constantly instructed. It may be asked, how are they to be obtained? and to this I answer, that all the trouble that is now given to collecting a confused crowd of Catechumens might well be devoted to searching out such young men as these. It is true that for some years this would not make so good an appearance, but it would be in this way that the seed of the Gospel would take firm root in those countries, and spread about to all around. Perhaps I think and speak like a fool, because I seem to speak of wishing to force a crop, to which as St. Paul says, God alone can give the increase. I answer:—surely, if Paul plants and Apollo waters in the very best way that they can devise, and remove as far as possible all hinderances, this cannot be called forcing the thing, but trying whether the talents entrusted to us would not produce more by applying them otherwise." The anonymous author concludes by requesting that the opinions of Francke and Benjamin Schultze should be taken on this affair.

Francke answered this with a detailed explanation. He goes through all the remarks, brings forward 14 heads, convicts the unknown author of several errors, and remarks truly enough that money cannot do everything as he seems to expect when he sees so little fruit from much seed: that the Missionaries would most willingly have formed such a Seminary for natives, indeed that they had done so, but that sometimes they could not get the right sort of people and that sometimes they degenerated. This explanation was sent to the Missionaries in Tranquebar, who agree in their remarks with nearly all that Francke says, but add a few particulars. In order to point out the original intention of the Mission, they give the words of the commission given to Ziegenbalg, which they say is to the same effect as what they have received. "We, Frederick the 4th &c. having graciously accepted and constituted, do hereby accept and constitute Bartholomäus Ziegenbalg to go as a Missionary to the East Indies, that he may apply himself with all diligence to instruct the heathen who are living in our dominions there or on its borders, in all holy doctrine as it is contained in the Word of God; and to bring them to a knowledge of salvation according to the further information contained in the Instruction &c. &c." but add they, "there is not one part of the Royal Instruction which says that a Seminary shall be formed, indeed we are not even told to take the trouble to establish schools; but the work amongst the heathen, and other duties incumbent on us, are principally insisted on." They go on to say that they have nothing to object against the work being carried on by natives. "If it should please the Lord to cause a great awakening amongst the natives of this country, and to kindle a greater light amongst them, for the appearance of which we long anxiously, we, who are so often oppressed, yea tortured, by the burden and heat of the day, are most heartily ready to return to Europe if it be God's will, and to leave the conversion of other heathens, and the future management of the congregations to native labourers."

So the Missionaries say; but no full confidence in the power of the Word of God amougst their converts is visible in them and much sad experience amongst their native Assistants discourages them; as when they say, "Some of the Natives are making good use of the pound with which the Lord God has entrusted them and try with faith and diligence to bring their brothers according to the flesh into the kingdom of Christ; but the greater number seek their own; indeed some by their open unfaithfulness have made themselves quite unfit for any further care of souls. Many of those who have been brought up in our seminary have not allowed the Holy Spirit to effect a real change of heart in them." They agree that it would be better if natives could do the Mission-work, but fear that it cannot be done, at least not at first. When Missionary John in 1784 puts the question," How can the heathen be more certainly brought to conviction and to the doctrine which alone can make them wise to salvation?" he answers without hesitations, "by skilful native labourers rather than by Europeans, though the latter will still be necessary for educating and guiding the native priests. Long experience teaches us that far fewer are gathered into the fold by the Missionaries than by their native assistants; and as there is such a want of suitable people amongst them, our zealous efforts should be in future directed to repairing it." John relates that he had often wished himself in the skin and dress of a native, that he might awaken less curiosity and more confidence: for in his conversations with the heathen, he found them either slippery, reserved or rude. Many of the obstacles which opposed Europeans would vanish before natives: they would not be occupied as unfortunately the Missionaries must be with the externals of the congregations, the schools and the correspondence; they would cause no sensation by their colour or dress, they could be on more confidential terms with the natives, they could speak their native tongue more fluently, and could som etimes sing something to their listeners from their native books, on which they place great value but which is unmanageable to the tongue and disagreable to the ear of an European. These native teachers might moreover live on a third of what an European requires, and while their number would be increased, the latter might be diminished." Thus we see that Missionary John knew very well how it ought to be; but the plan of making the natives help in Missionary-work always failed, most probably from a little fault on both sides. The same John whom we have already heard speak in 1784, expresses himself thus in 1800 when he touches on this subject in the Report drawn up by himself and his colleagues on the state of the Mission: "People in Europe commit a great mistake when they are surprised that more *native priests are not ordained*, and that christian congregations cannot be managed like those in the early days of Christianity, so as to support themselves and spread without external aid. This will scarçely be the case during the century which has now begun, nor until the whole nation has been raised to the same scale on which the Greeks and Romans stood when the Gospel was preached to them. For the following reasons we must expect that it will be a long time ere pious and able European Missionaries can be dispensed with. *Donum regendi*, or the gift of managing a congregation, not merely preaching to them, but also keeping them in order, is rarely possessed by a native. Even those native priests, catechists, and schoolmasters who are really pious and skilful men require constant attention, guidance and encouragement, for the national character is timid and vacillating; their enthusiastic fire soon changes into coldness, indolence and weakness. From this weakness in their character they cannot be so much respected as a sincere and clever European, for the difference must strike every one. Experience has shown that a very good and useful catechist becomes a less good and less useful priest so that doubts have been raised as to ordaining more and we prefer to be satisfied with catechists. Even the bringing up of Catechists has its difficulties, for as soon as they have received a superior education, they leave the Mission in order to obtain more profitable situations, to which they are encouraged in every way by their families, who wish to be supported by them."*

We are already acquainted with Rayanaiken (see Chap. XI) He continued to show himself untiringly diligent, and was especially useful in spreading the knowledge of Christianity in the dominions of the King of Tanjore, particularly at the time when the Missionaries themselves could not obtain permission to go into the interior. When Tanjore was besieged by the French in 1749, he could not fly, because it did not seem suitable to him that a shepherd should leave his flock, and God gave him courage to remain and to bear the hardships of the siege. He left the suburbs and took refuge in the fortress, and as his house, with many others, was pulled down by the King's command, he lost everything that he had, even his books, and was obliged for some weeks to preach without a Bible. During the siege he remained near the town ditches, and did not allow a

*I have found the following opinion given by Schwartz on the subject of native ministers:— "They are useful," says he, "and skilful enough to deliver a clear and edifying discourse. But they require some one to point out to them how they should manage this and that, who can receive a report of their work, and point out to them how they might have done better. If they were left to themselves, much confusion would ensue. The catechists would not be so obedient to them, especially if they were to see them make mistakes. Now on the contrary subordination is very easy, for the catechists know to whom to apply if the native priest has done wrong. I could prove all this to you by undeniable proofs." *Halle Reports.*

day to pass, without exhorting both Christians and Heathens. He performed Divine Service every Sunday and prayed for the King and for the citadel, which was saved. When the danger was over, nine Pariah suburbs of Tanjore chose him as their umpire in all their disagreements, and gave him full permission to publish the Gospel amongst them. He gave great joy to the Missionaries in Tranquebar by his zeal and talents, but there are traces of this joy not being unalloyed. Shortly after being chosen as umpire, he allowed himself to be appointed by the King of Tanjore as head-man of the people that burn the dead. As this brought him into close contact with heathen ceremonies, the Missionaries were displeased, and kept back his salary. When the Moravians came to Tranquebar, he became very intimate with them, though the Missionaries told him that they did not approve of it. These are the causes of the discontent which prevailed against him, but it is difficult to form any judgment on the affair from the slight notices we have. In 1766 he was severely ill for eight weeks, and he informed the Missionaries that "during this illness the Holy Ghost had wrought on his soul powerfully, and had shown him how much insincerity existed in him, that he had therefore determined to free himself from everything, and be sincere for the future." By Schwartz's advice he was removed from Tanjore to Arentangi, where he lived for some years in full activity, and died on the 29th September 1771, aged 71. His death took place on Sunday, after he had performed the service and visited a sick man. In the afternoon he was attacked by severe pain, which though it seemed at first to give way to the remedies that were applied, returned with increased force. He died with these words on his lips, "Lord Jesus, receive my spirit," after serving the Mission for more than 40 years. He possessed a clear understanding, an excellent memory, a pleasant manner of speaking, and was well read in the Bible and well acquainted with the principal events of Church history. His zeal in the spread of Christianity was richly blessed by God.

I will now turn to a short account of the Native Priests ordained after Aaron. The first of them was *Diogo*. In the year 1713 when he was but eight years old, his mother, himself and his brothers and sisters were received into the Lutheran from the' Roman-Catholic Church; he made good progress in the Mission-school, was appointed a catechist in the town of Tranquebar, and in 1741 was ordained a priest. His duty lay at a distance from the town, and he was most diligent in visiting his remote district, till prevented by bodily weakness during the last 10 years of his life; he died in October 1781.— *Ambrose* was also received in 1713 while still a child into the Lutheran from the Roman-Catholic Church, and brought up in the Mission-school. He first learnt weaving, and then went to sea, but as he had no inclination for either of these modes of life, and found that a school-master was wanted at the Mission, he offered himself and was accepted for his ability and good temper. This was in 1733; in 1740 he was sent as Catechist to the Mission in Cuddalore, where he remained till 1748, in which year he returned to Tranquebar, and was ordained a priest in the following year, in which office he remained for 28 years exhibiting much cheerfulness and sincerity. During the last two years of his life he was not strong enough to undertake journies, but he continued to labour, as well as he could, on the spot. On the 8th of February 1777 he entered into his eternal rest.— *Philip* was born of heathen parents in the year 1731 in the neighbourhood of Negapatam. After the death of his father, he was deceitfully enticed away by a slave-dealer, who brought him to Tranquebar, whence he was to be shipped off to Acheen; but he found an opportunity of making his situation known to his friends. His mother came immediately to Tranquebar, but could not find him anywhere. She happened to be passing Jerusalem-Church one Sunday when the congregation was leaving it. She asked one of the passers by what building it was. "It is a Church of God," was the answer. The troubled mother turned towards the Church and prayed thus: "If thou, O God, who art worshipped in this Church, art the true God, show me my child." She then went on to the castle and there met her son, who was coming out with the other slaves. She flew to him and embraced him, and applied to the proper authorities to restore him. She was told that she could not get him back again, unless another were supplied in his place, and the affair seemed to progress very slowly. The poor woman thought that she could not do better than to return to the Mission-Church, lift up her hands and say, "O Lord who art worshipped in this place, if thou wilt make my child free in ten days, I and my children will come to thy Church and be thy servants." The boy was indeed free in ten days, but the woman forgot her vow, went into the country and sacrificed to the idols. Then one night she had a dream. It seemed to her that a man dressed like the Priest whom she had seen come out of the Church in Tranquebar, appeared to her and said, "You vowed that you and your children would come to our Church; why then have you not come?" She now overcame her fear of going to Tranquebar, was instructed there, and was baptized with Philip and his sister in 1741. The remainder of Philip's life is best described by a letter from Missionary Klein, which was written directly after Philip's death on the 6th of February 1788. "Our faithful assistant Philip," says he, "was taken ill the beginning of this year, and it pleased the Almighty, who is the only true God and the Lord of the vineyard, to call away this his true servant on the 4th of this month. I was very much affected when I preached his funeral sermon from John XII, 26. I have preached the funeral sermons of three native priests, of Ambrose in Bethlehem - Church, of Diogo in the old Jerusalem Church, and now in the same of Philip. Our dear Philip came here at the age of 10 years in 1741. I took him into my service and I thus gained an opportunity of grounding him better in knowledge, and of encouraging him to a pious life. He was afterwards made schoolmaster, then town-catechist, and finally priest in 1772. Herr Kohlhoff baptized and ordained him, and therefore he, like myself, feels his death very much. Oh how willing and unwearied was Philip in visiting the sick and the healthy of his congegation! We have certainly lost a great deal in him, and have no one whom we can put in his place with equal confidence. Oh how great is the want of faithful native labourers!" — *Rayappen* was born of Christian parents in 1742. His grandfather who was of high caste and had been a zealous worshipper of idols, was converted to Christianity with all his family, received the name of Mark at his baptism, and became a very useful catechist: he, fortunately for Rayappen, undertook the care of him, for his father, Andreas, was a very different kind of man. He made good use of his time at school and was taught the art of printing. He afterwards became teacher in the school at Tranquebar and was then sent as catechist to Tanjore, where Schwartz gave him a very good character. In 1778 he was ordained a priest, and was a very earnest worker. It has been already remarked that he introduced the Gospel into the South of India in 1789; but the Missionaries were not always pleased with him. Yet they remark that several domestic troubles, particularly the lingering illness of his wife, produced so favourable an effect on him that he won their confidence again, made progress in Christianity, and applied himself diligently to the duties of his calling. On the 25th of March 1797 he died suddenly, and was buried in the church-yard of Bethlehem Church. — *Schawrirayen* distinguished himself as a town-catechist in Tranquebar. Missionary John says of him in 1792 that he far surpassed Rayappen both in ability and activity, and besides this understood German; but that they would not ordain him for fear of displeasing Rayappen, and also because the hope of being some day ordained incited him to greater usefulness. Rayappen died and still Schawrirayen was not ordained, because he was too useful as head-catechist to be spared. The ordination of this excellent catechist was still delayed in 1809, though it had been approved of by the Mission-College for ten years, but he was sent round to the Christians in the country with permission to baptize and to marry. So far as I know he was ordained in the year 1813, but died in September 1817. After him I do not think that any Native was ordained in Tranquebar.

After this they began to ordain natives at the other Missionary-stations, but the universal experience was that they did not display any independent activity, but always wanted to be led by the Missionaries. The first Native who was ordained at the English Mission stations was *Sattianaden*, who was ordained by Schwartz on the 26th of December 1790 in the presence of Kohlhoff and Jänike. He was destined for the south of India, where he had already made himself very useful as a catechist, and where he continued very useful as a priest until his death in 1815. In 1811 Pohle and Kohlhoff ordained 4 native catechists *, and as two of them died soon after, three † more were ordained in 1817 to fill their and Sattianaden's places. I do not know anything of these native priests, nor of their usefulness, but it cannot have been anything remarkable.

* Njanapragasam, Adeikkalam, Vedanaigan and Abraham.
† Nallathambi, Abraham and Pakianaden.

CHAPTER XVI.

THE TRANQUEBAR MISSION AFTER 1740 (CONTINUATION). — THE MISSIONARIES IN TRANQUEBAR.—CHRISTOPH SAMUEL JOHN.—DECAY OF THE MISSION.—GLIMPSE OF LIGHT. — CONCLUSION.

Amongst the Missionaries who lived and laboured in Tranquebar after the year 1740, many true and faithful labourers are to be found, but not one who distinguished himself much above the rest, excepting *C. S. John.* I must however bring forward also the name of *O. Maderup*, not indeed because he surpassed the rest, but because he was one of the very few who thought of writing anything in Danish on the subject of the Tranquebar Mission; very little however has been printed and the greater part has scarcely seen the light of day.

Christoph Samuel John, the son of a Clergyman, was born on the 11th of August 1747 at Fröbersgrün near Greiz, in Voigtland. He was brought up in his parent's house in the fear of the Lord, then went to the school at Greiz, and afterwards to the university of Halle, where he instructed the youth at the Orphanhouse. In 1769 Professor Knapp sen. proposed to him to go as a Missionary to Tranquebar, and after some consideration, he determined, with his father's consent, to accept the call. He was ordained at Copenhagen, and arrived in India in 1771, and spent the remainder of his life there. He was both a clever and a christian man, but with an overwhelming love and ability for teaching. The Mission had from the first devoted itself especially to the schools, but under him this tendency reached its highest point, and it clearly proves that the greatest attention to all school-arrangements does not suffice for the well-being of a congregation that has been lately formed. The Mission-College had remarked his zeal and activity, and when it requested by letter that one of the Missionaries should be chosen to carry on the correspondence it was no secret that John was the person desired; and when he was chosen it was soon visible that he would not allow this opportunity for personal communication with the College to pass unimproved, so that we must expect to see the history of the Mission wind very closely round this pedagogue. In his very first letter he expressed his pleasure at the correspondence being confided to one individual, for though the Missionaries were united at heart, they were so different in age, temperament and feelings, that it would have been very difficult to compose a letter which should embody the feelings of all. A tone of complaint prevailed. The College had remarked this, and expressed its pleasure when a more cheerful tone than usual was perceptible. This, says John, made a strong and lasting impression on me; however much there is that is unpleasant and discouraging, there is also much that is good and excellent, which may well give cause for joy, praise and hope.

John's cheerful views were connected almost entirely with the instruction of youth, into which he threw all his powers and it was not only for the children of the Natives, but he opened his house to the children of the Europeans, making it a regular educational establishment. He was induced to do this by the pleasure that he took in it, and by the desire of obtaining a comfortable subsistence. During the first six years of his stay in India, his salary was only 250 Rix dollars, which obliged him, he says, to wear dirty clothes, and to make known that he was in want of linen, clothes, tea and sugar, and though his rich neighbours sometimes made him presents of these articles, he received them with inward shame, for he would much better have liked to give than to receive. He found an opportunity for marrying, and though on the one hand he was very fortunate, he was very unfortunate on the other, for their income was so small that the young pair had to sigh over their troubles; they presented them to God in prayer and wrote about them to Europe, but as help could not arrive for a long time, John went out and collected shells and such like curiosities, by which he made some hundred dollars which enabled him to pay off his debts. At last a more suitable means of earning money appeared, when his school-arrangements were set to work and brought him a regular income. His colleagues were not pleased with all this, as John himself writes:—"My European school met with opposition in our little circle six years ago, or the others, with very good intentions, thought it was not suitable to my profession, and that it might even be considered as hurtful to future Missionaries and to the whole Mission. These fears increased, when I bought a large school house at my own risk, kept a carriage and horses for the better class of children and my own family, improved my housekeeping so as to make it suitable to the rank of the children and my own income, received several families who had fled from Negapatam, allowed my house to be filled with their property, and besides my own eighteen European and nearly as many Malabar children, employed about 60 workmen from the Poor Institution in my garden, and even desired that several children out of our school should learn to work with them. I did not trouble myself about what any one might think of this, but only took care that no one should be able to accuse me of any neglect of my duty; though being then in the yearly receipt of 3000 Rix-dollars I might have dispensed with the Mission altogether. These advantageous circumstances enabled me to carry out comfortably various plans from which my bitter poverty had hindered me before, for I could now venture on doing good when I had not to reckon so very closely as to 50 or 100 dollars, and considering the poor and exhausted state of the Mission-chest, this was a great advantage in any proposition for the advantage of the Mission or the Native youth. But to humble my pride, one stroke came after another. I fell ill often myself; thirteen children lay ill at one time, and God took from me all my own three children in the space of one year, which so overcame my cheerfulness and joyous hopes, that I had written by that man-of-war which was wrecked, asking for my recall in most melancholy tones, for I considered myself as an useless burden for the future. It is no wonder then that I was pleased when the parents took away half my boarders, for I wished them all away, that there might be no obstacles to prevent me from returning to my sister at Fröbersgrün to grieve away my remaining days, which I fancied would be but few. But God had humbled me for my benefit and again has granted me health and cheerfulness and strength, also two children, a son and a daughter—I expect a third with the New year—so that he has made me quite a recovered Job and has blessed me."

John goes on to relate that he sold the school-house, which had now become too large for himself and nine children, and again occupied the smaller house in which he had lived before. "Besides this," he adds, "I have a little piece of barren sand outside the town, which has a beautiful prospect, and where I have laid out a garden; this when the house is finished will cost about 2000 dollars. I go there in the afternoons when school-time is over, and occupy the children with gardening and collecting plants and insects while I visit both christians and heathens. From the hill there I overlook the sea,, the town with its surrounding villages, gardens and rice-fields, and I think, "May I but be permitted to do some good here, and may the whole neighbourhood, yea the whole land be filled with the knowledge of the Lord, with happiness and with blessing!"— Our congregations and schools are now very encouraging and hopeful. There are still many worthless members in the congregations whom I cannot count as really belonging to the Mission, but yet many do really commence to walk worthy of Christianity or at least decently, to which I think our new arrangement of instructing communicants in the afternoons, throughout the week before the Communion and otherwise examining and exhorting them, has greatly contributed. We are especially careful with the preparation for baptism; we try those who wish to be baptized with various works, and press them closely as to a real inprovement. No doubt the number of baptized persons is diminished by this, but the spread of Christianity is advanced rather than retarded. We strive to keep those firm who have been baptized and therefore often converse with them. Our greatest pleasure is derived from our Tamil school. We do not know a single negligent or unwilling disposition there, and in many of the boys and girls a real earnestness and fear of God are to be seen. Many of the boys surpass their teachers, and the girls have excellent examples in their teachers and two subteachers. Modesty and diligence reign over all the school-children. We have done away with the afternoon-school for those who will have to support themselves, and substituted the knitting of stockings and making of mats, which seems to have given new life to them. The frequent illness, the cutaneous disorders and the dirtiness in dress which were formerly so troublesome have now almost entirely disappeared. The Europeans rejoice in the cleanliness which they see both in the church and in the streets. Our two great bare school-gardens are now pretty pleasure-gardens, which have been laid out by the great friend to gardens and children, Missionary Rottler, my Jonathan. When either of us comes into the school, the joy and the love of the children to their teacher and father is most visible. We very seldom require corporal punishment. Of those who were brought up in our house, one is now an excellent catechist in Tanjore, another is a skilful and highly-approved interpreter to government, two are servants and writers to European merchants, and two are useful assistants in the school, while others are going on steadily, and if not citizens of the kingdom of God they are at least useful citizens on earth. In many European houses the floors are covered with mats made at the school, which cost from 10 to 40 dollars the piece. Here and there are baskets made for rice? which cost about 4 dollars each. The Europeans like our stockings, of which 20 pair cost 30 Rixdollars, and we have now twenty pair making for Major General Abeste. Many of the inhabitants send chairs, beds, palankins and sofas to our school for us to put in the canework. Herr Rottler has laid the foundation of a stocking knitting establishment amongst the natives."

The pleasing prospects which are expressed in this letter, were soon shaded. That John meant most honourably with all his efforts in favour of schools, is undoubted, as also that he continued in the path he had marked out with great zeal and perseverance; but on the other hand one cannot wonder that his colleagues (excepting Rottler, who agreed with him) did not approve of his plans, and that his educating European children was an especial thorn in their eyes, for they might truly say that it was hurtful to the Mission even though it might be useful in itself, as it must unvoidably turn his attention and that of his colleagues from their legitimate objects. The first who complained of John was Missionary Hagelund, a Dane and theological candidate from Copenhagen, who came out to Tranquebar in 1785. "The time approaches," says he, "in which I can hope to take a share in the work of the Mission here; it therefore seems suitable to me that I should also take a share in the correspondence with the College. Till now I have been a silent spectator of all that the others, or rather that John has undertaken, and have also watched his desire of being master in everything." So Hagelund continues, but he received a grave reproof from the College, .and died the year after. But it is easy to see that he was not the only one who was displeased with John's school for European children. In a letter to the College he speaks of two hopeful boys in his school, Johnson and Lebek, aged 17 and 15, of whom he hopes that the first who wishes to become a Missionary; may receive the title of co-rector of the school after 1790, and excuses himself for calling it *my* and not *our* school, because his colleagues, and especially König, will have nothing to do with it, and consider it as quite foreign to the purpose of the Mission. Not long after König wrote as he says for the first time in 25 years to complain that John applied to his schools what was intended for the use of the Mission. The College turned to Profr. Schultze at Halle to explain this difference of opinion to them: he returned a lengthy answer and goes back to show that König and Klein had long been opposed to the reforms of John and Rottler: he does not altogether approve of John's conduct towards the elder Missionaries, but does not consider it to be the cause of their differences. He thinks that John's school is an useful institution to the country gnerally though not to the Mission, as the catechists who are brought up there leave the Mission-service as soon as they can do so with advantage. The school had not produced a single native priest. The school was disadvantageous to the other national schools, as John attracted all the most able young men. The work amongst the heathen suffered in consequence, for though John's extraordinary inclination for school-work had given new life to that department, the work amongst adults languished, for the country congregations were only visited by native priests and catechists, and the journies amongst the Heathen, which the Missionaries had formerly found so useful, were almost given up.

The only way by which John's school might have proved useful to the Mission would have been if some of the young men educated there had shown a desire and ability to take part in the Mission-work. But this was not the case; on the contrary Johnson and Lebek of whom John entertained such great hopes, thinking that in the first he had found a real Timothy, were indeed sent to Europe for their further improvement, but Lebek turned quite away from the Mission, and Johnson played some foolish tricks and then followed his example. "No one is more grieved about it than I am," says John, "for I had taken great trouble with them, and since 1790 had been their principal support." But the real great opponent not so much to John but to the whole cause of the Mission was the spirit of the times. A mission to the heathen was such a ridiculous idea at the end of the last and the beginning of this century, that it was exposed to universal derision; this contributed so much to its downfall that it could only drag on a miserable existence as a sort of school-institution. We shall point this out afterwards.

Already in the year 1774 Professor Freylinghausen of Halle grieves over the universal decay in the Church, and declares that it is daily becoming more difficult to find suitable and willing persons to send as Missionaries to Tranquebar. He expresses this opinion in the following letter, "It is true that in early times it was difficult to find Missionaries, but it is not to be wondered at that it is now still more difficult, as many learned men impress the minds of the young with ideas that are quite contrary to the Gospel, on which account the greatest care is necessary in the selection of candidates, for fear of being deceived. For if a man were chosen as a Missionary who secretly nourished the idea that a philosophical morality were sufficient for salvation, he would of course only teach the Heathen what he himself believed." When the Missionaries found that as the old ones died away, no new ones were sent out to replace them, because suitable people were not to be found, it naturally produced a depressing effect on them. "Our position," says Schwartz, "is rather sad, but God knows ways and means for sending labourers into his harvest, though in truth sincere labourers are very scarce. The condition of the Church in Germany is grievous: they have invented a gospel which was unknown to Paul and the other apostles: they cast aside the precious sacrifice of Christ, and the powerful workings of the Holy Spirit. Infidels first sought to overturn the very foundation of faith; they looked upon Christ only as a good teacher, while his reconciling blood which is the source of all salvation and blessing, was despised. What but insolence and carnal feelings could arise from this? But a Missionary must beware of being cast down and discouraged on this account; for here especially, it is like a poison to the body and extremely hurtful to the soul, because faith and love and hope are thereby decreased, yea even totally ruined; and when people see that we are discouraged it hinders our work amongst souls which ought to be our joy. If anything sorrowful occurs to me, I go and catechise for an hour; this occupation sweetens all that had been so bitter to me. A missionary must not give himself up to repining: we ought to be witnesses of our Lord and not only converters. One often wishes that a rich and visible blessing might follow our work, as when Peter's sermon converted three thousand souls: but there is a time for sowing as well as a time for harvest, and it is a question whether we could remain humble if so great a blessing were granted to us. It is best to work diligently, and so to pray that God may bless our work." Thus Schwartz comforted himself, but he could do it the more easily, as God had given him a cheerful heart, and his connection with England was much more consolatory than that of the Tranquebar Missionaries with Denmark and Germany, where the falling away from Christ was more general. moreover he was more fortunate in his assistants than they, never receiving such an unfit one as Stegmann, nor such a bad one as Früchtenicht.* He had moreover not to do with an unwilling (not to say an ill-willing) Government on the spot, which treated all mission affairs as a burden and a folly.

*I must unfortunately give a few lines here to describe that monster of a Missionary mentioned above, who caused so much trouble and did so much mischief. Früchtenicht was born in Hohen - Westedt in Holstein, where his father was a Clergyman; he studied at Kiel, and received the character of "Capable" when he was examined in 1797 at Glückstadt. Profess. Schultze at Halle accepted him as a Missionary, and says of him, "when he offered himself, I examined him both in preaching and catechizing, and both in these powers and in his character I have remarked such qualities that I cannot but entertain the best hopes for the future, and can recommend him to the College as a Missionary". In Feburary 1799 he arrived in India, but not at Tranquebar, for the ship landed him in Bengal. On the way he had preached at the Cape, and as he had refused a sum of money, the Colonists had supplied him

In connection with what I have said on the decay of piety and so forth I will here relate a few traits which will no doubt be seen to be characteristic.

In the year 1791 the Mission Surgeon Martini died, and eleven days after his death a son of Missionary Klein who had studied medicine in Europe arriving in Tranquebar, the Missionaries determined to appoint him Surgeon in the interim. As Klein had attended medical lectures in Copenhagen, the Mission-College applied to the Faculty there for their opinion as to whether this was a prudent step. Professor Kratzenstein was deputed to answer, which he did in the following words:—"I do not know Klein, but I think that it would be advisable to grant the doctor to the Missionaries who is proposed by

with wine and other necessaries. He had drunk deeply of this, and continued the habit at Frederiksnagore where it was soon reported that he was a drunkard and a bully, who had no objection to fight with pistols. He contracted debts and placed them to the account of the Mission, and did not arrive in Tranquebar until October, where his fame had preceded him. On his first arrival however he was very diligent and orderly, but he soon gave himself up to drunkenness again, and came into Church on Christmasday in a state of intoxication. All warnings were in vain. He united to this disorderly life, the greatest shamelessness in his pretensions, scandalized the congregation, disgraced the Mission, and in his drunkenness insulted and threatened his Colleagues in their own houses, so that in 1800 they thought it right to suspend him. Früchtenicht continued to live as before, and on the 30th of January 1801 quarrelled with two Englishmen in the public street, who horsewhipped him there, and he bore the marks of this chastisement on his face for a long time after. The other Missionaries now removed him entirely from his occupation and refused to give him any more pay, but the Government would not sanction this until the instructions of the Mission-College should have been received, often reminding the Missionaries that "they had never been willing to be placed under the Government." On the 23rd of February he wrote to his relations in Europe intimating that he was about to destroy himself. His landlord, to whom he gave the letter, sent it to the police, who sent people to apprehend him and found him standing up in his bed in his priest's robes with a knife in one hand and a bottle in the other:— in that dress he was taken into the Fort at midnight. They wished to send him off in the ship "Christian VII", but the owner did not like taking such a dangerous man on board. He was therefore still in Tranquebar when the English took the town in 1801, and was imprisoned by them for eight days for striking an officer. The Missionaries at last got rid of him by promising him a certain sum of money on condition of his giving up all claims on them, and he then went to Madras. How he was treated there by the noble Gericke has already been told in Chapter XIV. Even after his return to Hamburg in the summer of 1802 he caused considerable expense, for he received a sum of money to induce him to make an application to have his appointment cancelled.

themselves; for the situation of a medical man in Tranquebar is not an enviable one; it is something like a penitential parish here. Any one who wishes to obtain such a place must either be a zealous Pietist desirous of gaining a higher place in Elysium, or an enthusiastic Linnéanist, like König" (who had held this place before) "who after all became blind and died."

That a Professor should laugh at the Mission in this way in an official document seems somewhat surprising, but it had to bear with unfairness from those who were much more nearly connected with it. The Secretary of the Mission-College, Hee-Wadum, writes to John in these terms:—"It is quite certain that all Catholics and Jews who join our Church take the step in expectation of some temporal advantages, and my opinion is that any one, *whoever he may be*, who has been faithless to his religion, can never be trusted, and I think that he would not be ashamed, whenever circumstances might make it advisable, to change his religion again and again, and that he would be able to perpetrate all sorts of villainy." This must have been very edifying for John to read. It was certainly only the Secretary, who was writing this on his own responsibility; but yet it is placed in the letter-book of the College. In a letter to his successor in the secretaryship, Gude, John says, "We have painfully experienced all that you say about Hee-Wadum's indifference in the many years that he was connected with the College. His private friendship for me never gave me any satisfaction for I saw how shortly and coldly he dismissed the most important points, so that I could not but think that many things had never been laid before the Honourable College."

But now something from Tranquebar.—When the Catechist Schreyvogel, who was afterwards ordained as a Missionary, arrived there in 1804, he sent a report to the Mission-

College, in which he relates that public opinion was adverse to Christianity and more especially to the Bishop Balle. The Bishop, as one of the Members of the College, heard the report read, and I have found a short abstract of it. It was probably intended for the Bishop's note-book, but he must have left it lying by the report, where I found it. It runs thus:—

"*Schreyvogel.* In Tranquebar the Bible is a book of fables, and the doctrines of faith are despised. Every one believes what he likes, and acts as he likes.—The Bishop of Copenhagen is a superstitious man.—Behold, such is Rationalism!—I have known this for a long time."

It is not my intention to give an account of all the squabbles between the Tranquebar Government and the Missionaries, which arose from their old difficulties about their rights over the Mission-congregation and other subjects. The discontent was mutual and the two parties sent home accusations to Copenhagen. I have seen one document from the Government, with Major General Anker at the head of it, dated 15th October 1792, which attacks the Mission very severely. It says amongst other things that the converts only distinguish themselves by profligacy and disorderly lives, and that they all consist of the very lowest classes who present themselves as candidates for baptism in order to obtain temporal advantages; it is added, as if by way of excuse, but in reality to make the accusation, more biting, that this could not be attributed to the faults of the Missionaries, as they had always shown, and continued to show a *holy* zeal in the discharge of their duties.—On the other side the Missionaries say, "we must pay some attention to general rumours, for we know that it has been said in Europe that no one is so bad as our Christians and that they act worse than the Heathens. We have two answers to this; 1st. That the heathen natives settle their quarrels amongst themselves, while the Christians bring them before our judges. 2nd. It is right enough that more should be expected from Christians than from Heathens, but not satisfied with this, the Europeans expect more from our Christians than from themselves. Much that was Egyptian clung to the children of Israel in the wilderness. We feel this most, as the suffering Moses did, and willingly leave others to reason on it, which is an easy affair."

"We have a regular blacksmith in the Government now," John writes, "in the Privy-Counsellor Schmidt, who forges memorials against us, and seems now determined to use the pen, as he formerly used the stick when he was a sergeant. The English Missionaries without privileges are enviable in comparison with us who have such noble privileges. It would be better for us to suffer persecution, which at least would have an end, than thus to be roasted in the fire of chicanery."

This was in 1801. In 1804 the accounts are rather more cheering. They say that the greatest caviller, Schmidt, is dead, and that a letter from the College thanking the Government for its care of the Mission, has had the best effect, and that General Anker had drunk success to the Mission at a dinner on the King's birth-day. But the Missionaries rejoiced in better days rather too soon. It is true that Schmidt was dead, but Lindgreen was put into the Council in his place, and Rehling was made judge. These two united in annoying the Missionaries, and encouraged some natives to bring forward complaints against them. They sent a complaint to the King against the Court of judicature which they said the Missionaries held in Bethlehem Church, and against the punishments dealt out there. One of the Natives named Tiagappen, made an especial complaint, that the Missionaries had taken away his inheritance, that Cämmerer had given him four boxes on the ear, and that John had chastised a woman with his own hands. According to all probability the first accusation was without ground and false, but the accusations of arbitrary power were not without foundation. Cämmerer acknowledged that he had given Tiagappen a few boxes on the ear on account of his insolent way of speaking, and John said that he had given the woman a slight punishment, which in his opinion had prevented a much greater misfortune. Rehling now instituted an enquiry, and treated the Catechists and all the Natives, who were favourable to the Missionaries, so severely, that they in their turn complained to Government, by which their complaint was sent to Rehling. Rehling summoned them, and appointed a provisional judge. The natives were so frightened by him that they recalled all that they had said, and were fined two Rix - dollars, which the Missionaries paid for them. This affair annoyed the Missionaries extremely and impeded their usefulness; John wished to go to Copenhagen to defend their cause, but finding on his arrival in Madras, that there was no ship about to sail, he returned to Tranquebar.

This was the way in which the hundredth Anniversary of the Mission was celebrated in Tranquebar. In the English Missions it was solemnized by a special service. "The consequences," say the Missionaries in 1807, "are that we have become almost desponding, that our Churches are empty and that Baptism and the Lord's Supper are despised."

Under such circumstances we cannot be surprised to find the Missionaries expressing much sadness over their future prospects. Even so early as the year 1793 John writes, "A new honest Missionary would be a great comfort and help to us, but if no suitable man can be found, it is better to let us die out." Some years later his colleagues say, "When we consider the universal and growing irreligion in Europe and India which threatens to carry everything before it like a torrent, and which we cannot withstand, and when we see the decay of morality in this country, and that in spite of all exhortations, prayers and warnings it ebbs daily more and more in our congregations, we feel as if we must sink under these manifold troubles which we can only lay before God in prayer. We could bring forward many reasons which make us feel almost certain that the Mission is approaching its end. If this is the will of Providence we cannot withstand it, but can only grieve for our congregations, who will then be left without European teachers. Our christians in the country are the best, because they live at the greatest distance from Europeans; but there are many excellent men amongst the town christians also who give us great joy, and who are of course better known to us than they can be to strangers." "We have long known that those who convert the heathen are fools in the eyes of many, especially in these our days. It is true that much folly clings to us, but we shall improve. It is well for him who has the least of human weakness in him; but let him who is pure amongst you throw the first stone."

During these very sad times, the Missionaries tried to be useful to science. Botanical and other scientific remarks are most frequent in their accounts of their journies which were published at Halle. They were in many ways connected with learned men, more especially with such as were interested in Natural History, both in Europe and India. The botanical collection of Dr. Rottler, John's conchological and Klein's ornithological and entomological collections were of great importance. Eight different learned Societies voluntarily elected them as members. Profess. Rüdiger of Halle sent a contribution towards John's biography after his death, in which he expressed how very much he had been indebted to him during his 36 years correspondence for much light on the subject of Indian languages.

Now came the taking of Tranquebar by the English on the 13th of February 1808, which with the years of warfare that ensued, prevented all correspondence between Denmark and the colonies. The English Government in Madras (according to the articles of capitulation) gave some support to the Mission in Tranquebar, so that it was kept up by incurring some insignificant debts which were afterwards paid by the Danish Government. It is very pleasant to know that the King of Tanjore was one of those who assisted it in its day of necessity, for he could never forget what he owed to Schwartz, and was always a liberal contributor though he never embraced Christianity. John was now old, and weakened by sickness and anxiety, caused especially by the misconduct of his son; but even in his weakness activity was his delight, and schools were the apple of his eye. Five or six years before his death he founded some free schools for children of all classes in Tranquebar and Tanjore. These schools made progress, and the "Remarks on Indian civilization" which John published, attracted much attention; but they did not do any good to the Mission. His eyes had long been weak and at last he became quite blind, but was sometimes led into the pulpit that he might address the congregation. He longed for his release, spoke of his death daily, and only prayed to God that his sufferings might not be long. The prayer was heard, for he died suddenly from apoplexy on the 1st of September 1813.

After John's death Cämmerer managed the schools together with the whole of the Mission. In May 1820 (the Mission having been placed entirely under the Government) he gave up to the Society for Promoting Christian [Knowledge 1300 Christians, 11 Catechists, and 11 small Churches with the property belonging to the latter, as these natives were English subjects in Tanjore. "The Mission in Tranquebar," he writes, "the Mother of all others, must now sink down to be a small institution in one place only."

A great change was preparing in East Indian Missions, for many Societies had taken firm root there, and now carry* on their work on very different principles, but it is remarkable that a Missionary of the old stock remained till very lately at every one of the head-stations of the old Mission at Tranquebar, Madras and Tanjore. Rottler was in Madras; he first came out to Tranquebar in 1776, but after Gericke's death he went to Madras where he remained until he died in 1836, aged 87. Cämmerer was in Tranquebar; he had embraced the calling of a Missionary in 1789, and continued at his post till 1837 when he died, aged 70. And so far as I know the younger Kohlhoff is still (in 1843) in Tanjore, at least I have not heard of his death: he is a son of the old Missionary Kohlhoff who celebrated his jubilee at his son's ordination in 1787. The ministry of the father and son embraces a space of more than a hundred years. I hope therefore that however many things are to be tried in the Indian Mission field, messengers will still be sent out who will join the old Mission and continue its work. We Danes seem to have a particular call to this; a call which we must not neglect.

It was, however, very near being neglected. In 1824 the Tranquebar Government proposed nothing less than that the Mission should cease altogether as an institution for making converts, and that schools should be founded in which all use-

*See what Missionary Cordes says of the impression made on him by the activity of the various Societies in Madras: Dresden Mission Report 1841.

ful knowledge should be taught, and which would prepare the way for a real extension of Christianity amongst the natives at some future day. The Mission-College yielded to this proposal (which was not opposed by Cämmerer) so far as to agree that the schools should for the future be their principal object, but would not agree to the efforts for conversion being given up. The Government had suggested that the name "Missionary" should be retained, as being much respected in the country, and the College thought that on the same grounds the name "Mission" ought not to be given up. "Times may change," it was said, "and in better days more extensive efforts for the spread of Christianity may be united to this name. All history proves how much there often is in a name, and now that the attention of all, but more especially of Protestant European is turned towards Missions, and when they are more supported and favoured than they had been for the last thirty years, it would awaken an unpleasant feeling if this name were given up by the Danish Government." The Mission was then placed on a new footing by a Royal Resolution of the 18th of May 1825, by which the Pastorate of Zion Church and the office of the first Missionary were united, and in which it was declared that "the spiritual pastors who bear the name "Missionary" in Tranquebar are to make efforts for the conversion of the heathen only where they can hope to succeed and where the moral character of the persons seems to call for it, but they are not to expect any money to be spent on the *extension* of Christianity." Cämmerer had already petitioned for his discharge, but in 1821 he received the Royal permission to continue to work as a Missionary for his pension. Schreyvogel left in 1826, and entered the service of the English Society, which placed him in Trichinopoly. He sent a farewell-letter to the Mission-College, in which he called their attention to the sad condition of the Mission and schools, and to the fact of there being certain people in Tranquebar who were trying to destroy the arrangements of the Mission. The first Dane who was appointed as Priest to Zion-Church and as Missionary was *J. Ivarsen*, who died on the voyage in 1827. His successor, *K. E. Möhl*, did what he could from 1829 to 1835. What has been done by *H. Knudsen*, who left Denmark in 1837 and who still holds the office, is too recent to be matter of history. Thus much we can say, that affairs are looking brighter there, and we can certainly say the same of the interest that is now displayed in Europe towards the Tranquebar Mission.

It is true that the English have taken the charge of their stations on themselves, and therefore we can no longer hope to be assisted by English money. The connection with Halle may also be considered as over, for the Directors of the Francke foundation have thought right to give the sum which was at their disposal to the Mission to Borneo. But the *Lutheran Mission-Society of Dresden* has extended the hand of fellowship to the old Lutheran Tranquebar Mission, and its emissary, *Cordes*, is working in conjunction with Knudsen. Our Kings have never kept back their promised support, but have been willing rather to increase than to decrease it. The Mission-College has not only recommended the messenger from the Dresden Society to the Tranquebar Mission, but is earnestly contemplating such an enlargement of it, that at least one more ordained Missionary may be appointed: there is quite sufficient money for this, as the College not only has under its management the regular yearly allowance for the Mission, but the interest of all the legacies that have been left to it, especially of Scholz' legacy of which I will here give a short account.

Samuel Scholz was a rich merchant of Breslau, who when on the borders of the grave at the age of 78 had been thinking for many years of making some donation to the Mission; he consulted his Confessor, Archdeacon Thinkel, who prepared all the necessary forms for him, though he thought that it would all come to nothing. The old man was bowed down by weakness and illness, but in 1784 he came in to the town from his estate of Langenau, about a (German) mile and a half from Breslau, in order to strengthen himself by enjoying the ordinance of the Lord's Supper, and bringing with him 8000 Rix-dollars (equal to 10680 Rix-dollars in Danish currency), intending that the interest of this capital should pay a teacher who should faithfully and honestly preach the gospel to the heathen. He sent the capital to the Mission College with the remark that it might be increased by adding the interest to it until the plan could be carried out; but that he so much wished that something should be done speedily, that if a suitable person were selected during his life time, he would give 1000 Rix-dollars more. Scholz died the same year, and his plan, which would really have been the foundation of a new Mission, was never carried out; part of the interest of his legacy has been given from time to time to the Tranquebar schools; but as the rest has been added to the capital it will be a most important assistance in the proposed extension of the Mission.

The money therefore is ready; and we have lately had such convincing proofs that the christian people of this country are favourable to the continuation of the work, and that the clergy are giving more and more of their attention to it, that we need only point to this fact and not stop to give proofs of it.

But we suddenly hear from a meeting of the States at Roskilde:—it is best for us to sell Tranquebar, not merely when there is a good opportunity, but the sooner the better and to any nation whatsoever. I have gone through the reports on this subject in the States-Gazette, and must say that I have not found a thorough representation even of our political and commercial relations with Tranquebar; while our ecclesiastical relations with it are not touched upon in one single word, and they certainly would deserve some little consideration if the place were to be sold. The paternal care of the Danish Government has introduced the blessings of Christianity amongst a heathen people, but the congregation which it has formed has not developed so far as to be able to stand alone; on the contrary it will require the superintendence and protection of the Mother-Church for many years more. Under such circumstances, it would argue us to be very hard-hearted did we neglect the work which our fathers have begun, and expose the Mission, much weakened by its long and almost mortal sickness, to the chance-favours of the new purchasers of the town. I must say therefore, looking back on historical associations, and casting a glance on our present ecclesiastical connection with our colonies: Do not sell Tranquebar!

It may truly be said that the Mission proposed by Frederic IV has won for us a far-spread and European fame; but without overstepping the truth we may add to this, that we have in this particular received *more* honour than we deserved. I have shown in this history that the work was good and has been blessed. I have not hidden the faults and foibles of those who were engaged in it, but have described them as truth required me. For the future we will endeavour to deserve that honour which Europe has hitherto awarded but too liberally to the Tranquebar Mission.

APPENDIX I.

Royal Declaration and Instruction given by Frederick IV. to the first Missionaries.

(translated from an old Manuscript in Mr. Eibye's possession.)

We, Frederick IV etc., do hereby make known to all concerned, that We in Our Royal favour have engaged and appointed, and do herewith engage and appoint Mr. Bartholomew Ziegenbalg, to go as a Missionary from here to Eastern India, and there to apply himself with all diligence to instruct the heathens who dwell within Our territory and on the borders thereof, in the holy doctrine, as set forth in God's Word and professed in the Symbolic Books of this realm agreeing to the Augsburg Confession, and to bring them to the knowledge of salvation, according to the further terms of the Instruction, which We in Our Royal favour shall for that purpose communicate to him. Our greeting etc.

Copenhagen, 17. Nov. 1705.

A Royal letter, worded like this, was written for Mr. Henry Plütschau on the same day.

Instruction

according to which

We, Frederick IV, King of Denmark and Norway etc., do in Our Royal favour desire, that Mr. Henry Plütschau, born in Mecklenburg, whom we have resolved to send to Eastern

India as a Missionary, should with all submission conduct himself on his voyage out to and there in India, until Our further Royal orders.

1, He shall, on the whole voyage out, betake himself with all diligence to those on board ship, who have been in Eastern India ere this, and who are somewhat acquainted with the native language in order that he may learn from them something of that language.

2, Having by the grace of God safely arrived in the country, he shall, in the name of Jesus, heartily calling upon the same, at once begin the work for which he is sent out, and shall labour among the pagans, as existing circumstances shall make it practicable.

3, Although it is of some help, to improve the little rest of the knowledge of God, which men still have by nature, and thus to lead them to the knowledge of God which he has revealed in his Word,—and it is left to the Missionary himself to judge when and in what manner this may be done with advantage, — yet he shall always specially betake himself to God's Word, not doubting that God will make the power laid therein prove effectual among the heathens.

4, He must hold and handle there in Eastern India nothing besides the holy doctrine as it is written in God's Word and repeated in the Symbolic Books of this realm after the Augsburg Confession, and teach nothing besides it. And as Christ himself began his prophetic office by preaching repentance, and commanded his disciples to preach repentance and remission of sins, so also he must follow the same course.

5, He has to instruct the ignorant in the first principles of the Christian doctrine with all possible simplicity, so that the needful foundation may be laid the earlier.

6, In order that the poor blind heathens may understand that the Missionary himself has in his heart what he teaches, he must always show himself a pattern of good works, so that also by this his conduct they may be won over.

† 7, He shall not forget daily to pray for the cooperating grace of God and for every thing required that he may perform his office faithfully and carefully, and to call upon God in the name of Jesus, that he would bless our christian undertaking with abundant and happy successes to the salvation of many souls, and that he would grant to Our whole Royal house the reward of this pious work with every needful blessing for this life and the life to come.

† 8, He shall keep good friendship also with the Evangelical Pastors of the place, and shall gather from them, as from men acquainted with the country, all kinds of useful information.

† 9, He shall be content with what We in Our Royal favour have granted him for his annual pay and support, and not take any money from the people for the performance of his official duties.

10, Whenever a ship leaves India for this country he shall send letters therewith, reporting to Us according to his Christian conscience with all submission concerning his office, its successes and its hinderances. In the same way he may add his proposals suggesting how this new undertaking, which cannot be perfect at once, might, perhaps, be better arranged in future.

11, And finally he shall bind himself by a truthful promise as in the presence of God, to obey this Instruction, and with that intent he shall subscribe to a copy of it in his own hand-writing.

Given etc.

Copenhagen, 17. Nov. 1705.

Frederick R.

At the same day Mr. Bartholomew Ziegenbalg, born in Lusatia (Lausitz), received the same Instruction.

† The order of these paras seems to have been different in the original. We follow the order of the German translation.

APPENDIX II.

LIST OF EVANGELICAL LUTHERAN MISSIONARIES IN INDIA.

A. The old Lutheran Missionaries, mostly of the University of Halle.

1. *H. Plütschau*, born at Wesenberg in Mecklenburg, studied at Halle, was ordained at Copenhagen 1705, embarked from thence on the 29. Nov. 1705, landed at Tranquebar 9. July 1706, left India again 15. Sept. 1711 and died as Pastor of Beyenflieth in Holstein about 1746.

2. *B. Ziegenbalg*, born at Pulsnitz in Lusatia (Saxony) 24. June 1683, studied at Halle, was ordained and arrived in India with the former, went home 26. Oct. 1714, was appointed Missionary-Provost and was married at home, returned via England, landed at Madras 10. Aug. 1716, died at Tranquebar 23. Febr. 1719, and was buried the next day in New-Jerusalem-Church.

His widow remarried 1720 and went to Denmark. Of his 3 children 2 died early. The eldest was afterwards Professor of Mathematics in Copenhagen, then for a time Director of the Danish factory of Frederiksnagor, returned to Europe, and died 1758.

3. *J. E. Gründler*, born at Weissensee 7. April 1677, studied at Halle, was ordained at Copenhagen 1708, embarked there 17. Nov. 1708, landed at Tranquebar 20. July 1709, married 1716, died 19. March 1720, and was buried the next day in New - Jerusalem - Church.

4. *J. G. Bövingh*, a Westphalian, studied at Kiel, was ordained and arrived in India with the last mentioned, left the

Mission in 1711.—*P. Jordan*, sent out unordained with Gründler and Bövingh, went home with Ziegenbalg 1714 and remained in Germany.

5. *B. Schultze*, born at Sonnenburg in Brandenburg 1689, studied at Halle, was sent out directly from Halle via Holland and England, embarked at Deal 20. March 1719, landed at Madras 25. July 1719, was ordained at Tranquebar 1720, began the Madras Mission 1728, went home 1743, and died at Halle 25. Nov. 1760.

6. *N. Dal*, born at Anslet in Sleswick (Denmark) 2. April 1690, studied at Jena and Halle, came out with the last mentioned, was ordained at Tranquebar 7. June 1730, died (unmarried) 5. May 1747, and was buried in New-Jerusalem-Church-yard.

7. *J. H. Kistenmacher*, born at Burg in Magdeburg, came out with the two last mentioned, began to preach but died unordained 16. Febr. 1722; is buried at the same church-yard with the former.

8. *M. Bosse*, born at Nelben in Magdeburg, was ordained at Copenhagen 1724, embarked at Deal (England) 15. Febr. 1725, landed at Tranquebar 19. June 1725, married 1736, was in 1749 discharged and recalled to Copenhagen, where he died 1750.

9. *Ch. Fr. Pressier*, born at Perleberg 26. July 1697, studied at Jena and Halle, was ordained and arrived in India with the last mentioned, was married 15. Febr. 1736, died 15. Febr. 1738, and was buried the same day in N. Jerusalem-church-yard.

10. *Ch. Th. Walther*, born at Schildberg near Soldin in Brandenburg 20. Dec. 1699, studied at Halle, was ordained and arrived in India with the two last mentioned, married 1729, returned to Europe 1739, died at Dresden 29. April 1741.

11. *Andr. Worm*, born at Neubrandenburg in Mecklenburg-Strelitz about 1704, studied at Jena and Halle, was ordained at Copenhagen 1729, arrived in India 8. July 1730,

married 29. July 1732, died 30. May 1735, and was buried in N. J. church-yard.

12. *S. G. Richtsteig*, born at Landsberg on the Warthe, (Newmark, Brandenburg) 1701, studied at Halle, was ordained and arrived in India with the last mentioned, married 26. Dec. 1731, died 12. May 1735, and was buried in the same church-yard.

13. *J. A. Sartorius*, born at Laufenselten in Hesse-Rheinfels 21. Febr. 1704, studied at Halle, was ordained in London (by the Lutheran Court-Chaplain Ruperti) and arrived in Madras 1730, where he remained. He began the Mission in Cuddalore 1737, died and was buried there 1738.

14. *J. E. Geister*, born at Berlin, studied at Jena and Halle, was ordained in Wernigerode (county Stolberg) 1731, arrived at Madras 1732, went with Sartorius to Cuddalore 1737, returned to Madras 1743, left the Mission 1746, went to Batavia and there embarked for Europe, but died on the voyage 1746.

15. *G. W. Obuch*, born at Morungen in East Prussia 20. May 1707, studied at Halle, was ordained at Copenhagen 1736, arrived in Tranquebar 19. Aug. 1737, married 14. March 1740, died at Tranquebar 3. Sept. 1745, and was buried in the N. J. church-yard.

16. *J. Chr. Wiedebrock*, born at Minden in Westphalia 9. Febr. 1713, studied at Halle, was ordained and arrived in India with the last mentioned, married 27. Jan. 1740, laboured at Tranquebar nearly 30 years, died 7. April 1767, and was buried in the N. J. church-yard.

17. *J. Balthasar Kohlhoff*, born at Neuwarp in Western Pomerania 15. Nov. 1711, studied at Rostock and Halle, was ordained and arrived in India with the two last mentioned, was married the first time 15. Febr. 1741, the second time Sept. 1760, laboured at Tranquebar more than 53 years, died there 17. Dec. 1790, and was buried in N. J. church-yard.

18. *J. Z. Kiernander*, born at Linköping in Sweden

1. Dec. 1710, studied at Upsala and Halle, was ordained at Wernigerode 1739, embarked at Gravesend 1. April 1740, landed at Cuddalore 28. Aug. eod. a., laboured there till 1758, when he went to Bengal, where he commenced the Mission. For further particulars see pag. 241 etc.

19. *J. Ph. Fabricius*, born at Cleeberg near Frankfort on the Maine 22. Jan. 1711, studied at Giessen and Halle, was ordained at Copenhagen 1739, came out with the last mentioned, laboured at Tranquebar till 1742, when he became B. Schultze's successor in Madras, died there (unmarried) 24. Jan. 1791, after more than 50 years' residence in India.

20. *Dan. Zeglin*, born at Stettin in Pomerania 26. Aug. 1716, studied at Halle, was ordained with the last mentioned, and came out with him and Kiernander, was married 1. March 1747, laboured nearly 40 years at Tranquebar, died there 4. May 1780, and was buried in N. J. church-yard.

21. *Oluf Maderup*, born at Maderup in Funen (Fyen, Denmark) 29. April 1711, studied at Copenhagen (*not* at Halle), was ordained there 1741, embarked there (with his wife) 19. Nov. eod. a., landed at Tranquebar 1. July 1742. His wife died 22. Dec. 1749, he remarried, but lost his second wife 3. Jan. 1766, married the third time 9. March 1767, laboured at Tranquebar more than 34 years, died there 20. Nov. 1776, and was buried in N. J. church-yard.

22. *Jac. Klein*, born at Elbing in Prussia 20. Jan. 1721, studied at Halle, was ordained at Copenhagen 1744, embarked at London 29. March 1745, landed (after a long and dangerous voyage, the ship being driven to Batavia) at Negapatam 3. Aug. 1746, married 5. March 1761, laboured at Tranquebar nearly 44 years, died there 18. May 1790, and was buried in N. J. church-yard.

23. *J. Ch. Breithaupt*, born at Dransfeld in Hanover (a relative of the renowned J. J. Breithaupt, D. D.) was ordained at Wernigerode 1745, came out with the last mentioned, learned Tamil at Tranquebar, went to Cuddalore 1747, and to

Madras 1749, where he laboured and died 17. Nov. 1782, after more than 36 years' residence in India.

24. *Ch. Fr. Schwartz*, born at Sonnenburg in Brandenburg 26. Oct. 1726, studied at Halle, was ordained at Copenhagen 17. Sept. 1749, landed at Cuddalore 30. July 1750, laboured more than 11 years in Tranquebar, commenced (in 1762) the Mission in Trichinopoly, settled at Tanjore 1778, and died there (unmarried) 13. Febr. 1798, after more than 47 years' residence in India. (Compare Chapter XIII pag. 199—236.)

25. *Dav. Poltzenhagen*, born at Wollin in Pomerania 1726, studied at Halle, was ordained and came out with the last mentioned, was sent to the Nicobar-islands Sept. 1756, where he died 28. Nov. eod. a. (See pag. 263.)

26. *G. H. Conr. Hüttemann*, born at Minden in Westphalia 1728, studied at Halle, was ordained and came out with the two last mentioned, went to Cuddalore, married, returned to Tranquebar for 2 years (1758-1760), died at Cuddalore 1781.

27. *Pet. Dame*, born at Flensburg in Sleswick 22. May 1731, studied at Halle, was ordained at Copenhagen 1754, arrived at Tranquebar 1755, died on a journey at Tanjore 5. May 1766.

28. *W. Fr. Gericke*, born at Colberg in Pomerania 5. Apr. 1742, studied at Halle, was ordained at Wernigerode 1765, came out via Hamburg and England, landed after a long and dangerous voyage at Point de Galle 4. Dec. 1766, arrived, after some stay in Ceylon, at Tranquebar 6. June 1767, went to Cuddalore to assist Hüttemann, whose daughter he married, laboured at various places especially at Negapatam until 1788, when he became Fabricius' successor (and chaplain of the Female Asylum) at Madras, died at Vellore 2. Oct. 1803, and was buried at Madras. (See Chapter XIV.)

29. *J. F. König*, born at Könnern near Halle 26. Oct. 1741, brought up in the Orphan-house at Halle, ordained at Copenhagen 1767, arrived at Tranquebar 1768, died there 4. Febr. 1795, and was buried in N. J. church-yard.

30. *F. W. Leidemann*, born at Stadthagen in Lippe-Schaumburg 6. Jan. 1742, studied at Halle, was ordained and came out with the last mentioned (and with D. M. *König*), died 8. Aug. 1774, and was buried in N. J. church-yard.

31. *W. Jac. Müller*, born at Heringhausen in Waldeck 24. May 1734, studied at Halle, was ordained at Copenhagen 1769, arrived in Tranquebar 13. June 1771, died 30. Dec. eod. a. and was buried in N. J. church-yard.

32. *Ch. S. John*, M. A., born at Fröbersgrün near Greiz 11. Aug. 1747, studied at Halle, was ordained and arrived in India with the last mentioned, died after more than 42 years' labour at Tranquebar 1. Sept. 1813, and was buried in N. J. church-yard. (See Chapt. XVI.)

33. *J. Ch. Diemer*, born at Gundershofen in Alsatia (Lower-Rhine, France) 1745, studied at Strasburg and Halle, was ordained at Wernigerode 1773, arrived at Bombay Aug. 1774 and went to Calcutta 1775, married, returned to England 1785, came again to Calcutta 1789, where he died 1792. (See pag. 244.)

34. *J. W. Gerlach*, born at Schlitz near Fulda 1738, studied at Halle, was teacher in the Paedagogium at Halle, was ordained at Copenhagen 1775, arrived at Tranquebar 5. Aug. 1776, went to Calcutta 1778, where he died 1791. (See p. 245.)

35. *J. P. Rottler*, M. A., born at Strasburg (Lower-Rhine, France) June 1749, studied at Strasburg (not at Halle) was ordained and arrived at Tranquebar with the last mentioned. Laboured at Tranquebar till 1803, when he was provisionally sent to Madras, was unconnected with any Home-Mission 1806—1817, when he took charge of the Madras Mission under the "District Committee," died after 60 years' residence in India 24. Jan. 1836.

36. *J. J. Schöllkopf*, M. A., born at Kirchheim in Würtemberg 1748, studied at Tübingen (not at Halle) was ordained at Wernigerode 1776, arrived at Madras 16. June 1777, where he died 11. July eod. a.

37. *Ch. Pohle,* born near Luckau in Lower Lusatia (Brandenburg) 9. March 1744, studied at Leipzig (not at Halle), vicariated in the court-chapel at Wernigerode, was ordained at Copenhagen 1776, arrived at Tranquebar 1777, from whence—on Schöllkopf's death—he was sent to Trichinopoly, where he died, after more than 41 years' labour, 28. Jan. 1818.

38. *Lor. Fred. Rulfsen,* born near Haderslev in Sleswick 7. Apr. 1753, studied at Copenhagen (not at Halle), was sent (with two unordained assistants for Calcutta) to Tranquebar where he arrived 16. June 1780 and died of fever soon after.

39. *J. Dan. Mentel,* M. A., born at Strasburg (Lower-Rhine, France) 13. Febr. 1755, studied at Strasburg (not at Halle), was ordained at Copenhagen 1780, arrived at Tranquebar 1781, but returned 1784 for health's sake and was made Joint-Pastor at Barmstedt in Ranzau (Holstein.)

40. *Pet. Rubek Hagelund,* born (in Denmark) 1756, was sent out 1785, arrived at Tranquebar 1786, where he died 1. Oct. 1788.

41. *J. Caspar Kohlhoff,* son of J. Balthasar Kohlhoff (Nr. 17.), was born at Tranquebar (baptized 29. May) 1762, brought up by Ch. Fr. Schwartz and ordained by him at Tranquebar 1787, laboured at Tanjore till his death 27. March 1844.

42. *Jos. Dan. Jänicke,* (brother of the excellent Joh. Jänicke, Pastor of the Bohemian Church and Founder of the Mission Seminary at Berlin, who died 21. July 1827), born at Berlin 27. July 1759, studied at Halle, was ordained at Wernigerode 1787, arrived at Madras 1788, laboured at Tanjore and Palamcotta, and died at the former place 10. May 1800.

43. *Aug. Fred. Cämmerer,* M. A., born at Wusterhausen in Brandenburg 22. June 1767, studied at Halle, was ordained at Copenhagen 1789, suffered shipwreck at the Cape, arrived via Ceylon at Tranquebar 1791, where he was the only labourer for many years, died 22. Oct. 1837, and was buried in N. J. church-yard.

44. *C. W. Päzold,* born at Weuchau in Lusatia 1764, studied at Wittemberg, was ordained at Wernigerode

1792, came out married via England, arrived at Madras 1793, learned Tamil from Ch. F. Schwartz, assisted Gericke in Madras, went to Calcutta as Professor of Tamil in the College of Ft. William 1802, returned 1804 to Madras, where he laboured till to his death 4. Nov. 1817.

45. *E. Ph. H. Stegmann*, born at Cassel 1773, studied at Marburg (not at Halle), was ordained at Copenhagen 1795, arrived at Tranquebar 1796; being unfit for Missionary - work he returned 1797, but came out again as Pastor of Zion-church 1799; went home a second time, was Pastor first in Jutland and then in Funen, where he died.

46. *W. Tob. Ringeltaube*, born at Scheidelwitz near Brieg in Silesia 1770, studied at Halle, was ordained at Wernigerode 1796, went out via England to Calcutta, where he arrived 1799, returned to England 1799, joined the London Mission Society, came again to India, and is said to have been killed on a journey into the interior of Africa before 1820.

47. *Im. Go. Holzberg*, born at Oberneuendorf near Görlitz 28. Apr. 1770, studied at Leipzig (not at Halle), was ordained with the last mentioned, arrived in India 1797, laboured at Tanjore till 1803, and then at Cuddalore, where he died 19. Dec. 1824.

48. *Lamb. Ch. Früchtenicht*, born at Hohen-Westedt in Holstein 1772, studied at Kiel (not at Halle) was ordained at Copenhagen 1798, arrived at Tranquebar 1799, a vicious man, got rid of 1802. (see pag. 296-297.)

49. *Christoph H. Horst*, born at Willenburg near Schwerin 1761, studied Medicine at Göttingen, joined the army and arrived with his regiment at Madras 1787, joined the Mission and was made Catechist ("Lector") at Cuddalore 1792, removed first to Tranquebar 1803, then to Tanjore 1806, where he was ordained by Pohle, and died 18. July 1810.

50. *Dan. Schreyvogel*, born at Lindau in Bavaria 16. Jan. 1777, was sent out unordained as Catechist to Tranquebar 1803, arrived 1804, was ordained at Tranquebar 1813, resigned and joined the English Church by reordination 1826, died at Pondicherry 16. Jan. 1840.

51. *Christl. Augustin Jacobi*, born at Olbernhau in Saxony 26. May 1791, studied at Leipzig and Halle, was ordained at Copenhagen 1812, embarked in England 1813, arrived at Tanjore, but died already 21 Febr. 1814.

52. *J. G. Ph. Sperschneider*, born at Blankenburg in Schwarzburg-Rudolstadt 1794, studied at Leipzig and Jena, was ordained at Halle 1818, embarked in England, arrived at Madras Nov. 1819, went to Tanjore where he laboured till 1826, when his connexion with the Patron Society was dissolved in consequence of his arbitrary expenditure of Mission funds.

53. *Laur. Pet. Haubroe*, born at Copenhagen 1791, studied there (not at Halle), was ordained at Roeskilde (Denmark) 1818, went to England, arrived at Madras Febr. 1819, laboured there till 1827, removed to Tanjore, where he died 1830.

54. *David Rosen*, born at Ebeltoft in Denmark 1791, studied at Copenhagen (not at Halle), was ordained with the last mentioned, and arrived with him in India; laboured in Trichinopoly till 1824, then at Cuddalore till 1829, then in Palamcottah till 1830, was at the head of the Danish colonization-experiment on the Nicobar islands 1831—1834, returned to Palamcottah 1835, went home 1838, was appointed Pastor of Lille Lyndby in Zealand, died 1862.

B. Danish Clergymen with the double office of Pastors to Zion church and Missionaries.

1. *J. Ivarson*, who died on his voyage out 1827.

2. *K. E. Möhl*, came out 1829, went home 1835.

3. *Hans Knudsen*, born at Copenhagen 11. Jan. 1813, studied at the same place, came out 1837, laboured faithfully and successfully for 6 years, fell sick and returned May 1843, but still continues to prove his lively interest in the Mission. He is now Pastor at Bregninge in Zealand.

C. Missionaries of (the Dresden or as it is called since 1848) the Leipzig Ev. Luth. Mission.

1. *J. H. C. Cordes*, born at Betzendorf in Hanover 21. March 1813, entered the Miss.-Seminary at Dresden 15. April 1837, was ordained at Greiz 26. Febr. 1840, arrived in India 27. Dec. 1840.

2. *C. E. C. Ochs*, arrived in India 11. Dec. 1842, left the Society June 1859.

3. *J. M. N. Schwarz*, born at Hagenbüchach in Bavaria 21. March 1813, entered the Miss.-Seminary at Dresden 2. Sept. 1839, was ordained at Greiz 27. April 1842, arrived in India 25. Dec. 1843.

4. *Ern. Dav. Appelt*, arrived in India 6. Sept. 1845, left the Mission Oct. 1860, and went to South-Australia, where he obtained a Pastorate.

5. *A. Mylius*, born at Baneik in Hanover 20. Nov. 1819, studied at Göttingen, was ordained at Ratzeburg 1846, arrived in India 5. March 1847, was disabled by sickness and returned to Europe Sept. 1850, is now private and Prison Chaplain at Hanover.

6. *K. H. Schmeisser*, born at Fürth in Bavaria 19. July 1819, entered the Mission-Seminary at Dresden Sept. 1842, arrived in India with the last mentioned, was ordained with Appelt (Nr. 4) and the following two at Tranquebar 18. Oct. 1847, died at Madras 3. June 1848, and is buried in the church-yard of the London Mission at Pursewaukkam.

7. *Ch. Fr. Kremmer*, born at Smalkald in Hesse-Cassel 8. Sept. 1817, entered the Miss.-Seminary at Dresden 23. Dec. 1843, arrived in India and was ordained with the last mentioned, laboured at Madras from 1848 till 1858, when he removed to Tranquebar (Poreiar.)

8. *A. Fr. Wolff*, born at Wittlohe in Hanover 19. Jan. 1819, entered the Miss.-Seminary at Dresden Sept. 1843, arrived in India and was ordained with the foregoing two.

9. *Jul. Glasell*, arrived in India 9. March 1849, returned to Europe 1851, is Pastor in Gothenburg (Sweden.)

10. *J. C. G. Speer*, born at Hohndorf in Silesia 1824, entered the Miss.-Seminary at Dresden 1845, was ordained at Breslau 23. Aug. 1852, arrived in India 26. Dec. eod. a., but returned (consumptive) May 1853 and died at his birthplace 22. April 1855.

11. *Ed. R. Baierlein*, born at Sieraskowie in Poland 29. April 1819, entered the Miss. - Seminary at Dresden 31. Dec. 1843, was sent out as Missionary to America 1847, where he was ordained, arrived at Madras 17. Dec. 1853.

12. *C. Al. Ouchterlony*, born at Stockholm 12. Oct. 1826, studied at Lund, was ordained at the same place 1852 and sent out by the Swedish Mission-Soc. of Lund, but this Soc. uniting with the Leipzig Mission, he arrived at Madras 9. Dec. 1853.

13. *G. E. Lundgren*, arrived with the last mentioned but returned to Europe Jan. 1855, is Pastor at Marbäck in Sweden.

14. *J. F. Meischel*, arrived in India 31. March 1854, followed a call to South-Australia Febr. 1860.

15. *And. Blomstrand*, M. A., born at Wexiö in Sweden 19. Dec. 1822, studied at Lund, was Lecturer in Lund's University 1846-1855, was ordained there 20. June 1849, arrived in India 12. Jan. 1858.

16. *H. W. Wendlandt*, came out (married) with the last mentioned, left India to join the Hermannsburg-Mission in Africa Sept. 1859, died at Emlalazi in the Zulu-country 24. June 1861.

17. *W. Stählin*, born at Westheim in Bavaria 1. July 1831, studied at Erlangen, was ordained at Munich 5. Nov. 1854, arrived in India with the foregoing two and the following two.

18. *G. Ch. Kelber*, born at Krautostheim in Bavaria 29. May 1828, studied at Erlangen, was ordained at Anspach 1857; arrived in India with the foregoing three, laboured at Madras, went on sick-leave to Europe in the "Cleveland" which left Madras in March 1861 but is not heard of since.

19. *S. Rydén*, born at Hestra in Sweden 24. Dec. 1825,

studied at Lund, was ordained there 1855, arrived in India with the foregoing four.

20. *Jul. Döderlein*, born at Erlangen in Bavaria 22. Aug. 1829, studied at Erlangen and Halle, was ordained at Anspach July 1853, arrived in India 27. Sept. 1860. With him arrived Mr. *Fred. Hobusch* to establish and superintend a Mission-Press at Tranquebar.

21. *And. Mayr*, born at Ratisbon (Regensburg) in Bavaria 20. May 1838, studied at Erlangen and Leipzig, was ordained at Regensburg 5. April 1861, arrived in India 4. Oct. 1861.

22. *H. Schanz*, born at Schöneck in Voigtland (Saxony) 8. Nov. 1834, studied at Leipzig, was ordained there 22. May 1862, arrived in India 8. Oct. 1862.

23. *Arn. Nerling*, born at Riga in Livonia (Russia) 11. March (27. Febr.) 1837, studied at Dorpat, was ordained at Riga 25. May 1862, arrived in India with the last mentioned.

24. *R. Handmann*, born at Oschitz near Schleitz 27. Febr. 1840, studied at Leipzig and Erlangen, was ordained at Schleitz 25. May 1862, arrived in India with the foregoing two.

Ev. Luth. Native Ministers.

1. *Aaron*, born of heathen parents at Cuddalore about 1699, baptized at Tranquebar 5. Aug. 1718, ordained by Pressier, Walther etc. 28. Dec. 1733, died 25. June 1745, buried in the old Jerusalem Church.

2. *Diogo*, born of Rom. Cath. parents about 1705, received into the Ev. Luth. Church 17. Nov. 1713, ordained by Obuch etc. 25. Dec. 1741, died Oct. 1781, buried in the old Jer. church.

3. *Ambrose*, born of Rom. Cath. parents 1709, received into the Ev. Luth. Church 8. Aug. 1717, ordained by Wiedebrock etc. at Poreiar 9. April 1749, died 8. Febr. 1777, buried in the church-yard at Poreiar.

4. *Philip*, born of heathen parents near Negapatam about 1731, baptized at Tranquebar 3. Sept. 1741, ordained by J. B. Kohlhoff etc. 28. Dec. 1772, died 4. Febr. 1788, buried in the old Jerusalem Church-yard.

5. *Rayappen*, born of Ev. Luth. parents at Poreiar 1742, baptized 3. Febr. 1743, ordained 1778, died 25. March 1797.

6. *Sattianaden*, ordained by C. F. Schwartz etc. 26. Dec. 1790, died 1815.

7. *Njanapragasam*, ordained by Pohle etc. 17. March 1811.

8. *Adeikkalam*, ordained with the foregoing.

9. *Wedanayagam*, do., died about 1813.

10. *Abraham*, do.

11. *Schawrirayen*, born of Ev. Luth. parents at Velipaleam (baptized 26. May) 1751; ordained 1813, died 25. Sept. 1817.

12. *Nallathambi*, ordained by Pohle etc. Aug. 1817, died 1857.

13. *Abraham*, ordained with the last mentioned.

14. *Pakianaden*, do.

15. *N. Nallathambi*, born 1801, baptized at Tanjore, licensed as Candidate 31. May 1849, ordained by H. Cordes etc. 27. June 1860.

16. *A. M. Samuel*, born at Madras 10. (baptized 18.) Febr. 1827, licensed and ordained with the last mentioned.